From 4-F to U.S. Navy
Surgeon General

D1478534

From 4-F to U.S. Navy Surgeon General

A Physician's Memoir

HAROLD M. KOENIG, M.D.

McFarland & Company, Inc., Publishers

Jefferson, North Carolina

LIBRARY OF CONGRESS CATALOGUING-IN-PUBLICATION DATA

Names: Koenig, Harold M., 1940– author.
Title: From 4-F to U.S. Navy Surgeon General : a physician's memoir /
Harold M. Koenig, M.D.
Description: Jefferson, North Carolina : McFarland & Company, Inc.,
Publishers, 2019 | Includes index.
Identifiers: LCCN 2019009727 | ISBN 9781476677323 (paperback. : acid
free paper) ∞
Subjects: LCSH: Koenig, Harold M., 1940– | United States. Navy—Medical
personnel—Biography. | United States. Office of the Chief of Naval
Operations. Surgeon General. | Admirals—United States—Biography. |
Physicians—United States—Biography. | Medicine, Naval—United
States—History—20th century.
Classification: LCC VG123 .K64 2019 | DDC 359.0092 [B] —dc23
LC record available at https://lccn.loc.gov/2019009727

BRITISH LIBRARY CATALOGUING DATA ARE AVAILABLE

ISBN (print) 978-1-4766-7732-3
ISBN (ebook) 978-1-4766-3589-7

The front cover photograph is of Harold Koenig (U.S. Navy). The artwork
is *Sick, Lame, and Lazy*, August 1971, Charles Waterhouse, acrylic on
canvas mounted on masonite, 25½ × 84 inches (courtesy Bureau of
Medicine and Surgery)

Printed in the United States of America

McFarland & Company, Inc., Publishers
Box 611, Jefferson, North Carolina 28640
www.mcfarlandpub.com

To Deena, a wonderful Navy wife
who raised our three sons, all of whom
became Navy officers and made us proud

Acknowledgments

I mention the people who encouraged me to write this book in the foreword. There were several people who helped as the writing progressed, people who read every word soon after it was written, found errors, suggested corrections. These were Nancy Tomich, Heather Wood Ion, and my wife, Deena. Our three sons also read some sections and offered corrections and additions. Joan Engel, David Fisher, Sheila Graham, and Tracy Malone reviewed sections concerning my tenure as Surgeon General. Ed Martin edited the section on my four years as a DASD. Don Coullahan reviewed the entire manuscript and suggested many corrections and improvements. Andre Sobocinski, the historian at The Bureau of Medicine and Surgery (BUMED), provided some photographs and recommendations on finding a publisher. I am most grateful to all of them.

Table of Contents

Preface

I retired in 1998 after a 32-year career as a physician in the U.S. Navy. My final assignment was as Surgeon General of the Navy. Upon retirement, having spent eleven years in Washington, D.C., Deena, my wife, and I moved to the other side of the country, to San Diego.

Though I had been assigned in San Diego twice during my career, it had been 11 years since we had last lived there. When we returned we moved into a home built in 1927 on Marlborough Drive in Kensington, a neighborhood established in 1910. Many of our neighbors have spent the major part, if not all, of their lives here.

Few of them have military experience and none have been involved in government at the highest levels of the Department of Defense. We have made many new friends here, and during social gatherings I shared stories about my Navy medical career and experiences in Washington. Often my new friends would say, "You should write a book." And always I would reply, "No, I have other things to do."

My cousin Katie Nelson, a niece of my mother, changed my mind. For a long time I ignored her encouragement to look into my genealogy, but she persisted and told me things about my mother and her family I was unaware of. Then, with my permission, she looked into my father's side of the family. Soon she called me and said, "Oh, my God, Harold, you have to look at your paternal grandmother's side of the family." It is extraordinary—my paternal grandmother's ancestors were pilgrims! I wish I knew more about them. Then I thought, *The same applies to me. I've had an interesting life, but if I don't write about it how will my descendants a few generations on know what it was like?*

My life has been filled with unusual experiences. I hope it gives you, dear reader, insight into life during my time and into the rewards and pitfalls of public service.

1

1

Life Before the Navy

I was born on February 28, 1940, in Salinas, California. Both my parents were teachers in the local schools. My sister followed three years later. At the end of the school year in June 1943 my father volunteered to join the Navy, his initial assignment training in Boston. We traveled to Boston and lived there for several months and then moved to Madera, California, and lived with my father's sister. When my father was assigned to Guam we moved to an apartment in Richmond, California.

After the war ended my father left active duty, but stayed in the Navy Reserve. We returned to Salinas and he resumed teaching at Salinas High School. For several months we lived in a one-room cabin, awaiting completion of our new home. My mother also returned to teaching after a few years. I had a happy childhood. Besides my academic pursuits, I was involved with church activities and the school orchestra, in which I played the violin. I also had a paper route, became an Eagle Scout, played Little League baseball and was on the high school wrestling and football teams. During the summer of 1957, before my senior year, I worked in agriculture at the Ferry-Morse Seed Company. During that summer my father developed acute leukemia and passed away in early October.

I had been accepted at Stanford and received a full tuition scholarship, and I had also applied to the U.S. Naval Academy in Annapolis. I had not been accepted there by the time I graduated from high school, but two weeks after graduation I received and accepted a last-minute appointment to the Naval Academy. Induction Day (I–Day) was on June 30. By November some first classmen began to notice that I did not hear them when they asked me a question, so I went to sick call to have my hearing checked and learned I had a hearing loss in my left ear. Serial audiograms over the next few months showed my left ear hearing acuity was continuing to decline. I had to be discharged but was allowed to finish the academic year so I could get college credit. I left the Naval Academy with a 4-F draft card in my wallet, which

meant I was medically unfit for military service and not subject to the draft.

I then attended Brigham Young University (BYU) and majored in chemistry. I had become interested in medicine during my hearing evaluation at Bethesda Navy Hospital and thus also took the required classes for admission to medical school. At the beginning of my senior year I was accepted to Utah and Baylor medical schools and chose Baylor. Orientation at Baylor began in September 1962. The dean, James Roy Schofield, MD, told us what to expect over the next four years. The subject he started out with was the military. He told us that the military recruiters would offer programs to pay our tuition, expenses, and a stipend during our senior year. He warned us not take the bait. He said there wouldn't be much need for military doctors in the future and so none of us should worry about being drafted.

There were 84 students in our class, all white—four women and no minorities. The first two years were didactic lectures and labs. We were required to wear slacks, a white shirt, and a tie to class. About three-quarters of the class were tobacco users, but

Top: **Me as a young boy with my parents, Fillmore and Dolores, and sister Elaine, 1945.** *Bottom:* **Midshipman Harold Koenig, 1958 (courtesy U.S. Navy).**

smoking was not allowed in the classroom. While smokeless tobacco was permitted, those who used it had to sit in the back of the room, spit into 16-ounce Dixie Cups, and properly dispose of the contents during breaks. Baylor was a private school, heavily subsidized by the Southern Baptist Church, and tuition was the same for both in-state and out-of-state students. At that time the school was named Baylor University College of Medicine, but the connection with the university campus in Waco would end soon and the name became Baylor College of Medicine.

Academics are similar in all medical schools, as the American Association of Medical Colleges (AAMC) dictates the curriculum. For the next two years we would spend most of our time sitting in classrooms, listening to lectures, taking copious notes, and reading textbooks. Physiology was one of our first-year courses with labs. One day the lab involved a classic experiment with an isolated, perfused rabbit heart. This is a difficult experiment to set up. Twenty-one rabbits were sacrificed for the experiment that day and only one was successfully set up—mine. Word spread throughout the research labs and several professors came by to see this. One was Professor Arnold Schwartz, a PhD in pharmacology who was doing work on cardiac drugs. He offered me a summer job setting up rabbit hearts and testing a number of agents on them, so I stayed in Houston that summer working for Dr. Schwartz.

One of my classmates, Burton Silverman, was a graduate of Rice University, which is just across Fannin Boulevard from the Texas Medical Center and Baylor. He had a friend at Rice, Lansing Prescott, who had a younger sister, Deena, who had just completed her first year of college at Lamar Tech in Beaumont, Texas. Burton and Lansing were looking for some classmates to take her out on blind dates. I was the last one they lined her up with. We went out several times and when the school year reconvened we corresponded and talked on the phone and she came home as often as she could on weekends.

David Ball and I shared a one-bedroom apartment with a large living room and a tiny kitchen that proved of little use other than to keep beer cold in the refrigerator. We mostly ate in the hospital dining rooms. The apartment had one air conditioner—in the living room—so it did not take Dave and me long to convert the living room into our bedroom and the bedroom into storage. We lived in that apartment for the next two years. More accurately, Dave lived there. I slept there but spent most weekends with Deena. At the end of the second year I stayed in Houston and did a preceptorship at the VA hospital in the Pathology and Laboratory Services Department along with my roommate, Dave, and another friend, Larry Walker. In gross anatomy our professor made sure all of us observed the black lungs of smokers and the pink lungs of nonsmokers. In pathology we learned about the changes Chronic Obstructive

Pulmonary Disease (COPD) and cancer caused in the lung. Most of the class gave up smoking, including my roommate, Dave. Most of the smokeless tobacco users also abandoned their habit.

America's involvement in Vietnam was increasing. Dean Schofield's prediction that none of us need fear being drafted was beginning to appear shaky. In early August 1964 Deena and I were watching the local TV news with her parents on Houston's CBS affiliate, KHOU-TV. The local anchor, Dan Rather, announced that the first American naval aviator had been shot down during a bombing raid over Haiphong and captured. He was identified as Lt (jg) Everett Alvarez, Jr., from Salinas, California. Everett had been three years ahead of me at Salinas High and had been one of my father's favorite students. Everett endured eight years and seven months of brutal captivity.

At the end of my second year, Deena and I became engaged. She transferred from Lamar Tech to the University of Houston and enrolled in summer school, intent on completing college and getting her teaching certificate as soon as possible. We wouldn't be able to get married until at least one of us was working and generating an income, and she would be the one who could get there first.

The third year, we were out of the classrooms and beginning our clinical rotations. Each rotation was six weeks, and there were eight rotations a year. We did get time off at Christmas and could take a couple of weeks of vacation in addition. There was no summer break; the rotations continued to graduation. Soon after Christmas of my third year I got an official-looking letter from the draft board in Salinas, where I had registered in accordance with the law when I turned 18. The letter informed me that they knew I was 4-F and medically unqualified for the draft. But, it continued, in compliance with the draft law, they had received a letter from Baylor saying that I was expected to graduate in June of 1966. It said there was an exception in the draft law for physicians who were 4-F and upon completing internship I would be reclassified as 1-Y and become draft eligible. I showed this letter to Deena and told her the Navy had a program I was interested in, called the Senior Medical Student Program. If I got it they would make me an Ensign on active duty for my entire fourth year of medical school. I'd get Ensign's pay and they'd pay my tuition and other fees. In return, I would agree to serve on active duty after my internship for three years instead of the two years required under the draft law. We had not yet set a date to get married, but this seemed to be a way we could move ahead.

I applied and soon received a letter from the Navy congratulating me on being accepted to the Senior Medical Student program. We set a marriage date of September 1, 1965. Dean Schofield was not happy with my decision. In June I went on active duty in the Navy as an Ensign. I had an ID card, no uniforms, got my paycheck every two weeks, and the Navy paid my tuition.

Deena and I at our wedding, September 1, 1965.

Deena found an apartment we could afford and I moved into it. Deena and I got married on September 1, 1965.

One morning during my senior year I was on Dr. Michael DeBakey's surgical service preparing for the first case of the day. The operating room nurse supervisor told Dr. DeBakey that the astronaut, Colonel John Glenn, was in the waiting room while his wife was having elective surgery. The nurse said John Glenn would like to meet Dr. DeBakey if he could. Dr. DeBakey broke out of scrub and told the rest of the team to go on in to the OR and get started. He turned to me and asked me to come with him. Dr. DeBakey invited Colonel Glenn to come see the procedure. Glenn accepted, saying he had always wanted to be a doctor, but World War II and the Korean War had gotten in his way. Dr. DeBakey told me to help John Glenn get a scrub suit, wash up, and take him into the OR. After the case was finished John Glenn and I went back to the physicians' dressing room and went to the small cafeteria there and had a cup of coffee. He asked what my plans were and I told him I would be going into the Navy after graduation and internship. We had a nice chat about military service and said good-bye. We would meet again in thirty years.

My final medical school rotation was obstetrics at the Jefferson Davis Hospital. There were about 750 deliveries a month there, all to indigent patients, most of whom had no prenatal care. The obstetrics program was short of residents, because so many had been called to service as the Vietnam conflict escalated. Medical students were thrown into the breech. It was see one, do one, teach one. We worked right up to graduation day and the hospital hired the four of us on the service at the end of the academic year to keep working the night shift until beginning our internships. We were paid $100 a night and I made $1,000. I lost count of the number of deliveries I attended.

When I crossed the stage to get my diploma from Dean Schofield he shook hands with me and said, "Congratulations, Dr. Koenig. We enjoyed having you with us." (Dean Schofield and I would meet one more time, in 1996 at my class's 30th reunion and his class's 50th. Each year Baylor chose two past graduates as Honor Graduates. That year Dean Schofield and I were the two chosen. He did remember me and knew that I was now an Admiral.) I was through medical school and would have an income. I had borrowed no money to pay for my education.

I had been accepted to a straight pediatric internship in the Baylor program. Internship started on July 1, 1966, and ended on June 30, 1967. As the end of my internship approached I learned from the Navy I had been assigned to Sasebo in Southern Japan, about 40 miles north of Nagasaki. My wife could go with me and we'd be there for the three years I owed for the Senior Medical Student program. I called Deena and gave her the news. Her parents weren't happy because we would be gone so far away for so long. I was happy. I would not be going to Vietnam. At the end of the internship year Baylor had a graduation ceremony for all the interns. Awards were given for the outstanding interns in the various specialties. I got the award for pediatrics—a plaque and a check for $100.

2

Back in the Navy

I had one week before I was to report to Corpus Christi Naval Air Station for "orientation." We could bring only clothing and personal items with us to Japan. Deena packed us out while I was in Corpus Christi and moved in with her parents. I flew to Corpus Christi, signed in at the hospital, and quickly realized they had no orientation program for the new medical corps officers planned. They sent me to the pediatric clinic instead.

There was one pediatrician there, Lieutenant Commander Ricci Larese. The other pediatrician had detached and his replacement wouldn't arrive for a month. They gave me an office and I went to work. This was my "orientation" for the first week. On Thursday I asked what I should do on the weekend. Ricci told me to go back to Houston, just be back to start work on Monday. On Monday a Lieutenant junior grade Medical Service Corps officer came to the clinic and said patients were reporting there was a civilian doctor working there. I said that was probably me and showed him my orders. He took me to the Navy Exchange and told me to buy khakis, saying I could get the whites and blues when I arrived in Japan. The LT (jg) took a copy of my orders and got the transportation arrangements made, so that by Friday Deena and I were ticketed on a Military Air Lift Command charter flight from Travis Air Force Base, California, to Yokota, Japan, the first week of August. He told me to arrange my own travel to California and get reimbursed on my travel claim. My plan was to do the three years I owed the Navy in Japan, come back to Houston, where I would do just one more year of pediatric residency, and then go into a growing practice in the affluent River Oaks section of Houston with one of my colleagues from Texas Children's Hospital.

Deena and I left Houston for California after a tearful farewell with her parents then took a bus from the San Francisco airport to Salinas and spent a few days with my mother.

3

Sasebo, Japan

Station Hospital, Sasebo

Station Hospital, Sasebo had 44 authorized operating beds, seven Navy nurses and eight doctors. Half of the doctors were detaching that summer. I was the second new doctor to arrive. The first new one was the Senior Medical Officer, a Captain who had come into the Navy during World War II. He was an orthopedist but was no longer clinically active. He would come to the hospital only about once a week. Most of his time was spent antique shopping.

I soon learned why there had been such a large turnover of personnel at one time. Some of the doctors had run a weight loss program that depended on their dispensing large volumes of amphetamines, powerful appetite suppressants that have a lot of undesirable side effects. Many patients got "hooked," and everyone involved was sent back to the States.

In addition to the Senior Medical Officer we had an internist, a surgeon, an obstetrician, a pediatrician, and three General Medical Officers (GMOs). Because I had a lot of OB experience in medical school I was made the assistant to the obstetrician. Normally that would be the surgeon, but our surgeon had trained in a VA hospital in Harlem. He claimed to have never taken care of a female patient and knew nothing about OB. As a result, the Senior Medical Officer decreed that the obstetrician could not go more than one hour away from Sasebo until he trained me to do cesarean sections, which he promptly did. I performed one with the pediatrician assisting me. I was also the assistant to the pediatrician and assisted the surgeon on all his OR cases because he and the obstetrician did not get along. The other GMOs didn't want to do anything except military sick call, so I did all the other stuff, plus military sick call when I wasn't otherwise occupied. I got a lot of good clinical experience.

The hospital was a four-story building with a single elevator that worked most of the time. It had been a Japanese Imperial Navy Hospital before and during World War II. There were still some Japanese Nationals working at the hospital who had been there during the time it was a Japanese facility. One Japanese National employee was Mr. Kubo-san. He rode his bicycle to work at the hospital for forty years. It didn't matter to him who was running the hospital. He spoke little English but was a superb bacteriologist. One day he called me into his lab and showed me some screw-top culture tubes growing out some sort of bug. He identified the organism as an avian form of tuberculosis that had come from a young Japanese-American boy we had admitted two months earlier with meningitis. He had died in a few days despite our efforts to treat him. He had acquired the organism from a pet bird the family had in the house. Avian forms of tuberculosis are notorious slow growers in culture; it amazed me that he had held on to these cultures so long and made the identification.

I had several other challenging clinical experiences in Sasebo. On two occasions I had to escort seriously burned individuals on medical evacuations to the burn unit at Camp Zama, near Tokyo. The first time was a shipboard accident that occurred a few days before Christmas on the aircraft carrier USS *Ranger* as it pulled in for five days of R&R (Rest and Relaxation) from the waters off North Vietnam. The evacuation required a helicopter ride from Sasebo to Itazuke through a heavy winter storm, then a three-hour flight to Tachikawa in a C-54, an ancient four-engine prop aircraft known as a DC-4 in civilian aviation. We never exceeded 500 feet elevation, flying over the water all the way to keep the plane as warm as possible and the oxygen levels high. My two patients were in critical condition, with more than 50 percent total body burns, and were on IVs and under heavy narcotic sedation to control pain. The final leg of the trip was another helicopter ride at night across Tokyo in the same storm that was hitting southern Japan. Both patients survived. I had a similar experience early in the summer when a schoolteacher tried to ignite a charcoal fire on a hibachi, using duplicating fluid as a fire starter. Duplicating fluid contains a lot of ether and is explosive. She also survived.

I saw hundreds of sailors and Marines with gonorrhea; there were new cases every day in military sick call. Many of these young sailors lost their virginity in Sasebo. They would get "the drip" and show up at their unit sick call. Their unit corpsman would send them to the hospital sick call, where the diagnosis would be confirmed. Our corpsmen were not above having a little fun with some of these young sailors, especially those fresh out of boot camp, often asking the sailor to sign a form letter that would be sent to his mother informing her of his transgression or telling a sailor there was a Navy regulation that three episodes of a sexually transmitted disease (STD) in a single enlistment was grounds for discharge. The latter part about three episodes of STD during an enlistment was true (but not mandatory), but notifying mothers was just hijinks. We never saw syphilis because we would treat the gonorrhea so early with large does of penicillin that it would wipe out the syphilis spirochete before it could become clinically manifest. My sponsor, Bert Gregory, ran the source-tracking part of the STD program. He had a three-ring binder for each bar in Sailor Town with pictures and names (both the Anglo name the girl used and her Japanese name) of all the girls who worked in each bar. Before the sailor left he had to tell us what bar he met the girl in and then identify her picture. It was rare we didn't have a picture of the girl. Bert would call the Japanese Public Health office, which would go get her to culture and treat her. After that she could only serve drinks until she was documented to be culture negative—then she went back to "full duty."

Ed Brown, the pediatrician, and I had a challenging case one evening. A toddler was brought in whose mother said he had just swallowed a metal button. An X-ray confirmed it was lodged in his mid-esophagus. Our surgeon had no idea what to do. There were no Japanese physicians in the area with pediatric endoscopy experience. We sedated the child, slid a #12 Foley urinary balloon catheter into his esophagus to a distance we calculated to be below the button, injected 4 ccs of radio-opaque dye into the catheter and did a repeat X-ray to make sure the balloon was below the button. We gently pulled the catheter out and there was the button! We kept the child in the hospital overnight to make sure he was in no distress, and after he ate a full breakfast the next morning we sent him home.

In another case, the eight-year-old daughter of our obstetrician fell out of a tree and broke a femur, the biggest bone in the body, the one in the upper leg. I got X-rays confirming the fracture. It was not compound (breaking through the skin) but was displaced (the fractured ends had separated and overlapped). This was the one time I convinced the Senior Medical Officer to look at an X-ray and provide advice. I put her in a bed in skin traction, gave her a lot of painkillers and muscle relaxants and in a couple of days the two bone fragments realigned. I put her in a long leg cast, and six weeks later she was as good as new.

In October 1967 I was asked to temporarily relieve the medical officer on the USS *Epping Forrest*, MCS-7, because his wife was going to have a baby during the ship's scheduled deployment. The *Epping Forest* was a converted World War II Dock Landing Ship that had originally been commissioned on October 11, 1943. It had a large well deck that carried 10 LCMs (Landing Craft Mechanized), small boats used for in-shore minesweeping. On October 26 we got underway for Yokosuka, Japan. The ship had just come out of dry-dock after a million-dollar overhaul. A typhoon had stalled over Okinawa, but since we would be headed north the Captain was not worried about it. The next day the winds climbed to 80–90 mph and there were 30–40-foot waves. Over the next several hours the LCMs broke loose from their mooring chains and by early evening all were lost. General Quarters was sounded and the ship's deck log reported: "Ship is considered to be in Grave Danger." When the seas started to calm the ship headed into Japan's Bungo Suido Channel, where divers inspected the hull and saw that it was still intact. The well deck was pumped dry and the *Epping Forest* returned to Sasebo, arriving at 0900 on Monday October 30. Decommissioned a year later, the *Epping Forest* was sold for scrap. While underway during the worst of the storm many of the sailors became seasick. I got a couple of Corpsmen, all the needles, syringes, and Compazine (an injectable medication for severe motion sickness) I could find and we went around the ship injecting those suffering from mal de mer (seasickness).

Early in the evening a sailor was brought to sickbay with a traumatic amputation of the last digit of one of his fingers, the result of a hatch slamming shut on it. I got out a suture kit, strapped him to the operating table, and cleaned up and sutured the stump. It did just fine and I removed the sutures two weeks later. The last evening at sea another sailor came to sickbay complaining of severe right lower quadrant abdominal pain. I examined him and suspected appendicitis, so I started an IV and pumped him full of antibiotics. When we came into the pier the next morning we took him off in a Stokes stretcher and transported him straight to the hospital, where the surgeon told me I could do the case. I opened the sailor up (with the surgeon as my assistant) and there it was, a red-hot appendix. That was the first "sea-duty" of my naval career, and it lasted about 100 hours.

In January 1968 the USS *Enterprise*, CVN-65, the first nuclear powered aircraft carrier, made a five-day R&R visit to Sasebo. This was the first visit of a nuclear powered surface ship to nuclear-phobic Japan. Demonstrations against it were planned and the police were ready. So were the college students, who were each given one thousand Yen and a bottle of sake by the local Communists and told where and when to demonstrate. The police knew where to be and showed up with their shields, helmets, face screens, Billy clubs, and water cannons. These confrontations were pretty one-sided but they made for good theater. The Japanese TV companies covered the activity from dawn to dusk, and a lot of their footage made it to the U.S., where Walter Cronkite and his colleagues retold the story. I was assigned to spend much of that time at the Marine barracks with a couple of Corpsman manning a clinic there should our services be needed. I remember waking up in the middle of the night and hearing my brass door handle jiggle. I got up and opened the door. There sitting on the floor was an enlisted Marine with a rag and a can of Brasso, polishing my door handle.

The *Enterprise* finished its R&R and departed. The following day another ship whose presence had gone unnoticed during the *Enterprise* visit got underway from Sasebo. It was the USS *Pueblo*, AGER-2, a *Banner*-class environmental research ship that was attached to U.S. Navy intelligence and served in a spying capacity. On January 28, 1968, it was attacked and captured by North Korean forces. One of its 83 crew members was killed in the attack. The *Pueblo*'s Corpsman's wife was Japanese and she and her son lived in Sasebo. I took care of both of them during the Corpsman's time in captivity. In the end, all 82 of the surviving members of the *Pueblo* crew were lined up and marched one by one across the "Bridge of No Return" at the Joint Security Zone of the DMZ (Demilitarized Zone) on January 23, 1969.

About halfway into my second year in Sasebo a message was sent to all Navy Medical Facilities asking that any medical officer interested in doing a residency in the Navy respond. I had already decided pediatrics was what I was going to do, so the pediatrician, Ed Brown, who had trained at Bethesda, encouraged me to apply. He said there was no real reason for me to stay in Sasebo doing GMO work for another year and that I ought to get on with my training. I responded that I would like to be considered for either one of these programs and listed San Diego as my first choice. The next day I had a response back from Washington that I was accepted for the San Diego program and should report there in July. That meant that my total tour in Japan would be cut from 36 to 22 months. It also meant I probably would be staying in the Navy for a lot longer than I originally anticipated.

Life in Japan, 1967–1969

Early in the spring we learned Deena was pregnant, and near the end of June my mother came to spend part of her summer break with us. Deena and I traveled by train to Tokyo to meet her flight and spent a few days seeing the sights there then traveled on the bullet train to Kyoto, the ancient capital of Japan. In Kyoto we stayed at a Japanese Riokan recommended by our MWR office called Inn Rakutosu, or to Americans "Three Sisters Inn." The three sisters all spoke English. Besides being wonderful hostesses they helped us get around the city to see the sights on pubic transportation.

Following Kyoto it was back to Sasebo for the summer. My mother didn't think she would be able to stay long enough to see the new baby, but it turns out the obstetrician was off by a month in his calculation of Deena's expected due date. Early in the morning hours of August 15 Deena began to have contractions. I thought these were just false labor, but she insisted they were more than that. She couldn't sleep, which meant I couldn't either. I turned on the light and started reading another chapter in James Michener's *Tales of the South Pacific*. The "false labor" contractions became more regular and suddenly the bed was wet. Deena's water had broken. I called the obstetrician and told him I was going to bring her in. In the hospital a nurse checked her and said she was crowning. The obstetrician was already in the delivery room getting ready to deliver another woman when the nurse informed him Deena was about to deliver in bed. He had her rushed into our second delivery room and told me to go in and deliver the other woman's baby, which I did. When I finished, I was a father. Steven Fillmore Koenig had arrived in the adjacent room weighing in at a healthy 8.5 lbs. He had picked an auspicious day to be born; in Japan it was Oban, an annual Japanese Buddhist event for commemorating one's ancestors. My mother got to be there for the birth of her second grandchild and her first grandson. Three days later I put her on a flight back to Salinas.

4

San Diego

Pediatric Residency: First Year, 1969–1970

The American Board of Pediatrics had recently placed the residency program in San Diego on probation. The program director had to fix the problems of the program during the following year or it would lose its accreditation. Those who had begun training would be allowed to continue and become board eligible, but new accessions would not be allowed.

The Navy transferred Commander Jack Schanberger from Philadelphia to San Diego to become the departmental chairman and residency program director. He had been in the same position at Philadelphia Naval Hospital. New staff were brought in: two Berry planners, Jerry Kaplan and Jack Resnick, both of whom had superb recommendations as teachers. Jerry had come from Los Angeles Children's and Jack from the University of Minnesota. Ray Skoglund was brought in from Navy Hospital Oakland, where he had trained in pediatrics. Doug Cunningham, who had just completed his residency in San Diego, was kept on as staff. John Mace, who had completed training in 1968 in San Diego, was the one staff holdovers. There was a pediatric allergist and a pediatric cardiologist, but they stayed in their respective specialty clinics. Overall this was a pretty small group—six residents, a chief resident, and six staff general pediatricians.

Jack Schanberger tied the Navy program to the University of California San Diego (UCSD) program, which was just getting started. UCSD had recruited a world-renowned pediatrician, Bill Nyhan, from the University of Miami to be its pediatric department chairman. He brought some superb teaching staff, principal among them Lou Gluck in neonatology and Faith Kung in hematology-oncology. There were a number of outstanding Navy Reserve pediatricians who came to San Diego to do their two weeks' active duty each year. Soon Jack Schanberger and Bill Nyhan had developed two strong pediatric residencies that had no problem getting full accreditation.

Pediatric residencies are all similar. The first-year residents rotate through the inpatient services, nursery, and clinics. There is no time for electives. We held teaching conferences every weekday from 0700–0800; the rest of the day was clinical work. Saturday mornings we had an outstanding joint conference at UC San Diego led by Bill Nyhan.

Night and weekend duty was every fourth night for the three first-year residents, the fourth night taken by a second-year resident. When on duty (in the Navy we call it having the watch) we were busy. We'd cover the nursery and ward and answer consults from the emergency room when there was a patient they needed help with. Our pediatric staff worked in an evening clinic that ran until 10:00 p.m., and we usually would get a couple of admissions every night. The nursery was always a challenge. We had a small unit we called the premie nursery where we put the premature babies and the full-term babies in distress; there were no Neonatal Intensive Care Nurseries (known now as NICUs). This was no different from what I had experienced at Jefferson Davis Hospital in Houston three years earlier. There really wasn't much we could do for these babies except put them in an Isolette incubator, keep them warm, give them IV fluids, raise the oxygen level in the incubator, and hope for the best. This is where over the course of the next few years Lou Gluck, a pioneer in establishing NICUs, made a huge difference.

Routine deliveries occurred in a part of the hospital near the pediatrics ward and clinics. C-sections were deliveries done some distance away in one of the main operating rooms in the second basement of building 26. We'd go to the OR carrying an aluminum box that looked like an over-sized lunch pail. It had sliding windows on each side and a port that could be hooked up to an oxygen source should the baby be in distress. A hot-water bottle warmed it. Once the baby was delivered and stable we'd carry it up a flight of stairs to the emergency room, where there was supposed to be an ambulance waiting to take us through the compound to the nursery. The ambulance was not always there. It took me only a couple of experiences waiting for the ambulance to realize I could do this a lot faster on foot than by ambulance. I'd run up the stairs carrying the baby in the box and go across the compound to the nursery. I could do this in a little over a minute, far less than it took the ambulance. I never had a problem with a baby while I was doing this and I did it dozens of times. Soon everyone did it this way.

The ward could hold 21 patients and we always stayed close to full. We could handle routine problems requiring hospitalization, but there was no intensive care capability. There was an internal medicine ICU relatively close by and we began to poach beds in it for children who needed continuous monitoring. This wasn't accepted well by some of the internists or nursing staff, but we wouldn't take no for an answer. One day I ran from the clinic carrying a young boy who had profound slowing of his heart, who was cyanotic (blue) and near death. I had done an EKG that showed he had a condition known as Wolf-Parkinson-White Syndrome, which periodically causes a profound slowing of the heart. I carried him into the adult ICU. Doug Cunningham, a staff pediatrician, joined me and we pulled the child through. Afterward Doug said to me, "Someday we are going to have ICUs just for kids."

The staff had a couple of half-days a week when they could see patients by appointment in follow-up. This is where they'd see the kids with chronic problems like diabetes, cystic fibrosis, kidney diseases, neurologic conditions, cancer, leukemia, and so on. As residents, when we were on a clinic rotation we'd go to the staff doctor's office to see these interesting cases and learn about the conditions.

We did not have to do all the lab tests ourselves as we did in medical school, but we still plated throat cultures on blood and chocolate agar, put them in a candle jar, and read the cultures daily looking for Strep. We did most of our own dipstick and microscopic urinalysis and finger stick hematocrits to check for anemia. We did all the EKGs, a single lead at a time, unheard of today. After-hours we would often have to hold babies for X-rays and do the initial readings on the films.

About halfway through my first year Jack Schanberger told me the American Board of Pediatrics was offering the written portion of the boards in a couple of months and he wanted me to take them. Normally we weren't allowed to take them until late in our second year. Jack reminded me I had a straight pediatric internship and two years as a GMO and the board allowed someone with that amount of experience to cut a year off their residency. I passed. The American Board of Pediatrics required two years between taking the written and oral boards, which meant I could take the second portion of the boards in 1972. I did, and again I passed.

During this year I was promoted to Lieutenant Commander (LCDR). I found out because a list had been posted on a bulletin board of all the Lieutenants who had been selected for promotion. It was annotated with a note from the CO's office that said we all could start wearing our new rank immediately. I told Deena and she asked when we would get the pay increase.

Pediatric Residency: Second Year, 1970–1971

I was assigned to the nursery and we took delivery of a new type of ventilator—called the "Bournes Ventilator" for the company that made it—designed especially for newborns with Infant Respiratory Distress Syndrome, which was the leading cause of death in premature infants and infants of diabetic mothers. What was special about this ventilator was that it was a volume ventilator, not a pressure ventilator. We could set it to deliver a precise volume of air enriched with a specific amount of oxygen to an infant's lungs rather than blow air in until it reached a certain pressure. Doing the latter quickly destroyed the alveoli, the tiny air sacs of the lungs, and the infant would die. To that point all ventilators were pressure ventilators, made only for adults. Though we had tried to use them on infants, they had never worked. We were told—and I have no reason not to believe this—no baby who had ever been placed on a pressure ventilator survived.

September 1 was our fifth wedding anniversary and Deena and I wanted to celebrate. We hired a babysitter for Steve, now 2, and went to George's at the Cove in La Jolla. We got through dinner okay, but as we were ordering dessert the maître' d came to me and said there was a call and it was urgent. I thought something might have happened to Steve, so using the restaurant phone (there were no mobile phones then) I called home. The babysitter told me Dr. Doug Cunningham had called and needed to talk with me right away. A baby had been born at the Navy Hospital with severe respiratory distress; it was a good-sized baby, probably an infant of a diabetic mother. They needed me to come in and put the baby on the new Bournes ventilator.

No dessert.

I dropped Deena at home and took the babysitter to her house on the way to the hospital. I got the baby on the ventilator and he began to stabilize. Doug called Lou Gluck, the neonatologist at UCSD who didn't have one of these ventilators at UCSD yet but wanted to be part of the action. The three of us sat through the night with the baby. It took a couple of days for the baby's lungs to stabilize, but we were able to get him off the ventilator and subsequently send him home. He was the first baby born in San Diego ever to go on a ventilator and survive. There have been thousands since.

That should be the end of the story, but it is not. These ventilators required special handling for cleaning and sterilization. After being wiped down in the nursery they had to be gas sterilized in the hospital's central sterilization unit. In the nursery the charge nurse dutifully wrapped this particular ventilator in sterilization sheets, but instead of following the written instructions on the machine to mark it for gas sterilization only she used the standard markings. The steam sterilization destroyed the machine, which came back a melted blob. Somehow Jack Schanberger got the Bournes Company to replace it.

In November I was off to Los Angeles County for two months. I was on call there every sixth night but had backup every third night. The clinical experience there was incredible. Throughout LA, cases of suspected meningitis were sent to the county hospital. We'd get three to six new cases a day and I got really good at doing spinal taps. The nurses always had the first dose of antibiotics prepared to push in the IV the moment we finished the spinal tap. We saved a lot of lives. We also saw a lot of other infectious diseases including diphtheria, tetanus, typhoid, whooping cough, and even some polio cases. We saw some really severe cases of chickenpox that had been sent to us to rule out smallpox. I cared for some polio patients who went on iron lungs, a holdover technology from the pre-polio vaccine days. One night I admitted several kids with whooping cough. On rounds I asked Dr. Werle why they weren't immunized, and I never forgot his response. Their parents had brought these kids here illegally. Though there were neighborhood clinics nearby and the immunizations were free, the parents wouldn't bring their kids in for fear of being deported.

Our second son, Scott, was born on September 11, 1971, nine months after my rotation in LA ended. Back in San Diego Jack Schanberger told me he didn't think I needed to spend any more time on the wards, nursery, or clinics, but he would appreciate my doing four things:

1. Continue to stand the watch (on-board night duty) until July 1, 1971, but always with an intern or first-year resident to supervise and teach.

2. Take over the care of children with hematologic disorders and cancer. He said the American Board of Pediatrics was going to require that all program accreditation reviews beginning the next year had to have a single person overseeing the care of children with these problems. He felt I had the aptitude for that.

3. Agree to stay here for at least another year, until July 1972, doing the hematology-oncology care while they searched for someone with training in that subspecialty.

4. Do this in the role of Chief Resident, so that I would not have to bother with on-board watch as other residents did or the staff watch in the evening clinic that ran until 10:00 p.m. during that year.

What a deal! No watch for a year and all I had to do was take care of the kids with blood disorders, cancer, and leukemia.

Hematology-Oncology Training: First Year, 1971–1972

About 80–90 percent of childhood leukemia was Acute Lymphocytic Leukemia (ALL). Life expectancy was about two years, the same as it had been when I finished my internship five years earlier in Houston. Children were treated with a single drug to get them into remission (free of disease) and then that drug was continued until they relapsed then the process was repeated with the next drug. This treatment approach was called sequential single-agent therapy. A new approach was being tested that used more than one drug at a time to induce remission, and then once that was achieved several agents that had efficacy were used together for maintenance of remission. Periodically (quarterly or semiannually) another round of induction therapy was sometimes given, then it was back to the maintenance regimen.

Faith Kung, who came to San Diego along with Bill Nyhan, was the pediatric heme-onc doc at UCSD. She took me under her wing, and I attended the clinics she ran at UCSD and San Diego Children's Hospital. She had all the patients on multi-agent protocols with a national study group. She encouraged me to get all the Navy patients on these protocols, and I did. Children started surviving two years and beyond—a scary point for parents, because they all had been told initially that this was as long as could be hoped for. We lost some along the way, but more started making it past two, then three, and then four years. When they began reaching four years disease free we started asking when should we stop, and if so, should it be cold turkey or a gradual decrease? The lead investigators discussed this and decided to randomize discontinuing or continuing treatment by alternating that decision at the study group headquarters. Those who randomized to remain on treatment would do so for one more year and then stop. I watched all my patients very carefully, checking their blood counts every month and their bone marrows quarterly. None of them relapsed when treatment stopped. Kenneth was one of the first children I stopped treatment on after four years. He was only one year old when he presented. In 2014 I reconnected with Kenneth's parents and learned he is now an attorney in San Diego and is married and has five daughters.

About 10–20 percent of childhood leukemia is not ALL. Some children have AML, Acute Myelocytic Leukemia, which is much more common in adults. Bobby came to us as a four-year-old with this disease. The condition was so rare in children there were no pediatric treatment protocols then. Faith Kung called the study group headquarters and they suggested we enroll Bobby on the adult protocol they had for AML. Bobby stayed in the hospital for two months, suffering through induction therapy and its ravages. He intermittently was on and off huge doses of antibiotics. Finally his blood counts began to rise, his infections cleared, and we were able to send him home. We treated him with a maintenance protocol for five years, then called the study group headquarters and talked with the director of the protocol Bobby was on. He said more than 400 people had been enrolled on that study and Bobby was the only one who survived. We stopped treatment. We pulled all the original slides from when the diagnosis was made and had several experts review them. Everyone agreed; he indeed had AML. When Bobby got married I attended his wedding. Later he had three children, went to college, and obtained a degree in electrical engineering. He never relapsed.

In January Jack Schanberger approached me with a new plan sweetened by another "opportunity." The new plan was to have me stay two years; the Navy had approved the Internal Medicine Department to have a hematology-oncology fellowship. They'd put me in that for a year, then I'd have two years of training. The year after that the American Board of Pediatrics was going to offer an examination in pediatric hematology-oncology for the first time, and those who passed would have board certification in this subspecialty. He wanted me to take that exam.

The Navy was now sending one senior resident from each training hospital on TAD (Temporary Additional Duty) for six weeks to a prominent civilian medical institution. The Navy would pay all fees, travel, and per diem for the period. Jack thought it would be a good opportunity for me to spend six weeks with a well-known pediatric hematologist-oncologist. He contacted Howard Pearson, department chairman at Yale and another well-known pediatric hematologist-oncologist, who had trained with Dr. Diamond at Harvard and had done his pediatric residency in the Navy at Bethesda. Dr. Pearson said he would be glad to have me, so arrangements were made for me to go there during July and August, when most of the undergraduate students were on vacation. I began my second year in heme-onc at Yale.

Six Weeks at Yale: Summer 1972

When I got to New Haven Dr. Pearson had arranged a room for me in one of the dormitories adjacent to the hospital. The dorm was virtually vacant given the time of year, so I took most of my meals in the hospital cafeteria. Weekends I was free to explore New England. On two weekends I visited Mike and Debbie Bohan; Mike was the internist in Sasebo while we were there. He was now Assistant Chief of Medicine at Chelsea Navy hospital just outside Boston. While visiting them one weekend the three of us made a day trip to New Hampshire to visit our now retired Senior Medical Officer from Sasebo, who during his four years in Japan had spent his time antique hunting, not practicing medicine. We discovered he had a large house with a basement full of Japanese "antiques" he could not sell.

I'd make inpatient rounds with Dr. Pearson each day and on clinic days see patients with him. Many of the conditions I saw at Yale are not common—so unusual in fact that even most pediatricians today have little understanding of them. There were a lot of children of African ancestry with sickle cell disease and other inherited hemoglobin disorders. There were also a large number of children with another group of disorders known as the thalassemias that were common in people of Mediterranean origin. Some of the children with this were permanently blood-transfusion dependent and so had complications from that. There were children with red cell enzyme defects and some with red cell membrane defects. All of these conditions had some effect on their health and well-being, some chronically and others just intermittently. Most community hospital labs did not have the capability to test for these conditions. Dr. Pearson had set up his own lab at Yale, where he could sort them out. That is where I spent the majority of my time. I'd stay there late at night learning how to run all of these tests. In six weeks I mastered this and was prepared to go back to San Diego and do just what Dr. Pearson had done, set up my own lab.

Dr. Pearson also took care of every boy in Connecticut with hemophilia and other blood coagulation disorders. Hemophilia is a genetic disorder that affects only boys. It is a lifelong disorder, quite painful and disfiguring. There were a few boys with it I knew of in San Diego who had been cared for by general pediatricians. They were treated only when they had a hemorrhagic event. Dr. Pearson taught me to put these boys on prophylactic home therapy so they did not have to come to the hospital for care.

There was another fairly common blood disorder that fortunately ran a short course of a few weeks to a few months called ITP, Idiopathic Thrombocytopenic Purpura. It can be quite worrisome because in its clinical presentation it can look a lot like leukemia. I learned how to quickly differentiate these disorders and then manage affected children in a much more humane fashion than was the common practice in most of the land, which was to put them in the hospital confined to bed until their blood platelet count returned to normal.

Dr. Pearson took a technician from his lab with him to clinic. The tech would do the tests right in the clinic while the patient was there. Chief among these was to make peripheral blood and bone marrow slides, fix them in alcohol, stain them, and then look at them on the spot. It would take our hospital lab in San Diego days to get this done and the report sent back to the doctor. I learned the value of looking at blood and all bone marrow specimens myself and not relying on someone else's written report. I subsequently was able to teach a lot of pathologists things they didn't know about blood disorders.

Dr. Pearson knew a lot of pediatricians from the nation's medical schools and introduced me to many of them. I went with him to a meeting of the Society for Pediatric Research in Washington, D.C., for three days, and he introduced me to many of these colleagues. Among them was Dr. Louis K. Diamond, who had trained Howard Pearson.

The six weeks I spent with Dr. Pearson were the most productive clinical learning experience of my entire medical career. When my six weeks ended, Deena flew in with the boys and we started our trek west. We were able to visit three families we had been stationed with in Sasebo—Mike and Debby Bohan in Boston, Bill and Gerri Labunetz in Philadelphia, and Ed and Nancy

Brown in Cleveland. We stopped in South Dakota and saw Deena's brother, his wife Linda and their two sons. We went through Yellowstone and saw the geysers and bears, then turned south to Provo, Utah, and visited the Nelsons, my landlords from my years at BYU.

Hematology-Oncology Fellowship: Second Year, 1972–1973

I resumed seeing oncology patients and started recruiting lab techs from the hospital's Clinical Investigation Center (CIC) to work with me in the clinic staining peripheral blood and bone marrow slides so I could examine them there. The parents of the patients liked this because they didn't have to wait days for the results. I asked Jack Schanberger to get a dual microscope for our clinic so two people could look at slides at the same time and I could teach them what they were looking at. This proved useful in teaching others how to examine peripheral blood smears. This had become a lost art with increasing lab automation. It is amazing how much can be learned from examining a peripheral blood smear, saving both time and money. Many of our residents and interns were going to be assigned, at least for a while, to remote places, as I had been in Sasebo. They wouldn't have all the fancy lab equipment and the staff to operate it like we had in San Diego.

The number of our clinic patients rapidly increased. Families with children with cancer were being transferred to San Diego because of our capability to care for them. We started finding many children with hematologic disorders, like abnormal hemoglobins such as sickle trait, enzyme and membrane defects, and hemophilia. I started to find many Filipino children who were being treated with oral iron for anemia and they were not responding. I looked at their peripheral blood smears, and the smears looked a lot more like those of the Greek and Italian kids I had seen in Dr. Pearson's clinic with the milder forms of beta-thalassemia trait. I pursued this and showed that these kids had a condition called alpha-thalassemia trait, a condition similar but not identical to what the Greek and Italian kids had and also relatively benign. It required no treatment. I got hundreds of children off of unnecessary oral iron therapy.

I set up several lab tests in the clinical investigation lab that I had learned to do at Yale, including some enzyme tests, membrane tests, and tests to determine what sort of an abnormal hemoglobin a patient had. This caused some friction with the hospital's main lab initially, but after some discussion we came to agreement and on I went. Soon I was doing tests for the adult heme-onc doctors as well.

During this year that I was a fellow in the internal medicine heme-onc program there was also one internist in the program, in his first year. I had been transferred on paper to the Internal Medicine Department, so I was asked to attend their heme-onc clinic once a week. I got to see some conditions that are rare in children. There was a Berry Plan internist, Sam Armstrong, with us who had spent a year in heme-onc training at the University of Washington. He was very sharp, and the three of us got along quite well together. There was also a senior officer who reminded me of my senior medical officer in Japan. He was so worthless we were glad he was more interested in talking on the phone with his buddies than seeing patients. We didn't want him messing the patients up.

I had another interest. Several months before I went to Yale there had been a Filipino baby stillborn at the Navy hospital with what looked like hydrops fetalis. This is what babies with severe Rh incompatibility with their mothers die of. This was this mother's first pregnancy and her baby did not have an Rh incompatibility with her. I had managed to get a tube of his blood from the placenta and stored it in a refrigerator. While at Yale I mentioned this case to Dr. Pearson. He said it might be a case of a very rare condition he had never seen, a severe form of alpha-thalassemia that is lethal in utero called Bart's Hydrops Fetalis. It was characterized by very rapid migrating hemoglobin on electrophoresis called Hemoglobin H. When I returned to San Diego I did the electrophoresis on it, and it was pure Hemoglobin H.

Dr. Pearson told me there was a Hong Kong–born Chinese hematologist at the University of California, San Francisco, who was familiar with these disorders, Yuet Wai Kan. I called him and told him about the case. The first thing he told me was to call him just Y.W., as it was easier. So from then on he was Y.W. to me. He asked if I could reach the mother and get a sample of blood from her and her husband. I tracked her down and they agreed to give me a sample for analysis. She also told me she thought she was pregnant again and wanted to know the chances of having the same result as with the first pregnancy. I told her I thought the chances were probably 1 in 4. I also told her I thought Y.W. could help us determine early on in the pregnancy if the baby would be affected or not. I asked if they would like to pursue that and they said yes. I called Y.W. with the news and we made arrangements for me to draw blood, take it to the San Diego airport and express-ship it to Y.W., who picked up the fresh sample at the San Francisco airport himself and did the tests. Those tests confirmed that the chances of another stillborn baby were about 1 in 4. To determine if the fetus was affected we would have to get a sample of fetal amniotic fluid cells. To achieve this I sent the parents to San Francisco.

On completion the study predicted that the fetus would survive and that it was a girl. She would have a mild form of the disorder, which would manifest as a moderate anemia that could be mistaken for iron deficiency. When the baby was born, I was present at the delivery. I got another blood sample from the placenta and sent it to Y.W. The placental blood sample showed he had been spot-on in his prediction from the amniotic fluid cells. The baby girl grew up just fine, and for several years I followed her and another sibling born a few years later. As far as we know this was the first time a hemoglobin disorder had been diagnosed in utero. We published a paper on the case and Y.W. and I collaborated on many more research efforts over the next several years. He became very well known internationally in hematology and served a term as president of the American Society of Hematology.

My interest in abnormal hemoglobins led me to seek out a research expert at UCSD, Dr. Harvey Itano. I spent time working in his lab and learned more about the interface of hematology with biochemistry. Dr. Itano had an MD degree but had never practiced; instead, he pursued a PhD in biochemistry at Cal Tech under Dr. Linus Pauling, the only two-time winner of an unshared Nobel Prize and only one of four people ever to win two Nobel prizes. Dr. Itano had a postdoctoral fellow, Tom Vedvick, whom I became close friends with. Tom and I produced several research papers during my remaining years in San Diego.

As this second and final year of my heme-onc training was concluding Jack Schanberger approached me with two more requests and a question. The first request was that he wanted me to take the American Board of Pediatrics Hematology-Oncology subspecialty boards, which were going to be given for the first time in the fall of 1974. I thought I was through with board exams, but Jack said this was really important. I started studying very hard about 18 months in advance.

His second request was that I take Al Lightsey, a pediatric resident, as a fellow in pediatric heme-onc starting the summer of 1973. That meant I would go from being a student to a teacher overnight. Al had been a brilliant pediatric resident, and his superb performance continued as he progressed through heme-onc training.

Deena and I completed our move to 5555 Calle Miramar and again became house-poor. The house came with no landscaping, but the community covenants required that new occupants have an approved landscape plan and have it underway within six months. Thus, I went back to the lessons I had learned from my father at 28 Cedros and St. Paul's Episcopal Church in Salinas.

FEP is an acronym for free-erythrocyte protoporphyrin. I won't go into the biochemistry here, just trust me, measuring FEP is a good test for differentiating iron-deficiency and lead poisoning from the benign condition alpha-thalassemia trait. During the 1960s some very significant advances were made in devices that automated blood counts. From a small sample of blood it became possible to count the number of red and white blood cells in a blood specimen, as well as very accurately measure the size of the red blood cells (RBCs) and their hemoglobin content. Before then, the best we could do was run separate tests for the amount of hemoglobin in blood and measure the percentage of red cells in a sample of whole blood, called the hematocrit, by spinning a sample of the blood in a high-speed centrifuge. These were time-consuming tests and not as accurate as the new automated machines. Normal values for blood's hemoglobin content and hematocrit had long been known, but the size of RBCs was something skilled observers guessed at by looking at blood under a microscope. The new devices were very accurate at measuring the size of RBCs. Normal values for all these parameters were now well established and were printed on the laboratory report chit that would be returned to the doctor who ordered the test and the patient's medical record.

Our pediatricians at the Navy hospital were finding many children with RBCs that were smaller than normal and had slightly low total red blood cell counts, hemoglobin levels, and hematocrits. One reason for small RBCs was iron deficiency anemia. A lot of kids were thus placed on supplemental iron, but many did not improve. Of course, parental noncompliance was often suspected, but mothers insisted the children were getting their Fer-in Sol drops (oral liquid iron—children hate the taste of it) just as the doctor ordered.

I started looking at these children and realized a lot of them were Filipino. I also remembered Dr. Pearson telling me that in New Haven whenever he saw a child with anemia and small RBCs, he'd check for lead poisoning. He certainly had good reason to do this, because many houses in New England were quite old and had been painted many times with lead-based paint, which would crack and peal and kids would chew on it. He told me that a colleague, Dr. Sergio Piomelli, in New York City had developed a simple test for screening for lead poisoning that was a lot simpler than doing blood lead levels. I contacted Dr. Piomelli, and he told me how to set up a pretty simple test called the FEP.

One of our lab techs in the Clinical Investigation Center set up the test, and every day would go to the lab, get the leftover samples of blood from tests done on kids with small RBCs, and do FEP tests on them. We found a lot of children with small RBCs but normal FEPs. Most of these were Filipinos. We also found some with small RBCs and moderately elevated FEPs, but not nearly as high as Dr. Piomelli was seeing in children with lead poisoning. We did tests for blood iron levels on them to determine if they were iron deficient. We also sent blood from them out for lead levels but found none with elevated levels. Now I knew we had two groups with small RBCs: those who were iron deficient and needed treatment, and those who had something else. I tested this latter group for what Dr. Pearson saw a lot of in New Haven, beta-thalassemia trait, which is also a cause of small RBCs. None had beta-thalassemia trait. I was convinced that these kids had the less well-known and generally benign form of thalassemia called alpha thalassemia trait. We proceeded with some special tests for that and proved that indeed was the case. There was no treatment needed for this. Mystery solved.

Tom Vedvick and I published an article in the *Journal of Pediatrics* in which we showed that 5 percent of American-born Filipino children had alpha thalassemia trait. In fact, we were able to show that almost all of the Filipino children with mild anemia and small RBCs had alpha thalassemia trait. We published a subsequent paper in the *Journal of Pediatrics* that showed a quick and easy way to differentiate children with alpha thalassemia trait from kids with iron deficiency was by measuring FEP. If the FEP was elevated, they needed iron; if it was normal, their mothers were instructed to not let any other doctor put them on iron. Over the next seven years I published five more articles about FEP and anemia in the peer-reviewed medical literature and gave many talks to physician groups about being sure that any child they put on iron supplements really needed it and that they weren't dealing with a benign genetic condition, alpha-thalassemia trait. As I have mentioned before, oral iron is no fun to take.

In the fall of 1974 it was time for the American Board of Pediatrics' first-ever examination for board certification in hematology-oncology. It was given in three localities. The one closest to me was at the University of California, San Francisco. I had been studying hard for this, and Jack Schanberger said I was ready. We left Steven and Scott with Grant's godmother, our neighbor, Virginia Gistaro. My mother drove up from Salinas the day of the boards, which I took along with about a hundred other people. We had four hours to complete it. After two-and-a-half hours I was done. No one had left, so I went through it again checking my answers. Finding nothing to change I was the first to turn in my test to the proctor.

That evening my mother joined Deena and me for dinner in downtown San Francisco. I wanted to have a drink to celebrate that this ordeal was over. Deena told me she didn't want a drink. She said the smell of alcohol made her sick to her stomach, but she had not mentioned it before then. She said she knew then she was pregnant. One thing I learned as a physician is that the best way to know if a woman who has been pregnant once is pregnant again is to ask her—she knows. My mother and I were thrilled. A week later I got a letter from the American Board of Pediatrics saying 450 people had taken the exam and less than 300 had passed. I was one of those who passed. Grant was born on May 29, 1975.

I had been asked to do a presentation at a small invitation-only meeting in Finland on my work on FEP and how it was useful in differentiating alpha-thalassemia trait and iron deficiency. The Navy Medicine policy at that time was not to fund travel to international meetings, but the hospital's Commanding Officer (CO), Rear Admiral Will Arentzen, made an exception for me. This was the first time I had ever traveled to Europe; my only other international travels were while we were stationed in Japan and trips to Tijuana and Canada. I wanted Deena to go along.

Grant was only four weeks old when we took all three of our sons to Spokane, Washington, to stay with my sister and her family. We went to Finland, and I gave my presentation. We then visited Sweden, where I gave pediatric grand rounds on FEP and childhood anemia at the University of Uppsala, the second oldest medical school in Europe. We visited Bergen and Oslo, Norway, then flew back from Copenhagen to Spokane to pick up our sons. When we got there Grant was six weeks old and had doubled his birth weight. He was as plump as a Thanksgiving turkey. All the neighbor women had wanted a chance to feed him, and he really got his fill.

Dr. Louis K. Diamond

I found a few young children with profound anemia that was not due to disordered hemoglobin synthesis, RBC membrane or enzyme defects, or the even more rare situation where an antibody had developed and was destroying RBCs. One of these conditions always presented in the first year of life and was permanent; the other usually presented a little later in childhood and would resolve spontaneously in a few weeks or months. This latter condition is known as Transient Erythroblastopenia of Childhood (TEC).

In 1938 Drs. Diamond and Blackfan described the condition that presented in the first year of life and was permanent, calling it "congenital hypoplastic anemia." Now it is known as Diamond-Blackfan Anemia, or DBA for short. Only about 25 to 35 new cases are diagnosed in the U.S. each year. These children all present during the first few months of life. The few RBCs their marrow does produce tend to be larger than normal and contain more of the fetal form of hemoglobin (Hgb F) than normal. Recently, a number of gene mutations have been described in children with this condition. About 45 percent of the new cases have an affected parent, and the rest appear to be a spontaneous mutation. Affected individuals have a much higher chance of developing certain cancers of blood and bone-forming tissues. Initial treatment consists of oral corticosteroids in high doses. About 80 percent of children will respond to steroids, then the dose can be tapered, sometimes to a very low dose, even every other day, but it can't be completely discontinued. For children who do not respond or who won't continue corticosteroid treatment, RBC transfusion becomes their only viable option.

My first case of DBA was Kelly, whom I followed until she was in her late twenties. She graduated from college and became a schoolteacher. She was always short for her age, but we did not identify any other congenital anomalies. A few years after Kelly's birth her brother was born, and we followed him closely through his first year of life. He never showed any signs of DBA and grew and matured normally. During the years I was in San Diego a few more DBA cases were referred to me from other military medical centers. I followed four cases, one of whom was transfusion-dependent and eventually died of iron overload from his multiple transfusions.

Nicole was an example of TEC. Previously healthy, at the age of 12 months, when she was to be given a routine immunization, she was noted to be remarkably pale. Her hemoglobin level was 5.9 g/dl, about half the low end of normal for a child that age. Her peripheral blood reticulocyte count (reticulocytes are new red blood cells that have entered the circulation in the last day) was 0.1 percent (normal is 1 percent) and her bone marrow contained few RBC precursors. Her Hemoglobin F level was elevated at 4.8 percent. Over the next seven days her hemoglobin level fell to 4.4 g/dl, so I transfused her with 100 ml of packed RBCs and started her on low-dose steroids. Nineteen days later her reticulocyte count was 8.1 percent. Over the next month her hemoglobin level rose to 12.1 g/dl. Steroids were discontinued, and she remained hematologically normal. (Her dad was a career Navy psychologist who worked with me later in our careers, so I had continuing follow-up on her. The last time I saw her was at her wedding in the California Mission in Carmel when she was in her mid-twenties.)

Nicole was an unusual case in that she was profoundly anemic and presented at an age when she could have been a late presentation of DBA. I contacted Dr. Diamond, who was fully retired and professor emeritus at Harvard, the University of California San Francisco (UCSF), and Stanford. He and his wife Rose had moved to San Francisco so they could be closer to their only child, Jared Diamond, PhD, who is a professor at UCLA. Dr. Diamond said he would come to see Nicole and my other patients. He spent the day with us—we had a full house of patients. Faith Kung came with some of the pediatric residents from UCSD, and we had a great pediatric hematology teaching day. Dr. Diamond told me he had heard about a doctor in Vancouver who had a novel system of growing RBC precursors in culture. He wondered if I might be able to visit her and learn the techniques and apply them to the study of children with some of these bone marrow failure states, like TEC and DBA.

I contacted Dr. Connie Eaves and her husband Allen, who were the directors of the Terry Fox Laboratory for Hematology-Oncology Research. They welcomed me to their lab and taught me how to set up and to grow RBC precursors in culture. One requirement for growing cells in this system is a 5–10 percent carbon dioxide (CO_2) environment, so that meant I had to get a new incubator for the CIC lab. Once again I got help from the Navy

Surgeon General, Vice Admiral Will Arentzen, who told one of his deputies, Rear Admiral Mel Museles, also a pediatrician, to find the money in the research budget.

A CIC laboratory technologist had been very helpful in supporting our pediatric hematology clinic. I asked her to take on the bone marrow culture studies, and in short order she had them up and running. We were able to study the effect of serum samples from four children with TEC to see what effect it would have on development of RBC precursors in culture. We showed that serum from children with TEC routinely suppressed RBC precursor development in cultures. We were able to take this a step farther and determine this inhibitor was in the IgG fraction of serum. We showed that TEC is due to transient immune suppression of RBC precursor development.

I did a study with Dr. Diamond using the bone marrow culture technology and presented it at the Society for Pediatric Research (SPR) annual meeting in 1981. It had a catchy title: *Congenital Macrocytic Anemias (CMA) of Mice and Men.* I did many other studies using this bone marrow culture system over the next five years and eventually got it into the research lab at the Navy hospital in Oakland.

Training Fellows

Al Lightsey was my first "fellow." In addition to having to teach him what I knew and what I would come to know, I now had the responsibilities of every other staff pediatrician. I had to take my two half-days each week in the Pediatric Acute Care Clinic (PACC) and the Evening Pediatric Clinic that ran until 2200 (10:00 p.m.) every day all year.

The PACC was a walk-in clinic. Bea Schwab, the department secretary, at the end of each month reported our clinic workload to the command. That number always hovered around 2,000 visits, plus or minus a hundred or so. I did not believe her, so I gathered up the last year's daily patient logs, analyzed them, and noted that we seldom saw fewer than 100 children a day. That meant we had at least 3,000 visits a month. I asked why the difference? Her response was that she had been working as the secretary in pediatrics for thirty years and she knew how many children were seen. I showed the patient logs to Jack Schanberger, who realized I was right. He and I had been here for four years now, and this was the first time he knew the workload his staff was handling and the inaccuracy of the data that was being reported. This shortfall in data reporting affected both our staffing levels and our funding.

The evening clinic was an extension of the daytime clinic. We had an hour off to make rounds on our hospitalized patients, get something to eat, and get back to work. This was not an appointment clinic but walk-in; patient flow was slower, but there were always patients to be seen. We'd have this duty about three times a month—no compensatory time off for the evening or weekend time worked. It was in this evening clinic that I had one of the most tragic experiences of my career. I was on the way to my car a few minutes after the clinic closed at 10:00 p.m. and the nurse came running after me shouting, "Come back! I think we have a dead baby!" I returned and indeed he was. He was about ten months old and had been brought in by his mom and dad. Something did not look right to me. I asked them to have a seat and said I'd be back in a few minutes. I carried the baby to the radiology department. The radiologist, CDR John Marriott, was closing up also. I showed him the baby and told him we needed a total body flat-plate X-ray. We did it, and counted 22 fractures. I went back to the clinic, told the nurse to call the police, and then talked with the parents. I told them the baby was dead but could not tell them why. Of course, there was a grief response and I just let them cry and comfort each other. Soon the police showed up, and the father confessed to beating the child because he couldn't stand the crying. He was arrested on the spot. We got a friend of the mother's to come and take her home. In court the father pleaded no contest and was convicted of manslaughter. He was discharged from the Navy and sent to state prison.

I did the pediatric evening clinic until 1975, when I was promoted to Commander. The new Commanding Officer, Rear Admiral Will Arentzen, had a different way of doing business. Commanders stood the Medical Officer of the Day (MOOD) watch. That meant beginning at 1630 (4:30 p.m.) we ran the Emergency Room until 0800 (8:00) the next morning. There were other doctors there, some of them GMOs and other Lieutenants and Lieutenant Commanders who were in specialties that did not have evening clinics. This was before emergency medicine had become a common specialty. The practice of using other specialists to work in emergency rooms was soon to end but not before I had done my time at it. Certain specialties were exempt, like radiology, general surgery, most of the surgical subspecialties, OB-GYN, and anesthesia, because they were on call for emergencies in their clinical areas. This watch was no clinical challenge for me because of my Sasebo experience as a GMO, but it was for those who hadn't had that sort of experience. I'd have the duty about twice a month, but it was all night—again with no compensatory time off.

Hematology-Oncology: Trainees and Research, 1973–1979

Al Lightsey also became quite involved with research. While my major interest was in RBC disorders, his interest developed along a much smaller component in the peripheral blood, the platelet. Platelets are organelles, remnants of the shattered cytoplasm of very large cells in the bone marrow called megakaryocytes. Mega means big and cyte is cell—so "big cells." They are a critical part of the process of blood clotting and of maintaining the integrity of the vascular system.

Al spent time with physician-scientists outside the Navy hospital. He formed a strong relationship with Dr. Robert McMillan at Scripps Clinic and Research Institute in La Jolla. He published a paper on platelet disorders in the *Journal of the American Medical Association* documenting the life-saving management of a very severe case of ITP that required the use of some of the agents used in inducing remission in leukemia to get the process to enter remission. In the *Journal of Pediatrics* he published two articles that showed ITP was associated with the production of an immunoglobulin that bound to platelets, probably causing their destruction. Al stayed on as staff in San Diego, passing the peds heme-onc boards and running the training program until the mid 1980s. He then transferred to the Uniformed Services University of the Health Sciences in Bethesda, where he received the best teacher award in 1987, which was presented by President Ronald Reagan. He retired to Georgia, where he was on the faculty of the Medical College of Georgia until he completely retired.

Two more pediatricians were sent to our training program, Bill Thomas and Rick Ellwanger. Bill came from Bethesda, the National Naval Medical Center, completed the training program, and returned to Bethesda. He passed the peds heme-onc boards, returned to San Diego in 1980, and stayed there until he retired. He then moved to Tacoma, Washington, where he remains in practice to this day. Rick Ellwanger came from Portsmouth Naval Hospital, completed the program, returned to Portsmouth, passed his boards, and practiced there until he retired. After he retired he trained in radiation oncology and practiced that specialty in the Tidewater area of Virginia.

There were three general pediatricians at Navy Hospital San Diego who became interested in heme-onc. They spent a lot of time with me and went on to train in civilian programs, all becoming board certified in pediatric heme-onc.

Tom Vedvick, Harvey Itano's postdoc in the biochemistry department at UCSD, and I continued our collaborative research efforts. We published six articles in the medical literature, most having to do with biochemical properties of hemoglobin. My association with Y.W. Kan continued. Along with him and others in his lab we published four articles on alpha-thalassemia in the refereed literature, one that appeared in *Nature*, one of the premiere scientific journals in the world. I published others involving interesting case reports with staff at the Navy Hospital San Diego. All told, I published more than 30 articles in the peer-reviewed medical literature.

Hematology staff and fellows at dinner in Tijuana, 1979. Left to right: Laurel and Rick Ellwanger, Deena and me, Al and Nancy Lightsey, Fran and Bill Thomas.

One other relationship needs mention. John and Pat Spinetta were child psychologists who had done their graduate work at Los Angeles Children's Hospital. They moved to San Diego, where they were on the faculty of San Diego State University and also spent clinical time at San Diego Children's, UCSD, and in our clinics. The Spinettas had been pioneers in modernizing the psychological approach to treating children with life-threatening diseases. The practice earlier was always to hide the diagnosis from the children and to never use words like death, leukemia, or cancer around the child. Once the diagnosis was suspected, children were hospitalized and remained so for a long time. Children are smart; they figure out this is not normal and there must be something terribly wrong. So both the children and the rest of the family knew something was wrong, but they hid the fact that they knew from each other.

The Spinettas taught us that it was best to stop this subterfuge. We needed to use real words. Kids could handle it. We didn't need to tell children they were going to die, but we needed to tell them what they had. Based on their level of understanding they would gradually incorporate this into their understanding of their disease. The Spinettas also taught us that just because children had these conditions didn't mean they were fragile or they would break. The best place for them was at home and out playing with their friends or back in school, if at all possible. That's how we approached management of the children, their families, and the schools. School officials were often reluctant to have these children back in class. The Spinettas were invaluable liaison persons for us with the schools. When we had problems they were there to intervene and help out.

Organizations such as Candle-Lighters and Make-A-Wish weren't available to us then. We did a lot of those things ourselves. I had one boy in his early teens with ALL who wanted to go see a major league baseball game. I called the San Diego Padres, and they gave me a private box to take him to. When we arrived, there was a large box of souvenirs for him. He lasted to the 7th inning stretch, when he said he was tired and asked to go home. He died less than a week later.

I had a preteen boy who had pulmonary fibrosis from chemotherapy he had developed in infancy following radiation treatment for Wilm's tumor that had spread to his lungs. The fibrosis was progressing, and we knew it was going to take him soon. He told us he wanted to go for a plane ride. I had a neighbor who was an American Airlines pilot, and I asked him if there was any way we could pull this off. He set it up. I flew with the boy and we went first class to Los Angeles and back on a shuttle flight. I had a canister of oxygen to keep him from becoming low on oxygen during the trip, and he had a great time—couldn't stop talking about it. He died within a month. Something I learned later on was that my pilot friend had purchased the two first-class tickets himself and arranged the whole thing with a pilot colleague of his without letting the airline administration know.

The Spinettas had friends in their field. One was the Swiss psychiatrist Elisabeth Kübler-Ross, the author of the book *On Death and Dying*, in which she defined the five stages of grief: denial, anger, bargaining, depression, acceptance. She had retired and was living in Escondido. The Spinettas got her to come to the Navy hospital to see what we were doing with dying children, and she gave a presentation to our entire department. These were among the most valuable lessons I ever learned. I worked hard at keeping kids at home and active as long as they could be. Very few of my patients beyond the mid–1970s died anywhere but home. It was better for them and their families.

More Responsibility and Change of Duty Orders: 1980

As the summer of 1979 approached I got called to the hospital Commanding Officer's office. Rear Admiral Bill Cox told me Captain Vic Viewig, a cardiologist and former Navy line officer, was retiring. Vic had been running the Medical Officer Indoctrination Course for interns to prepare them for operational assignments that most of them would go to upon completing internship. This was a didactic series of lectures that covered flight surgery, submarine medicine, surface warfare medicine, duty with the Marines, shore-based GMO duty—just about any assignment an intern could expect. There were lectures by clinical specialists on common problems they would see in these environments. The lectures were held on Saturday mornings for about two hours. The interns called it "Boat School." It wasn't popular with some of them, but by the time they finished their operational tours most agreed it had been of significant benefit.

Admiral Cox told me he wanted me to take over the course. The sweetener for me was that I would be off all watch lists. What a deal! One thing he suggested was that we make the sessions attractive by providing donuts and coffee. The interns wouldn't want to pay for it, so he said he'd split the cost with me, $5 a week; the head of the hospital galley said that would cover the cost of consumables to make the donuts and the coffee. (One of the interns in that group was Lt. Bill Roberts, who went on to become a Rear Admiral, Upper Half.) Now I had a new and additional title, Intern Director. On my next fitness report Admiral Cox, as he departed the command to become the Navy Surgeon General, ranked me number one out of fifty commanders at the hospital. Little did I realize how much impact that would have on my future.

In October Tom Vedvick and I went on a four-day fishing trip off the coast of Baja California. We got home midday on a Saturday and Deena told me the Chief of Pediatrics who had replaced Jack Schanberger when he retired, Bob Biehl, had called and said they wanted me to go to Bethesda for the Graduate Medical Education candidate selection conference that began Monday morning. He said they wanted me to help select the next heme-onc fellowship candidate because there were several applicants. I took a shower, got part of a night's sleep and on Sunday was off to Bethesda. I was in a small meeting room with the chiefs of pediatrics at the four hospitals with pediatric residency programs. They gave me a handful of records to look at on pediatricians interested in peds heme-onc. It didn't take long to winnow them down to a first choice. Then they told me to start helping them rank applicants for general pediatric residencies, so I lent a hand with that.

Rear Admiral Mel Museles came in. He had been Pediatric Chief at both Portsmouth and Bethesda and had, at Vice Admiral Arentzen's direction, helped me get the CO_2 incubator I needed for my research. He asked them, "Have you told him yet?" There was dead silence. He said, "I will, then. The reason you are here is we want you to move to Oakland next summer to become the Chief of Pediatrics and run the residency program." This would blow up my plans to complete my 20 years of service and retire in San Diego.

The chairman in Oakland was retiring and the program was in trouble. He was a good doctor but did not like the administrative aspects of running a residency program. He had taken the position with reluctance and the program had suffered, failing its last accreditation review by the American Board of Pediatrics. The residents were not performing well on the in-service exams, which are like the written boards but administered every year during training to assess program progress. There were a couple of first-year pediatric residents who, despite good records in medical school, performed below the 30th percentile on the in-service exam, an unheard-of low for military pediatric residents.

Rear Admiral Museles told me the Navy had been really good to me. It had paid my way through my senior year of medical school; I had a great GMO tour in Japan; a pediatric residency; a hematology-oncology fellowship; and support for my research interests for the last seven years. Now it was payback time. He encouraged me to take a day trip to Oakland as soon as I got back to the West Coast. A new hospital he said was really nice had been built and occupied in 1968. He told me BUMED would support my research there and provide for any equipment I needed that they did not have already.

I went to Oakland, met the head of the Clinical Investigation Program, Steve Lewis, who was very helpful and said he would assist in getting my research going. I met the pediatric staff and toured the spaces. One thing that bothered me was that in addition to the current chairman there were three other captains in the department. All of them knew that I had been nominated for the position and they assured me they would have no problem with me as the chairman. One of the three was Ricci Larese, who had been the pediatrician in Corpus Christi I worked with when I came into the Navy from internship in 1967, thirteen years earlier. He was now a pediatric cardiologist.

I was introduced to the hospital executive officer, who was one of the most arrogant medical officers I ever met. He had nothing good to say about San Diego and said he couldn't understand why BUMED was sending a Commander to take over Oakland's residency program when they had three Captains on staff. I don't think he was even aware their pediatric program was on probation. He told me he would be departing Oakland to become Commanding Officer at the Navy Hospital, Charleston, South Carolina, before I reported to Oakland. He made it clear that he thought he would be in Charleston only two years before he was selected for promotion to Admiral. Charleston had the reputation of being a hospital where Commanding Officers were selected for Flag Rank. I wasn't offered a chance to meet Admiral Lonergan.

The rest of the year I wound down my activities in San Diego and prepared for the move. In late August I drove to Salinas, spent a night with my mother and then drove on to Oakland, where I stayed with Del and Pat Pascoe. Del was a retired Navy Captain and had been Chief of Pediatrics at Oakland for many years. He kept a close eye on the residency program and filled me in on more details of the problems in the department, from his perspective.

5

Oakland

My first departmental meeting was with all the pediatric physicians: interns, residents and staff. They had done their homework and knew my history and reputation. I told them that, although I did not know as much about each of them individually as they did about me, I was well aware of the issues facing the department. I told them I planned to rectify these problems, and they were all going to have to do their part. I discussed the probationary accreditation the program had received during its review by the American Board of Pediatrics and the poor performance of the trainees on the in-service exam.

The ward charge nurse told me there had been no patients on the pediatric ward for the two weeks preceding my arrival, that the residents had been sending children needing hospitalization either to the University of California, San Francisco hospital or Oakland Children's. This was demoralizing to the nurses; they felt the doctors lacked confidence in them. I told the residents they couldn't learn if they did not have patients to treat, and so from this moment forward no patient would be sent to another hospital for inpatient care without my approval. If I were away, I would designate a senior physician to approve any transfer in my place.

I told them that all patients admitted during the preceding 24 hours would be presented at morning report the following day at 0745. Also, any newborn with problems would be presented. Attendance for all residents and staff at this meeting was mandatory Monday through Saturday. On Sunday the report would be given to the staff pediatrician on watch. I was aware that it had become departmental practice that when no patients were admitted there was no morning report, and because there was no morning report there was no teaching conference. That situation was over; there would be a didactic presentation on an assigned topic at every teaching conference. I told them I had no doubts about why residents had done so poorly on their in-training exam. There was little teaching going on and because of that they weren't learning.

Then I addressed the ambulatory clinic. Each of the specialists held their specialty clinics by appointment, but acute care was walk-in. I told them we would convert acute care to same-day appointments as soon as possible and we did, in less than a month. We would have one staff pediatrician on duty until 2000 (8:00) every night, with a first- or second-year resident on board every night. Interns would not be allowed to stand duty alone.

Departmental policy reserved one hour every Thursday morning for detail people (drug company representatives) to come and present their wares to the doctors in the clinic from 0900–1000. During that time walk-in patients were directed to the emergency room. The detail men had a calendar on which they signed up to bring sweet rolls and jelly donuts for the doctors to snack on during this time. That was now over. If a drug company representative had something to present to the department it had to be cleared with me—and no food was allowed.

There was a large closet in the clinic that the drug representatives kept fully stocked with their products. Most popular were the ready-to-feed bottles of baby formula—just pop the sterile cover off the nipple and plug it into the baby. The drug reps were told to clear all of the formula out by the end of the week or it would be thrown out. We were trying to teach mothers that breast was best, but by passing out free formula we were sending a different message.

Two of the three first-year residents had just completed a straight pediatric internship and done poorly on the in-training exam. I put them on a special program in which they had to read an entire chapter in the *Nelson Textbook of Pediatrics* each week and then spend an hour discussing it with me. When the in-training exam was given again later that year, both of these residents raised their scores from below the 30th percentile to above the 80th. Both of these residents had issues. One was a female who had married a surgical intern during their internship. He had gone to sea as a GMO, decided he had made a big mistake in marrying, and filed for divorce. The resident was angry with me for not taking this into account in my dealings with her.

The other was a male who was Jewish and demanded to be allowed to wear his Yarmulke with his uniform, be served kosher meals in the hospital galley, not be assigned duty during Shabbat, have all the Jewish holy days off, and serve only his equal share of federal holidays, including Christmas Day. The previous chairman had agreed to his demands, which caused problems with the other residents. I told him I did not object to his wearing a Yarmulke. The galley was ordering frozen kosher meals for him and charging them to the pediatric departmental budget. I told him that was over and he could bring kosher food from home and heat it in a microwave. He said he needed to spend Shabbat with his wife and baby son. I said fine and told him we had a Navy Lodge on base where they could stay and walk between there and the

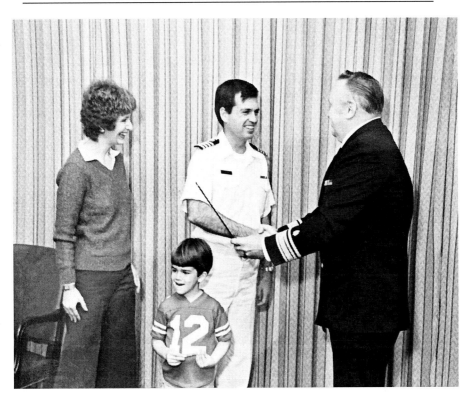

My promotion to Captain at Naval Hospital Oakland, 1980, with Deena, Grant, and Rear Admiral Walter Lonergan (courtesy U.S. Navy).

hospital building to observe Shabbat together. The Navy Lodge had a nominal charge for its use and it was seldom full. I told him he would have to make a reservation and pay for it out of his own pocket. I also advised him that every Jewish holy day he took off would count as a holiday for him. Rear Admiral Mel Museles, who was also Jewish, met with him and told him my rules were reasonable.

With all this completed, I went to the Commanding Officer's office and was promoted to Captain.

Personnel Issues

The two first-year residents decided to get even with me along with two pediatric staff physicians who were angry about their own personnel issues. The first staff physician was fellowship-trained in infectious disease and had come on active duty to pay back obligated service for assistance with his educational expenses. After reporting to Oakland before my arrival, he had been assigned three months' TAD aboard a civilian-manned spy ship. This sounds intriguing, but it was really pretty dull. It was a ship that sat in the middle of the ocean and tracked Russian ballistic missile launches. A doctor was always assigned for extended deployments but had very little to do. This staff physician was in a foul mood from then on because he felt this was a waste of his time and talents.

His wife had divorced him and taken him to the cleaners financially. He was sloppy in his personal appearance and in keeping his office clean and he was always grumpy. His uniform was dirty (we wore whites most of the time, so this really showed). His office was so messy that patients complained about it. I kept after him to clean himself and his office up but made no progress. Finally I took it up with the hospital executive officer. He said to let my department know that on Friday he would come to the pediatric clinic and do an inspection. This physician did nothing to clean his uniform or the condition of his office. The executive officer gave him the weekend to prepare for a repeat inspection. If he failed he would be taken to mast (an administrative disciplinary proceeding) before the commanding officer, Admiral Lonergan, and could expect the loss of half his pay for two months and being placed "in hack." That's when an officer is given a room in which to live and not allowed to leave the base. If that did not bring about the needed changes he would face a special court-martial. He complied but not without a lot of grumbling.

The second officer was a civilian-trained general pediatrician the Navy had assisted financially with his medical school tuition and expenses. He owed the Navy four years for this. Oakland shared the responsibility to provide a pediatrician—on a rotational basis with other West Coast Navy hospitals—to a Navy clinic on Adak Island, Alaska, far out in the Aleutian chain. The assignments were for six weeks. Only general pediatricians were assigned, not those with subspecialty training. This rotation schedule meant that each hospital would have the responsibility to provide a pediatrician to Adak annually. Our turn was coming up, and I nominated this officer for our six-week assignment. He told me he would not go. I reported this to the executive officer, who told the officer he would find himself in irons (handcuffs) and be transported there against his will.

The officer contacted an Oakland attorney who had assisted other physicians in getting released from obligated service on the grounds that they had become a conscientious objectors. He had successfully helped a San Diego pediatrician get released from his service obligation by claiming conscientious objector status when he was asked to take a rotation in Adak. The Oakland officer was to be a repeat performance for this attorney—who already had a written script. The attorney threatened to go to the press with a story that

Oak Knoll was providing substandard care. This was similar to charges of substandard care brought against the hospital in the mid 1970s by an anesthesiologist who wanted to be released from his obligated service. It had resulted in a lot of local negative publicity for the hospital. This attorney charged that premature babies were dying at Oak Knoll who should have survived. Once this became known within the department the others with an axe to grind joined in.

The divorcee resident cooked up an additional new accusation—sexual harassment by me. I had told her to clean up her uniform appearance when it had become unacceptable. I specifically told her to either polish her brass belt buckle or get a new one. One day I was in the Exchange buying a new buckle for myself so I decided I'd get one for her also. I took them both back to the clinic and put mine on. The nurses saw it and remarked how nice it looked. I told them I had gotten one for this woman as well. She was not there at that time, so I asked the nurses if they would give it to her since I had to leave and to tell her she owed me 75 cents. The nurses decided to have a little fun, so they found a small box, put the belt buckle in it, and wrapped it with gift paper, complete with a bow and a tag that said from Captain Koenig. The box the nurses used was for a small number of tampons (we kept a few handy for patients or staff who might need one). She said this was embarrassing to her—and so she charged me with sexual harassment.

All of these accusations were rolled into a single Navy Medical Inspector General investigation. The investigating officer was the chief of urology, a physician with stars in his eyes who had come into the Navy from private practice—and who wanted to be an Admiral in the worst way. But in face of the facts the accusations melted away. The nurses said I had nothing to do with the wrapping of the belt buckle in the tampon box. The Jewish resident's accusations dissolved in the face of Admiral Museles. The grumpy infectious disease doc's complaints were seen as unjustified.

That left the "killing babies" accusation. An outside neonatologist was brought in who spent a month reviewing our outcomes with premature infants. We had a new and really enthusiastic neonatologist on staff who had done wonders to clean up the mess created by the department's previous neonatologist. The outside neonatologist's conclusion was that we were doing very well given the condition the infants were in when we received them from Obstetrics. He noted that the Obstetrical Department needed to do a better job of managing the delivery of premature infants and get them promptly to the nursery.

The Navy Medical IG came to Oak Knoll, reviewed all the reports, and told me I was not guilty of anything and that I was doing a good job. The Commanding Officer decided not to send the officer who brought the charges to Adak but rather give him a discharge from the Navy under conditions other than honorable. This meant he was free to go, owing the Navy nothing for the financial support he received during his training—but in the future he would have no VA benefits. That may not seem like much—unless some day he should need them.

As a result of the cases in which medical officers claimed conscientious objector status as a way of getting out of six-week rotations to support the clinic in Adak, the Navy decided to send a pediatrician there for two years, starting the following summer. One of our finishing residents, Lieutenant Wayne Easter, drew that assignment and did a superb job. The Navy base at Adak was closed in 1997 as part of the Base Realignment and Closure process.

When the Jewish resident had completed his training and was preparing to detach I had to sign off that he had met all his obligations and was cleared to transfer. I told him I was going to take a look in medical records to make sure he had none left to complete. I looked in the pediatric file drawer to see if there were any with his name on them stuffed in any of the other resident's folders. There were not, so I signed off and away he went. A few days later medical records with his name on them appeared in the pediatric drawer. He had taken them out before my inspection and returned them afterward. I discussed this with the Executive Officer (XO), and we sent a message to his new command requesting that he be sent back to complete his obligation. But his new CO said they were really short on help and this would inconvenience them. So I dictated the records. I also included a notation about this in his detaching fitness report, which was signed by Admiral Lonergan. A year later he was due for selection for promotion to Lieutenant Commander. Virtually all doctors are automatically selected for promotion from Lieutenant to Lieutenant Commander. He was not. This cost him the difference in pay between a Lieutenant and a Lieutenant Commander for the next year, several hundred dollars a month.

I had three other officers who had career-ending issues. The first was a rotating intern who was on pediatrics early in the year and began showing signs of schizophrenia. He had been a Navy scholarship student in medical school and during that time was diagnosed with the illness. He had been placed on medication and done well enough to graduate, but he did not disclose this to the Navy, nor did his school. He stopped taking his medication during internship and relapsed. He was discharged medically with the finding of "condition existed prior to enlistment."

The second was another intern, a woman who had been in the Navy Medical Service Corps and was accepted to the Uniformed Services University of the Health Sciences Medical School and graduated. She had been a marginal performer in medical school but they decided to let her graduate and see how she did. Four months into her internship she came to me and said she wanted to quit. She was redesignated a Medical Service Corps officer and reassigned.

The last instance involved one of our staff pediatricians from India. He was a nephrology specialist (kidney diseases). One day another medical officer asked to see me about a sensitive subject. He told me that the mother of a patient he was seeing told him that this foreign-trained doctor had previously seen her and her baby. She felt that he was making sexual advances to her during the exam and that she knew several other women with similar experiences. We called in the Naval Investigative Service, which investigated and substantiated these accusations. We checked with state and local authorities and found that two parents of babysitters for this officer and his wife had lodged complaints about his actions while taking their daughters home. No formal charges had been filed. We held formal hearings, reported him to the California State Medical Board, and discharged him from the Navy. The State Medical Board issued a warning to him that further reports could result in his losing his license as well as bringing criminal charges.

The Changing of the Guard: 1982–1984

In the summer of 1982 Rear Admiral Lonergan retired. He had been at Oak Knoll from 1977 to 1982. Our Executive Officer was off to Navy Hospital Okinawa to be the Commanding Officer. Our new Commanding Officer was Rear Admiral Robert Elliott and our new Executive Officer was Captain Jim Sears, who had been chief of psychiatry in San Diego before coming to Oakland.

The pediatric department and training program were moving along well. We had some new staff, most prominently Lieutenant Kevin Shannon, who came to us directly from residency at the University of Texas, Southwestern, in Dallas. He proved to be a superb teacher but also was very interested in research. Captain Steve Lewis, the Clinical Investigation Center director, had been very supportive in helping me secure all the equipment I needed to get my lab set up again, and we had a dedicated lab technician. I taught the lab tech how to do many of the specialized tests I had set up in San Diego, but I also now had direct access to my colleagues Y.W. Kan and Bill Mentzer in San Francisco. I introduced Kevin to my lab, and he was a natural, spending many hours there while I was increasingly busy with other hospital and Navy activities. Kevin designed and carried out numerous studies. He also became friends with my San Francisco colleagues and in a few years began a Navy-sponsored fellowship in heme-onc with them. Upon completing that, he returned to Oakland to finish his obligated service and then became full-time faculty at UCSF. He is now a full professor there with a CV as long as his arm.

I took stock of what my pediatric residents at Oakland accomplished. Kevin Shannon was staff, not a resident, but I'll take credit for getting him interested in peds heme-onc. I also helped interest two Oakland residents in this subspecialty, Joe Torkildson and Paulette Bryant. Joe trained at Los Angeles Children's and returned to Oakland, put in twenty years in the Navy, retired, and is now a neuro-oncology specialist at East Bay Children's in Oakland. Paulette did her heme-onc training at Stanford and now is on staff at a St. Jude's-affiliated hospital in Charlotte, North Carolina. All told, there were twelve doctors I helped to train or influence to become interested in peds heme-onc. They all gained board certification.

Some Oakland pediatric residents did quite well in other areas. Barry Cohen was an intern my first year and spent his entire residency with me, stayed in the Navy, and reached retirement. He became one of the Navy's experts on managed care as the Tricare program matured. Henry Wojtczak became a pediatric pulmonary specialist, put thirty years in the Navy, and still works at the Navy Hospital San Diego as a civilian. Dave Moyer put in a full career in the Navy in allergy-immunology and remains in the East Bay. Wayne Easter, who was the first pediatrician to fill a two-year assignment in Adak, later became chief of pediatrics at the Kaiser hospital in Redwood City. Bryan Barnett eventually did a second residency in dermatology, stayed in the Navy to reach retirement eligibility and now is in private dermatology practice near Tracy, California.

The Navy Surgeon General, Vice Admiral Bill Cox, was also busy. The Navy Secretary had decided that the span of control for BUMED was too great. He wanted Navy Medicine regionalized, so Bill spent his time working on that. Navy Medicine was split up into eight regions, six in the continental U.S., one in Europe, and one in the Pacific. A Rear Admiral was put in charge of the four stateside regions that had admirals as hospital COs; these were the four with large teaching hospitals: Bethesda, Portsmouth, San Diego, and Oakland. The other two in the continental U.S. had senior post-command Captains. Europe and the Pacific also had Admirals heading them. In addition to having these "regional commanders," the new commands had large administrative staffs to oversee the hospital activities. Along with that was a decision to reduce the span of control for hospital COs so they wouldn't have so many clinical and administrative departments reporting directly to them through the XO. The new alignment called for there to be five "directorates" in each hospital, each with a senior officer appointed as director. The five directors would be responsible for all the departments in their directorate and they would provide the interface with the XO and CO.

There had always been a chief nurse, who would now become the director of Nursing Services. There had always been a director for Administration but now there would be three new directorates—Medical Services, Surgical

Services, and Ancillary Services. Medical and Surgical are self-explanatory. Ancillary Services included radiology, laboratory, nuclear medicine, and clinical investigation. This reorganization meant that Rear Admiral Elliott would be the hospital CO for less than a year. He had to move out of the hospital building to one of the original 1940s "temporary" redwood hospital buildings. The XO, Captain Jim Sears, was named the new CO. It fell to Jim to determine who would be the directors.

I thought the director jobs would be just another assignment on top of being a chief of service. Jim had other ideas; he wanted them separate and would pick them from among the current departmental chiefs. Since I was still "junior" amongst chiefs in what would be the medical directorate, I felt I was "safe." Wrong. I was "it." In preparation for assuming these new responsibilities Jim had me and the other two clinical directors attend a four-week course at the Naval School of Health Sciences in Bethesda. This course was originally designed to prepare medical corps officers to be XOs and COs. This turned out to be a very good course preparing us for our new responsibilities.

The Joint Commission was due to come back to Oakland after two years because of the hospital's poor showing in 1982. That meant they would visit again in early 1984. Captain Jim Sears said he wanted one of the directors to be in charge of preparation for the survey. I thought that would mean the director for Administrative Services. Wrong again. I was it. Captain Sears told me the Joint Commission had a three-day training program about how to prepare for a survey, and he told me to go to it. The next one was in Dallas in just a few weeks. I went and what I learned scared me silly. I found there was a lot I did not know about hospitals. The Joint Commission had a "bible" on how to prepare for the survey that was the syllabus for the course. I read it so many times I could recite it in my sleep. I assigned responsibilities to our subject matter experts and then checked and rechecked that everything we needed to have squared away indeed was, and that they knew the correct response to questions the surveyors would ask. I made sure they knew what deficiencies had been identified in their area the last time the Joint Commission had visited and that these issues had been corrected.

The time for the survey came. The surveyors had a meeting in the auditorium for the senior staff, introduced themselves, told us they would be aboard for two days and the following afternoon they'd reconvene with us and tell us what they found. They poked around clinics, operating rooms, doctors' offices, and medical records; they checked fire doors and interviewed patients and junior staff. The next afternoon at the appointed hour we reconvened in the auditorium. The head surveyor announced he wouldn't beat around the bush with us. We had passed and gotten a score of 99 out of 100, the highest they had given that year. This time we got a full three-year accreditation. BUMED was overjoyed. A few months earlier Bethesda had gone through a survey and received a provisional passing grade with a revisit scheduled in one year.

Not long thereafter, the Navy announced the results of that year's Flag selection board. Captain Jim Sears was one of those selected. That meant come summer he would be detaching, and there would be another changing of the guard. That was not all. Dave Lichtman was given orders to Bethesda to be chairman of orthopedics; Jim Winebright, our director of Ancillary Services, was to go to Camp Pendleton as XO. Dave and Jim had both been at Oakland for at least ten years. I figured they would go, but I would stay. Wrong once again. I was to go to Portsmouth, Virginia, as XO. Portsmouth was one of the "big four" Navy teaching hospitals. In preparation for this, the Navy wanted me to attend a month-long course on Shore Facility Management in Northern Virginia. This wasn't a Medical Department course; it was a "Big Navy" course for prospective XOs and COs of large installations. The course convened near the end of April, and my orders said I was to attend the course "en route," which meant I would detach from Oakland before attending the course. That was less than a month away! I had only a short time to get ready. We put our house on the market, anticipating it would take at least a few months to sell. It sold in seven days.

I went East and took the course. As with most Navy courses, the sessions lasted all day, were detailed, and had plenty of assigned after-hours reading. There were more than fifty captains in the course, most of them line officers nearing the end of their careers, and they didn't seem to be very interested. I finished the course and went back to Oakland to help pack out for our move East. Deena, Grant, Ginger—our ever faithful cat—and I flew to Washington, stayed overnight, and then headed 200 miles south to Portsmouth in a rental car. Our other two sons stayed in Oakland to attend Scout Camp with their troop, then they followed us.

As we flew East I realized that the changing of the guard also applied to me. I was moving from clinical medicine to executive medicine, and if history was any guide the chances of my returning to clinical practice were small.

6

Portsmouth

We were assigned quarters in Portsmouth, one of two identical antebellum houses on the hospital grounds, and the Commanding Officer lived in the other. These houses had been well maintained through their first one hundred years. The CO, Captain John Rizzi, told me that the Naval Medical Command in Washington, Rear Admiral Joe Cassells, had called while I was in transit and told him to tell me when I arrived to "not unpack all the boxes." I was going to be in Portsmouth for only a year, not two years as my orders stated. The Commanding Officer at Camp Lejeune had decided to retire in the summer of 1985 and they thought I would be a good relief for him.

Transition to Executive Medicine

Portsmouth Naval Hospital was running extremely well under John Rizzi. He took on the job of preparing me for command by letting me run the day-to-day operations, watching and advising as I went. I started each day walking through Building-1, where Navy patients had been receiving care for 150 years. Pediatrics, including the nursery, obstetrics, and psychiatry, still operated in this building. The obstetrical service was quite busy, delivering about 300 babies a month. The pediatric ward maintained a census of around twenty children. One of my former peds-hem-onc fellows, Rick Ellwanger, was there, and he would ask me to drop by and consult on some patients.

From Building-1 I would head back past our house to the main hospital building, take the elevator to the 15th floor, and work my way down through all of the patient areas, checking to see if there was anything of note I needed to know before going to morning report at 0745. The directors—administration, nursing, ancillary, surgical, and medical—the Commanding Officer, and I attended morning report. The chief nurse would report on all the inpatient activities. Our chief nurse held herself in very high esteem. She was not used to the XO physically making rounds on all the inpatient areas before morning report and the fact that I knew as much, and often more, than she did about the condition of patients. The difference was that I actually went to the areas, talked to the nurses, and saw the patients, whereas she would just sit in her office and the area-supervising nurses would call her and report. Nothing beats your own eyes and ears.

I had a great secretary, Jodi Danin, who had been the XO's secretary for twenty years. She kept me on schedule and taught me a lot about the people at the hospital as well as how it worked. One task I had was the XO's screening mast. This was something I had learned about in the Shore Facilities Management Course before reporting to Portsmouth. I'd see all the staff that had charges brought on them under the Uniform Code of Military Justice. My job was to sort out the cases that needed to go higher—to the CO or beyond—and deal with the others myself. We had a superb command Master Chief who would brief me on each case. The Master Chief and I handled more than 90 percent of the cases, keeping them out of the CO's office.

During my tenure I had a few officers who got in trouble and I had to deal with them. One reported aboard from a civilian residency and failed his incoming drug screen, having cocaine in his urine. He said it had to have come from an injection of Lidocaine, a local anesthetic. The problem with this excuse is there is no chemical structural similarity between Lidocaine and cocaine. They do not cross-react. We kicked him out. There's no point in wasting time on jerks.

The second one was a neurosurgeon. He had five spine cases in which he had gone into the wrong intervertebral space. Our credentials review board recommended removing his clinical privileges to do anymore of these cases. He got a slick lawyer to plead his case. I was chairman of the credentials review board. We removed his privileges to do spinal cases and put this in his credentials file, which would follow him the rest of his career. He was fine inside the head; it was just spines where he shouldn't operate.

The third was a hotheaded ob-gyn senior resident. He made a video that he showed at the department's end-of-year party. Most members of the department and many of their spouses, most of whom were women, attended the party. Unfortunately, he had recruited a number of enlisted female staff at the hospital to have on-screen roles in the video, and many of the scenes were pornographic. He went to a general court-martial and was kicked out of the Navy, with this activity recorded in his credentials file.

John Rizzi thought that a necessary experience for me would be to be a member of a promotion board, so he contacted Washington and had me assigned to one. Just before Thanksgiving I was on an active component (in contrast to reserve component) Medical Corps captain selection board. The president of the board was Rear Admiral Bob Elliott, who had been my CO at Oakland for a year before becoming the Northwest Region Commander. There were five other Captains, all very senior to me. We had over 400 Commanders in zone eligible for promotion, and we could pick about half of them. This is no easy task. We reviewed their microfiche records and every member of the board had to look at and score every eligible officer's record before we could vote. The process took a whole week. It was quite laborious, but I learned a lot about how the Navy promotions system works and also a lot about the Navy's Bureau of Personnel.

John Rizzi nominated me for a course called the Interagency Health Care Institute for Federal Health Care Executives run by George Washington University. This course had been offered for twenty years and it is still being offered today, fifty years after its inception. It is a two-week course run by Dr. Richard Southby, a professor at the university. The course is sponsored by the five federal health services: Army, Navy, Air Force, Veterans Affairs, and U.S. Public Health Service. There are about 50 attendees in each class with a variety of graduate professional degrees and formal educational backgrounds. The attendees are selected by their respective agency because of their potential for senior management positions.

The course was held in a hotel on the Virginia side of the Potomac River overlooking Washington. One of the rules in the classroom was that no telephone messages would be delivered while classes were in session, rather they would be delivered during the breaks. The rule was not broken until Wednesday, when a clerk came in with a government telephone message slip. I wondered who could be getting a rule-breaking message? The clerk handed me a message that said to call Admiral Quinn at ComNavMedCom, ASAP. Worried that something had happened to Deena or one of the kids, I went down the hall to a coin phone (this was in the days before mobile phones) and placed the call. Admiral Quinn's secretary answered and said, "The admiral has been waiting for you to call." She put me through to him and he said, "Harold, congratulations. The Secretary of the Navy has signed off on your being assigned as CO of San Diego." So much for Camp LeJeune. On Friday, after the first week of the course, I took a short flight back to Norfolk for the weekend. The weather was nasty—rain and sleet. Deena was going to pick me up at the airport. John Rizzi told her to stay home—he would come get me. That was a real act of kindness on the part of a fine officer and gentleman.

The Flag selection board results were released, and John Rizzi's name was not on it. The two Medical Corps officers selected for promotion were virtually unknown to most of us in Navy Medicine. One had never been an XO or CO but had been assigned to the staff of the Surgeon General. The other had been Chief of Medicine at Bethesda and recently had become CO of the Naval Health Sciences, Education and Training Command at Bethesda. He had never served as an XO or CO of a hospital. There were several good candidates who had served as COs of Navy hospitals, some of them, like John Rizzi, at more than one.

I soon learned why Admiral Quinn had said to me, "You're going to San Diego. You're really going to need good luck—the place is a mess." On a subsequent trip to Washington I met with both him and Rear Admiral Joe Cassells, his boss. They told me San Diego had just failed a Navy Medical IG Inspection and that it had gotten a one-year provisional accreditation from the Joint Commission. In addition, the surgery residency, once Navy surgery's pride and joy, was on academic probation. The CO had been told to fire the chief of surgery because of his ineffectual leadership, but the CO lacked the will to act. The head of thoracic surgery needed to be decredentialed, and on the list went. I was given several hours of briefings on the situation. The new hospital construction was moving along ahead of schedule and there needed to be a lot of planning by the command in preparation for the move. However, there was no evidence that this had started. This was as close to a lose-lose situation as I could imagine.

The change of command was scheduled for July 12, so we had to leave in time to drive across country. We arrived in San Diego a few days before the change of command so I would have time to discuss the changeover with the detaching CO and my new XO. I went to the hospital to sign in so the clock would stop running on my leave. I was pretty relaxed and laid back by this point, having been away from work and the Navy for a couple of weeks. It was July, it was hot, and I was in shorts, sandals, and a tee shirt. I went into the CO's office and the secretary, Donna Mackenzie, who knew me only by telephone, said, "May I help you?" I said, "I came to sign in." Still not knowing who I was she told me I had to go somewhere else to do that. I handed her my orders, and I thought she was going to faint.

7

Return to San Diego

Before detaching from Portsmouth I was told I could choose my XO from one of two candidates. I chose Fred Sanford, a radiologist I had known for several years. I was also told I could select a new chief of pharmacy. The Navy had a list of senior Captain pharmacists for me to choose from. I consulted Dan Horan, who was chief of pharmacy at Portsmouth. He told me the best candidate was not a Captain, but a senior Commander, Noel Hyde. I picked him and after a little arm-twisting I got my way. I said if they could put me in as CO, junior to about two-dozen Captains, they could put Noel in as pharmacy head.

Fred had taken over as XO when I arrived. I told him my first concern was the chief of surgery. I didn't relish my first act as CO to be relieving the chief of surgery, but this was something that had to be done. Fred said that even the chief of surgery had anticipated this for some time. The Commanding Officer I was relieving was a surgeon, had been friends with this officer for years, and could not bring himself to do it. Fred said he would have the officer come to his office right after the change of command ceremony and inform him. Fred did that and gave him his orders reassigning him as a general surgeon at Naval Hospital Camp Pendleton. I chose Captain William Rowley, a vascular surgeon, to be the new chief of surgery.

Designated quarters for Deena and me were a two-minute walk from my office. The house was right under the flight path of planes landing at San Diego's Lindbergh Field, less than 60 seconds from touchdown. It was noisy and our first night there I thought I would never sleep, but we quickly got used to it.

I began my first day as Commanding Officer by walking through the hospital before morning report, just as I had done at Portsmouth. I did this until the day I left. One thing I noticed that first day was that there were cigarette vending machines on all the wards except pediatrics. For a quarter a patient could buy a pack of their choice of twenty brands. I told the command Master Chief to have the Chiefs form working parties and remove all the cigarette machines. I believed that by selling tobacco products in patient care areas we were endorsing their use. That was not a message hospitals should be sending. We had a Navy Exchange on base, and I called the Exchange officer and told him to remove all the tobacco products by Friday—smokeless, cigarettes, cigars, pipe tobacco, everything. The local head of the Navy supply system came to my office and told me I couldn't do this, and I told him, "Yes, I can." This was another lesson I had learned at the Shore Facility Management Course. I banned all smoking indoors and provided designated outdoor smoking areas.

The first visitor to my office was Capt. William J. (Joe) O'Donnell, CEC, USNR, officer-in-charge of construction for the replacement hospital. He was a Navy Reservist who had been quite successful in civilian life in supervising big construction projects. This $238 million project was made to order for him, and he volunteered to come on active duty to see the project through. He was a cigar-chewing, knee-slapping Irishman with a colorful vocabulary. He told me the history, size, and scope of the project and said he had one piece of advice for me: allow no change orders. He said I could expect a parade of supplicants asking for all sorts of changes. He told me that change orders were budget killers; they're where contractors make their money. He suggested I tell the staff that no change order requests would be granted and not to bother me with them. That was some of the best advice I received. Joe and I got along well.

Later that day the command Master Chief met with me to discuss enlisted mast. They did not have XO Screening Mast in San Diego as they did in Portsmouth; mast cases came straight to the CO. He told me there were about twenty cases a week on average and mast was held behind closed doors in the CO's office.

I said that I was changing that, effective today. I felt that twenty cases a week was a sign of failure of the chain of command, and the Chief Petty Officers were the most important link in the chain of command. I told the command Master Chief that in my view the Chiefs were responsible for enlisted discipline and I expected them to handle it. They should send only the most serious cases of repetitive disciplinary problems to me. I wanted that word passed to "All Hands." He broke out in a big grin, said, "Aye-aye, Sir." He left to pass the word. The Chiefs were reempowered the first day. I had told him we would no longer hold enlisted mast in my office. We'd hold it on the quarterdeck and it would be formal, all attending to wear their covers (hats), just as it had been done historically on Navy ships. All hands were invited to come and observe, but they would have to stand in ranks, remain covered throughout mast and wear the uniform of the day.

Nurses, Chiefs and leading Petty Officers soon caught on to the value of "Open Mast." They would assign enlisted members who were treading close to the disciplinary line to come to mast, stand in ranks, observe, and learn. After the last case at mast was heard the Master Chief would call "attention on deck" and all present would snap to attention.

The Quarter Deck had a double high ceiling; there was no second deck directly above. The acoustics were quite good, and sound carried well. The Master Chief and I would walk back to my office door and as we entered he would shout, "Dismissed!" At one of the early iterations of Open Mast, as soon as he said "dismissed" someone in ranks whispered, "Jesus Christ!" The area's acoustics assured that all present heard this. The Master Chief and I grinned at each other; we knew the message had been transmitted and received.

Open Mast and empowering the Chief Petty Officers had the desired effect. After the first month, weeks would pass without a Captain's mast case. I would see only the multiple repeat offenders, and most of those were people who tested positive in the urine drug-screening program several times. The Chiefs even gave those kids some slack. After their first positive they'd counsel them; after the second they'd warn them that they be fined and confined; one more positive and they'd be out of the Navy.

First Week: July 15–19, 1985

I made twice daily rounds to what I considered to be the high-risk areas of the hospital: the emergency room, the operating room area, the ICU, and the labor and delivery area. These are places where things can go sour fast and harm can occur. I reinstituted a policy that is universal practice in the operational Navy but for some reason had dropped out of practice here. I told the senior person on each unit to teach their staff that the first person to see me coming should call "attention on deck" so that all present would know I was there. Then I'd call "carry on," and they could continue with what they had been doing. I told them that I would address them by their rank or rate and last name, not by their first name, as my predecessor had done, and they should call me Captain Koenig. Respect runs both up and down the chain of command. I'd look for the staff member in charge and have them tell me what had happened since I last passed through. I wanted the staff to know I cared about them and for them to tell me if something was not right. I was not sneaking in to spy on them.

On my visits to medical and surgical wards, inpatient pediatrics, and the pharmacy we'd have the same routine. People knew I would be there each day. One time I had to go to Washington and didn't mention before I left that I would be absent for a few days. When I came back I had some explaining to do. The people thought I had stopped visiting them because I was unhappy with them. After that if I wasn't going to be able to make rounds the XO did it.

Morning report came at 0745, just as it had at Portsmouth. The command Master Chief joined me on pre-morning report rounds, two sets of eyes and ears rather than one. The directors picked up on this and they too started visiting their areas of responsibility without being told to. Our staff learned that we cared not only about what they did but also about them. At the end of my day I'd always visit the ICU on my way home. "Attention on deck!" "Carry on." "What's going on?" The ICU charge nurse would present every patient to me, a quick 30-second review. One of the ICU charge nurses was LCDR Kathy Martin. Her husband, Walt, had been a classmate of mine at the Naval Academy. In another year my oldest son, Steve, would be in the NROTC Unit at the University of San Diego, where Walt was the CO.

I always went to the pharmacy, where a huge amount of the command's budget was spent and where there can be a lot of patient dissatisfaction. This is why I brought Noel Hyde to be chief of pharmacy. Waiting times at our pharmacy were as long as four hours, and the waiting area was outdoors. The weather in San Diego is nice but not all the time. Quickly we identified one of the problems. DoD policy limited dispensing to a 30-day supply of most medications except for a few items, such as birth control pills, insulin, and seizure medications. Prescriptions could be written for three refills, and then the patient would have to see the doctor again. On my own I changed the policy to a 90-day supply with three refills. Workload went down, patient and staff satisfaction went up. Costs did not change. I thought someone in headquarters would raise hell because I did this. *Navy Times* published this good news story, and there was no walking it back. Headquarters remained silent. The rest of the system—Army, Navy, and Air Force—soon followed.

The hospital was delivering 450 to 500 babies a month, with a staff of seven obstetricians and nine residents. The American College of Ob-Gyn standard was no more than 15 deliveries per obstetrician per month—maximum. At our hospital there was seldom staff supervision for interns and residents. It was much like I had experienced during my OB rotation in medical school—see one, do one, teach one. The maternal morbidity and mortality rate was off the charts. There had been ten maternal deaths during the previous year and one the first week I was there. The acceptable rate for maternal deaths is zero. I immediately cut our delivery rate to 150 a month, sending the rest out on CHAMPUS (now Tricare). That was a popular move with the expectant mothers and the community physicians. After getting people retrained and comfortable with new policies and procedures, we gradually increased the delivery rate to 250/month. The rest of my tenure as CO we didn't have another maternal death or any other obstetrical horror stories.

An emergency medicine residency had been started the year before I got there. On the first day I discovered that the ER did not have a registered nurse assigned except on the day shift Monday through Friday. They were handling a patient load of 200 patients per day. They had hospital apprentice corpsmen (E-2's) screening patients. These were kids with only 14 weeks of hospital corps school training playing doctor. The first week I was there a woman sat in the waiting room for four hours with severe sub-sternal chest pain. She was having a heart attack. She died in that chair. I closed one of our four internal medicine wards and transferred the nursing and corpsmen staff to the emergency room. We had no more people die waiting to be seen during my tenure.

The ward I closed was called the Senior Officer's Ward—for commanders and above and their wives. Most of the patients were retired and the most common reason for admission was a "tune-up." "Tune-up" was "code" for drying out alcoholics, and it was a two-week process. I was asked what would be done with all the patients who needed this? A lot of them were repeat customers. I said unless they were active duty, and essentially none were, they'd have to go out on CHAMPUS and cost share (25 percent for retirees and their family members) for their care. That was a strong incentive to get control of their drinking.

An overworked corpsman on our second-floor high-risk psychiatry ward failed to lock a door. A sailor on suicide watch spotted that and went out the door to the balcony and jumped to his death on the cement courtyard below. I asked Captain Richard Ridenour, a psychiatrist and our director of ancillary services, to institute policies to prevent further occurrences like this. I moved more corpsmen onto that unit. No more patients committed suicide on our psychiatry ward.

Credentialing is a very important function for hospitals. It means checking to see that staff members really have the training and licensure they claim. That means we had to check with the issuing organization, such as their medical or nursing school or state medical board, to see that their diplomas and board certifications were real, not purchased from counterfeiters. We had a GS-13 who was assigned to run our credentials office. She was responsible for seeing that all this was properly done. Knowing the command was scheduled for a return visit by the Joint Commission in twelve months and this was an area they would examine closely, I called the hospital's head of credentialing to my office and asked, "How many staff doctors do we have?" She did not know. I said, "Give me a guess." She guessed and was off by a factor of two. She resigned later that day. I asked the head of graduate medical education, "How many doctors in training do we have at this hospital?" She did not know. We fixed both of these problems by putting a junior Medical Service Corps officer with a few enlisted staff in to help.

I asked about the medical readiness of our staff, the people who would have to deploy on the hospital ships and the fleet hospitals when conflict threatened. I learned that there were staff that had been at the hospital for twenty years and had no documented physical exam, no dental check-up, and no immunization records. I assigned another junior Medical Service Corps officer and some enlisted personnel to audit the medical readiness records of every active duty person at the command. If they were deficient, and most officers were, they were told that no special requests like leave, medical special pay, or travel to medical meetings would be granted until the deficiencies were corrected. Most of this was pretty simple; they just had to do it.

Another issue was personal appearance. For several years facial hair was allowed in the Navy, including full beards. This changed in 1984 so all that was allowed was a mustache not extending beyond the corners of the mouth. There was good reason for this; airtight seals could not be established with gas or oxygen masks with more facial hair than that. A couple of senior Captains objected, refused to comply, and so were asked to retire. I wished them "fair winds and following seas."

We found that the Navy-wide physical readiness testing that had existed for several years had not been implemented. It involved measurements of height, weight, and abdominal and neck girth. If all those measurements were within limits then there were measurements of upper body and core strength (push-ups or pull-ups and sit-ups) and a 1.5-mile run for time. A swim for time could be substituted for the run, but few chose that, as it was tougher than the run. The Chiefs would administer this for the enlisted. Most of the junior officers went for it with gusto.

Donna, my secretary, had been at the command for a long time, working in personnel before becoming the CO's secretary. She told me there were several senior Captains at the command who never showed their face around the front office, but she knew they were overweight and out of shape. So we scheduled individual examinations in private for the Captains at the command. The most senior Captain, Al "Shaky" Holmes, a legendary officer, conducted them. All the measurements were done, and if they met Navy standards then the physical fitness test could be taken. If not, then the people in question had to go on a weight control and physical training program until they could meet the standards before taking the test. A few retired (again, "fair winds…"), some made remarkable progress, and one lost more than 100 pounds.

One more story about Donna, who, at the time I am writing this (2018), is still the CO's secretary. But she now has a fancier title, something like Executive Assistant. She is the institutional memory of the command and still a good friend. When I got to the command, computer use in offices did not exist. Donna was a great typist, but even she would occasionally make a typo. She was a whiteout superstar. She could fix a typo so it would hardly show. But I knew IBM had a new typewriter with memory that could remember about 3 pages of text. It wasn't cheap, about $3,000 if memory serves me correctly, but I signed the purchase order and Donna took to the new machine like a duckling to water. Now she could give me a draft of a letter, I could edit it, and then she could produce a final copy for signature. Thus began the computer age in the front office, and it quickly spread through the command.

The Rest of the First Year: 1985–1986

Within a month of taking over as CO I was asked to talk to a group of retirees in a huge auditorium at the Naval Training Center, San Diego. There was mounting angst among local Navy leadership about perceptions regarding the availability and quality of care provided at the Navy Hospital. Many people were recruited into the armed forces with unauthorized promises, one being that when they retired they would have free health care for life from the military. Many of them had served in World War II and Korea and were now aging. Recruiters had made these promises and leadership reinforced them for so long that they were believed to be true.

What the law actually said was that retirees were eligible for care from military hospitals if the resources existed and were at the facility. The Commanding Officer had to determine if the resources existed. If the resources did not exist, then retirees were entitled to care from CHAMPUS until they reached age 65, when they would become eligible for Medicare. CHAMPUS and Medicare had been pretty good insurance until health care costs began to accelerate rapidly.

Retirees did not distinguish between the words eligible and entitled, most thinking of these words as synonyms. Congress and administrations in my opinion bore much of the responsibility for the misconceptions among the military retiree community because they had allowed these recruiting and retention promises to be made for so long that the belief they were enshrined in law had become pervasive. The problem was aggravated by the fact that care at military facilities was essentially free, except for a nominal per diem charge for inpatient care for other than active duty.

On the night of the talk Deena and I got onto Barnett Avenue leading to the Naval Training Center. There was a massive traffic jam. Navy Shore Patrol (SP) were trying to direct traffic and the city police were helping. I asked one of the SPs, "What's going on here?"

He said, "Some Navy doctor is giving a talk tonight on healthcare at the Navy hospital."

I said, "That's me."

He said, "Oh, we better get you in there then."

After being introduced I asked all the retirees to take out their ID cards and look at the backs of them. I pointed out that it said they were eligible for care from a military medical facility if the resources are available and that it was up to the commanding officer to make that determination (words I would find myself repeating for the rest of my career). I told them we couldn't do everything for everyone who wanted it at the Navy hospital. For example we couldn't give every retiree an annual eye exam, something we had frequent complaints about. We didn't have the staff. I said we would do only what we could do safely. It was unethical for us to try to do something when we knew we would not be able to do it safely. Our hospital was overwhelmed with patients desiring care. There were an estimated 400,000 eligible beneficiaries within a 50-mile radius of the hospital, and we were a referral center for active duty patients from a much larger radius than that.

COMNAVMEDCOM had directed hospital commanders to decrease the number of people being sent out on CHAMPUS for elective (nonemergency) surgical procedures, in order to decrease health care costs. I had already disregarded that direction by disengaging the majority of our expectant mothers to community care. In just my first few weeks in command I had learned that women desiring elective reconstruction of the breast after a radical mastectomy for breast cancer were being placed on a waiting list. There were several hundred women who wanted this elective (not emergent) procedure. The waiting list was growing faster than our ability to do the cases. I directed our local CHAMPUS office to contact every woman on that list and offer her a nonavailability statement immediately—and we did.

In the question and answer session there were many statements about the "broken promise" of free care for life. I responded that the government was not breaking a promise to them, that people with no authority to make the promise had made it, and that in no way obligated the government to fulfill it. I emphasized that I would do all I could to help them get the care they needed, but I wouldn't allow them to be stacked up on waiting lists anymore. If we couldn't do it in a reasonable time we'd give them a nonavailability statement. There would be a cost share for that care, 25 percent for retirees and their dependents. I encouraged them to all consider getting a supplemental insurance policy. Those over 65 would be covered by Medicare and there would be cost shares for them also, but less than under CHAMPUS. The retirees began to understand I was on their side. The press reported this, and confidence among retirees began to increase. The debate over the "broken promise" continued for nearly two decades after I addressed this overflowing auditorium of retirees in San Diego before finally being resolved in a series of federal court decisions and appeals.

The rest of the first year I spent following up on what I had started in the first week. Most of it was to improve access to care, make care safer, and prepare the hospital for the upcoming return Joint Commission survey and a return visit by the Navy Medical Inspector General. The Joint Commission came near the end of my first year and we were ready. We passed, with a score of 99/100, just like at Oakland. A lot of people worked hard to make this happen, and I gave them the credit.

Captain Al Holmes, MC, USN, was older than dirt. He was what was known as a pre–DOPMA officer, DOPMA being the Defense Officer Personnel Management Act. It governs promotion and length of service for officers. It did not apply to an officer who was still in the rank he was in before this act became law. This applied to Al Holmes. He had the nickname "Shaky" because he was. He was an old-time internist and still prescribed digitalis leaf for congestive heart failure rather than the pills that had become available. He was a good doctor, a really good one.

He had a clinic on the second deck of Building-1, and to be his patient you had to be a Navy Captain or higher or a Colonel from another service branch. Once you became his patient he was your doctor for life. He kept more than 6,000 medical records of patients he was caring for in his office. He was assisted by a couple of corpsmen, a receptionist, and a staff internist assigned to him. This was elitism at it best. But it was elitism at its worst in the view of a retired Navy Commander living in San Diego.

This officer had been writing letters to the local newspapers about this clinic for a few years, pointing out how discriminatory it was that many patients were being turned away to go out and cost-share on CHAMPUS but high-ranking officers had basically open access to a private doc at their beck and call. Shaky's clinic was well known to the Navy medical headquarters, the CNO, and the Navy Secretary. Before I arrived they had been told by Congress to shut it down. The Navy felt they did not take orders from Congress, so the letter writing and congressional interest continued. The local newspapers made it a cause. I was made aware of this and was told I would have to deal with it but was given no guidance as to how. I met with Shaky and told him we were going to have to make some changes. He didn't like it but understood. I cleared out some space in what was called Building-29, a relatively new (circa early 1960s) clinic building where the rest of the internal medicine clinics operated. I made Shaky turn over all his patients' records to the central records office, but I said he could continue to care for these patients. However, he and his colleague would have to accept new referrals from central appointments with no regard for the patient's rank. This would not quite compete with Solomon's actions several thousand years earlier, but it did quiet the commander and the local press.

I had a Captain thoracic surgeon who had been pressed into doing heart surgery. Before I tell his story, though, I need to address a situation on the other coast—at the National Naval Medical Center, Bethesda. There was a heart surgeon at Bethesda who had been recruited into the Navy. Bethesda had not checked into his record in civilian practice—in other words he had not been properly credentialed by Bethesda. When he was brought on board Commodore J.J. Quinn, who was the Commanding Officer, and Captain Lee Georges, who had been selected for promotion to Flag rank in 1985, were involved in his credentialing process. This heart surgeon had lost many patients in his civilian practice and was looking for a new venue, so he chose to come into the Navy. His patient outcomes at Bethesda were equally dismal. A prolonged investigation followed and in the process it was learned that this surgeon was legally blind in one eye. He was taken to court-martial and wound up serving four years in a federal prison. Commodore Quinn was asked to retire as a Captain or face a court-martial, so he chose to retire. Captain Georges was not promoted to Flag rank and retired. With that as background, here is what I had to deal with.

The thoracic surgeon in San Diego had earlier been sent to Stanford to be trained in heart surgery. He did not make satisfactory progress, so after several months was sent back to San Diego with a note in his credentials file that he should not do hearts. Nevertheless, pressure was brought on him by Commodore Quinn, who now was deputy commander at COMNAVMED-COM, to do heart surgery—and he tried. His outcomes were not good—about one-third of his cases did not survive the procedure. My predecessor had stopped the heart surgery program just before I arrived but dealt no further with this officer. I called the officer in and behind closed doors we had a discussion about his future. He was retirement eligible. I told him he could retire, but his credentials file would reflect that his clinical privileges to do heart surgery had been suspended and he should not do hearts in the future. He agreed and retired.

By this time four newly minted heart surgeons trained in civilian programs had arrived. The head of heart surgery at UCSD agreed to staff the next 100 cases done at our hospital. He would pick the cases that would be done at our facility and those that we would send to UCSD or one of the other facilities in the area doing hearts. The purpose of this was to build a "cushion" of good outcomes at our hospital. We did it: 100 consecutive cases without losing a patient. Then our surgeons were given permission to do cases on their own, but only low-risk cases—a step at a time.

I had two really bad enlisted problems while here. The first was a "bomber." This guy would call the Operating Room main desk, the labor and delivery deck, or my house and recite the following poem:

Roses are Red
Violets are Blue;
You better get out
Before the bomb gets you.

The calls would come at any time, but the ones to our house came only in the middle of the night. When that happened we would all have to get dressed, wake Fred Sanford, the XO, and his wife next door and wait there until the FBI had cleared our house with bomb-sniffing dogs. This happened before caller ID was available. To capture incoming call numbers back then the FBI had to get a judge's consent and bring in special equipment. We had it in our house for several weeks. We finally caught the guy, a junior enlisted member of our staff who had been dating one of the NIS agent's daughters! He went to a Special Court-Martial and got five years' hard labor in a Navy brig and a dishonorable discharge (bad paper). We found out during the court-martial that a judge in Idaho had dealt with him on some crimes he had committed there involving firearms. The judge had told him to either go to jail or join the Navy.

The other enlisted problem involved a junior enlisted sailor who had saved up enough money to fly home to the Philippines, get married, and bring his bride back to the U.S. A more senior enlisted volunteered to drive him to the Los Angeles airport. The junior sailor never showed up in the Philippines. Eventually his body was found in a reservoir in the mountains east of San Diego. The senior enlisted who had volunteered to take him to the airport owned a cabin there. He also owned a small house in Imperial Beach south of San Diego. There was an old refrigerator that had been tightly duct-taped shut on the back porch. It started to smell and neighbors complained. A sheriff's deputy opened it and found another decaying body. The sailor is serving a life sentence without parole.

The following is one of the most difficult situations I had to deal with. As a hematologist I had cared for many young boys with hemophilia. These boys all received multiple transfusions of plasma concentrates when they had a bleeding episode. When I returned to San Diego as CO every one of them had died from a "new" disease. We came to know this disease as AIDS, caused by the Human Immunodeficiency Virus (HIV). Many people were dying of AIDS because they had received contaminated blood or blood products administered before we began testing the blood supply for the presence of this virus, or they acquired it by using contaminated needles to inject street drugs intravenously or from having sex with an infected partner.

One patient I remember well, Mr. Martinez, had run the mailroom the entire eleven years I had been there during my first tour. He was a spiffy dresser, always wearing a bow tie and a matching vest. He was a World War II vet and had served with an uncle of my father, Captain Fillmore George Koenig, an aviator who had been in the Battle of Midway. Mr. Martinez and I became friends. Soon after I got the cardiac surgery program going again he had bypass surgery. He came through the surgery fine, but he became ill about a month post-op and was dead within six weeks. He had received blood during the procedure that was later found to contain HIV. He died of AIDS.

There were about 3,000 active-duty staff at the hospital and corps school. Every one of us had to be tested for HIV. Since there were so many to test, it was done in weekly batches. Navy policy was that positive reports had to be delivered sealed to the CO only and the CO had to personally and privately notify the individuals that they were positive. Then the person would be processed for discharge. No exceptions were allowed.

There was a superb lieutenant male nurse in our ICU for whom I had written a letter of recommendation to go into the Navy's nurse anesthetist training program, and he had been accepted. The day he detached he came to my office for his departure call and to thank me. Within one hour of his leaving my office the weekly HIV positive report came in, and he was one of the positives on the list. I asked my secretary, Donna, to see if she could find him. She did, and when he came to my office he said, "Skipper, you don't have to tell me. I know." I thought so highly of this officer I personally called COM-NAVMEDCOM and requested a waiver. The answer: "No exceptions." Donna kept track of this fellow and told me a few years later he succumbed to AIDS.

The Second Year: 1986–1987

At the end of my first year my XO, Fred Sanford, got orders to Naval Hospital, Newport, Rhode Island. He had done a wonderful job, and I was sad to see him go. But one thing I had learned about management: you never hold a good person back. I chose Bob Gibbs, director of surgical services at Portsmouth, to be his replacement. Bob was board certified in obstetrics and gynecology and general surgery. He could help me deal with a few of the surgeons at the command whose feelings had been hurt with some of the changes I had made.

I had some robberies to contend with that year. We had a Baskin-Robbins Ice Cream franchise on base that stayed open until 10:00 at night. The women who ran it would take the cash to the Bank of America on base and drop it in the deposit slot. They were held up a couple of times as they made the short trip from the parlor to the bank. We got the Naval Investigative Service involved. The robbers turned out to be boyfriends of the women transporting the money—an inside job.

We had a branch of the Bank of America that had been on base for decades. We also had a Credit Union, but the B of A had seniority. The Navy was trying to convince all personnel to have their pay deposited electronically into a bank account. They were making all new accessions do this, but a judge said they couldn't force people already in the Navy to do it. On pay day, which was every two weeks then, many of the staff who hadn't switched to electronic deposit would take their check to the bank and cash it—resulting in a line several hundred people long. That meant they weren't working at their jobs, and we were losing a lot of productive staff time.

I asked the Bank of America manager to put in some ATMs, which were rapidly gaining popularity. I figured they would be an incentive for people to enroll in electronic deposit of their pay. That way the staff could withdraw just the cash they needed. The bank manager refused. I asked if he would PLEASE put them in at the new hospital. He said no. So I called the manager of the credit union and asked her. She said, "Of course." When it came time to assign space in the new hospital I let the credit union have the space reserved for a bank and thanked the Bank of America for its years of service. All the staff are now on electronic deposit of pay and many use the ATMs on base to get cash when they need it.

The hospital ships were being built in San Diego while I was CO. I had an ancillary responsibility to visit the construction sites every few months and would walk through the *San Clemente*–class tankers in which the hospitals were being constructed. The two tanker hulls destined to become the *Mercy* and *Comfort* were converted at National Steel and Ship Building. These two hospital ships served in conflicts in the Persian Gulf and have supported many humanitarian and goodwill missions.

The Navy's fleet hospital program was getting underway at the same time the two hospital ships were under construction. This was a program that would provide transportable deployable hospitals. They were pre-positioned in storage areas around the planet near where a possible future need for them existed. They came in two configurations, 500 and 1,000 beds. They were self-contained, meaning they had their own galleys and enough supplies to operate 30 days without resupply, and they had the capability to make potable water from local water sources. Our hospital was tasked with conducting the Full Operational Test and Evaluation (FOT&E) for this program. To do this, we had to train 500 of our staff, myself included, about how to set up, operate, and take down a fleet hospital. We did this in groups of a hundred at a time at a special training site at Camp Pendleton. Each session lasted seven days. Once the staff were trained we took the entire group to the Las Pulgas area (Las Pulgas meaning "the fleas" in Spanish, the area was appropriately named), set up a complete 500-bed hospital, operated it with Marines performing the role of patients for a week, and then took it down and packed it up. While we were there we had several encounters with Western diamondback rattlesnakes. Our staff would find them curled up under their cots; one was even found in a sleeping bag. We had made sure staff members were aware that we were poaching on what was normally the snake's territory and had trained them to be aware and cautious. We got along fine with the snakes; none of us were bitten and none of them were killed.

Since then several fleet hospital deployments have been made to combat theaters in the Persian Gulf conflicts, in Zagreb, Croatia, during the conflict there, in support of activities at the prison at Guantanamo Bay and in humanitarian efforts after the tragedies in Haiti.

A Big Surprise

After accomplishing all this, I thought, they would leave me here for the opening of the new hospital. Commanding Officer tours at this time usually lasted three years. One afternoon in the spring I received a call from a friend in Washington who said he had seen the command slate that would be announced the following morning and my name was on it. I was going to Bethesda to be the Commanding Officer of the Naval Health Sciences, Education and Training Command (HSETC). HSETC was a big job. It had been a Flag billet until recently, but so had the Navy Hospital San Diego. I thought about retiring but after talking about it with Deena I decided to give it a try. This job would for the first time in my career take me completely out of medical facilities.

Before moving on to HSETC I addressed the graduating recruit classes at both the Naval Training Center and the Marine Corps Recruit Depot. It was an honor to speak at both of these events, but it was the Marine graduation that brought back memories. In the 1970s, when I was still a "real" doctor at the Navy Hospital, San Diego a black recruit had collapsed while his unit was doing a ceremonial run around the parade field at the Marine Recruit Depot—a distance of more than a mile in full battle gear. This soon-to-be Marine (they are recruits until graduation, then they become Marines) was the honor recruit of his company, so he got to carry the company flag in the run and was supposed to carry it in the graduation parade the next day. He made it through the run but collapsed then died. Postmortem exam showed massive sickling of red blood cells throughout his body. Our hospital CO, RADM Bill Cox, asked me to do the JAG Manual investigation and write the report. He knew me well enough to know I had insight in this area and that I would be thorough in my investigation and make good recommendations.

This young man had sickle cell trait. Normally this is a benign condition, but under severe stress individuals with sickle cell trait can have sickling events. Similar events have occurred in black athletes with sickle cell trait competing in contests at high altitude. Back then water restriction during extreme exertion by recruits was standard practice in boot camp. My findings were that this recruit had died as a result of a sickle crisis resulting from dehydration because he had not been allowed access to water during prolonged physical exertion. My recommendation was that all recruits be required to carry two full canteens on their belts at all times during physical training and that they be required to drink at least one of the full canteens every hour. This became Marine Corps doctrine and has been ever since. At the Marine Recruit Depot graduation ceremony I spoke at nearly a decade later I saw the two canteens on every recruit's belt as they passed in review on their way to becoming Marines. I said nothing to the Depot Commanding General, but I remembered.

Our new hospital was being built on land from both the original Navy hospital property and some new property acquired from the city in a trade. There was one portion of the land in the new hospital area that had been designated for a new Navy Exchange gas station and Minimart—a convenience store. Appropriated funds could not be used to build this, but the Navy Exchange system had plenty of money and it was their intention to proceed.

I had control of this piece of land, since it was on existing Navy property on our base. Again, I remembered my lessons from the Shore Facility Management Course. I said no, we would grade this land and pave it for additional parking. This decision was not popular with some staff because there was a gas station on the original hospital compound that was very convenient—and prices were 10 cents a gallon less than off base. I knew parking was going to be a major problem at the new facility because Congress had cut one of the originally planned parking garages out of the program to contain costs—a decision that all of us aware of the situation knew was very short-sighted. I felt the last thing we needed was people driving on to the base to get gas or groceries. We made this parcel a surface parking lot with hopes that some day a parking structure would be constructed there. Several years later Congress did provide appropriated funds, and a parking garage with a capacity of nearly 1,000 vehicles was built on that site, greatly improving parking on base.

Every year, the San Diego USO held a fundraiser to help with its budget. The first year I was commanding officer they had it in the well deck of one of the Navy's new amphibious ships, with Bob Hope as the speaker. About 300 people attended at $100 each. I was on the USO Board, and the next year they were looking for a venue that would be attractive. The CEO asked if they could have it in the new Navy hospital. Interest in the new hospital was high in the community, since it had been a controversial topic for many years and the progress of its construction was visible to the public. This was a chance for the Navy to open it up to community opinion leaders and hopefully make a good impression.

I checked with Captain Bob O'Donnell, the OIC of the project. The new hospital belonged to him, not Navy Medicine. It wouldn't belong to Navy Medicine for several more months. Bob was a good guy and said, "Hell, yes." The galley could seat 500 and the parking area near the galley was complete and could handle the number of cars expected. Bob had control of the access gates, so our problems were solved. We held the dinner in the new, never-before-used hospital dining facility. We sold all 500 seats at $100 each, 200 more than Bob Hope had drawn a year earlier. This year the theme was a Mexican fiesta. We had dozens of piñatas hanging from the overhead. A popular Mexican restaurant in Coronado catered the event for free, including margaritas.

I said a few words, introduced Captain O'Donnell and he said a few more. Numerous local dignitaries were there. One was a recently retired Commander, naval aviator Randall "Duke" Cunningham. Along with his Radar Intercept Officer (RIO), they became the only Navy flying aces of the Vietnam conflict. He was highly decorated, receiving the Navy Cross, the Silver Star twice, the Air Medal 15 times, and the Purple Heart. Following the war he became an instructor at the U.S. Navy's Fighter Weapons School, better known as TOPGUN, and commanding officer of Fighter Squadron 126 (VF-126) at NAS Miramar. He was planning to run for Congress. He had been politicking throughout the evening and polishing off margaritas like they were Kool-Aid. As the attendees were leaving, "Duke" took to the air again. He climbed on the dinner tables with a broom in hand and ran back and forth while riding it like a witch and occasionally swatting piñatas. With Captain O'Donnell and a few others, I got "Duke" back on the ground, out the door, and off the compound.

In 1990 Duke won election to Congress and served eight full terms and part of a ninth in the House of Representatives. He resigned from the House on November 28, 2005, after pleading guilty to accepting at least $2.4 million in bribes and underreporting his taxable income for 2004. He pleaded guilty to federal charges of conspiracy to commit bribery, mail fraud, wire fraud, and tax evasion. Sentenced to eight years and four months (a total of 100 months) in prison, he was also ordered to pay $1.8 million in restitution. On June 4, 2013, he completed his prison sentence and was released.

A memorable event was the stepping of the mast for the new hospital. Mast stepping is a nautical tradition, and being a Navy Hospital we elected to follow it. It is a ceremonial occasion when the mast is put in place, towards the end of a ship's construction. The ceremony involves placing one or more silver coins under the mast of the ship, which is thought to bring good luck. Rear Admiral Jim Sears, Captain Bob O'Donnell, and I each placed a silver dollar in the hole in which the flagpole would be placed. There was a story behind each coin. Mine was that it had been minted in my father's birth year. Once the coins were in place, the flagpole was raised by a large crane and lowered into place.

Two interns at the Navy Hospital while I was CO, Lieutenant Forrest Faison and Lieutenant Bruce Gillingham, became Flag Officers. Faison is now a Vice Admiral and the Navy Surgeon General. Gillingham is now a Rear Admiral, Upper Half (two stars), and is assigned to BUMED as Deputy Chief, Readiness and Health. One of our internal medicine residents was Connie Mariano. She eventually served as a White House physician, President Clinton's personal physician throughout both his terms. She retired as a Rear Admiral, Lower Half.

When I was at Portsmouth, Captain John Rizzi had told me that being relieved of your first command was a very emotional event. Not only would Deena and I be leaving San Diego for the second time, a place we had come to regard as home, we would be moving for the fourth time since 1980, and three of those moves would be cross-country. It also meant we would be leaving one of our children behind, Steve, to go on his NROTC summer cruise and then start his second year of college. The staff had a wonderful farewell party for me, and I received some nice gifts. The speaker at the event was my secretary, Donna Mackenzie. She was very kind in her remarks.

At the change of command Captain Carl Weslowski, MSC, relieved me and I was awarded the Legion of Merit.

This was the hardest job I ever had.

8

Bethesda

HSETC: 1987–1988

HSETC is an acronym for Health Sciences, Education and Training Command, pronounced H-SET-SEE. I took command in July 1987 and would be there less than a year. There were fewer than 100 staff in the command, compared to the 3,000 in San Diego, but they were senior officers, civilians, and enlisted. The place ran like a well-tuned top. The command's name is long but precise in its description of its purpose: Overseeing all Navy Medical Department education and training programs—a very large span of responsibility.

Several subordinate commands reported to me. There were two Hospital Corps Schools, a Dental Technician School, Flight Surgery Training, Submarine Medical Officer and Diving Medicine training for officers and enlisted, the Fleet Hospital Training Center at Camp Pendleton, and the Fleet Marine Medical Service Schools for Corpsman at Camp Pendleton and Camp LeJeune. Each had highly competent commanders, instructors, and administrative staff. During my tenure at HSETC I visited all of them. These visits seemed routine, but they proved invaluable to me in the future as my responsibilities changed. I had spent the first twenty years of my career in hospitals; now I was being exposed to the rest of Navy Medicine.

We also had the administrative responsibility for the Health Professions Scholarship Program that provided financial support for physicians, dentists and some allied scientists in medical, dental, and professional schools, with a year-for-year payback for each year sponsored with a minimum of three years. There were specialty-training programs for nurses in a variety of specialties such as operating room nursing, nurse anesthetists, and midwifery. There were programs for enlisted to become registered nurses and for Medical Service Corps officers to obtain master's degrees in healthcare administration.

We ran the Graduate Medical Education Selection Board annually in the fall, where all the training program directors selected their interns, residents, and fellows for the following year. I was now in charge of operation of this board and was told to have a presentation about the new hospital ships. I was also told I should have Don Sturz, a newly selected one-star admiral, to do the presentation. He had been the CO of the hospital aboard one of the ships when it made a shakedown cruise to the Western Pacific.

Since I was in charge of the program, I decided to also do a presentation about the Fleet Hospital FOT&E that I had been CO of during my final months in San Diego. I showed excerpts from video footage we made during the exercise. With help from my HSETC staff, I condensed more than twenty-four hours of video into a fifteen-minute presentation. Every one of the hundred or so captains in attendance had heard of the hospital ships, but few knew about the fleet hospital. Both of these platforms would soon become major responsibilities for the training program directors, who had to ensure that their trainees were prepared to work in them. Virtually every officer trained in a Navy program has a collateral assignment to one of these platforms after completing residency.

The first trip I made came in early September, and it was back to San Diego for the commissioning of the new Navy Hospital Corp School on the same compound as the Navy Hospital. I then made a visit to Great Lakes to see the Corps School and Basic Training (boot camp). I had been asked to be the reviewing official at the recruit graduation, an event similar to what I had done in San Diego both for the Navy and the Marine Corps. The graduation was impressive, but it was staying at the BOQ (Bachelor Officers' Quarters) that was the highlight. They had four VIP rooms. One was called the Souza Room, named after Lieutenant Commander John Philip Souza, known as "The March King" because of the marches he composed. He had spent many years conducting Navy and Marine Corps bands. During World War I, at age 62, he volunteered to come back on active duty and conducted the Navy Band at Great Lakes. The room was decorated with framed originals of many of his compositions. The real delight, though, was a clock radio with a cassette tape in it that I could set as an alarm clock and awake to his music.

The Hospital Corps Schools had both basic corpsman training, which was a fourteen-week program, and a host of specialty training programs, some of which lasted longer than a year. There were some technicians at HSETC who had developed an award-winning teaching aid that mimicked the popular TV quiz show *Wheel of Fortune*. They had even got that program's MC, Pat Sajak, and the host, Vanna White, to act in it. It was a forerunner of today's video games. Students used it to help perfect various parts of their academic training in Corps School, and it proved very effective.

On December 8 I was tending to business in my office, and Rear Admiral

Jim Sears dropped by unannounced to chat about the future of Navy Medicine for about an hour. When he left, my secretary, Effie Thompson, who was really well plugged into Navy Medicine's rumor mill, told me that the Medical Corps Flag selection board had met the day before and Admiral Sears was president. She said only one Flag had been selected this year, and that his dropping by to see me was "interesting." A few minutes later she told me that Admiral Bill Buckendorf wanted to talk to me. We talked for 15 minutes or so. When he started to sign off he said to me that soon I would figure out why he called. Effie told me he had also been on the board and was already back at his job in Norfolk. Obviously, the board had done its work quickly. Effie was certain I was the selectee. I just kept my mouth shut.

Deena and I were planning to go to San Diego at the end of January 1988 for the commissioning of the new hospital. The ceremony was going to be on a Friday morning, so we would fly out the afternoon before. We were about to leave for the airport when Deena decided she needed to go to the drugstore across the street and get something for the trip. She told me to be ready to leave when she returned. I was in my skivvies and the phone rang. It was Jim Sears, who asked, "Is this Admiral Koenig?" I said, "No, it's Captain Koenig." He said, "No longer. Now you are Admiral Koenig. The Secretary of the Navy just released the flag board results and you are it." Effie had been right.

The phone kept ringing; it was one well-wisher after another. Deena came back and said, "I thought I told you to be ready?" Scott was there and was yelling, "Dad made Admiral! Dad made Admiral!" I put Scott in charge of the phone, pulled on my clothes, and we were off. Of course, word spread faster than our plane traveled and by the time we arrived in San Diego people were tracking me down. There were more phone calls to handle. The next day it was more of the same at the commissioning ceremony that was a real big deal for the entire community. All of the living hospital commanding officers except one were there.

We flew back to Bethesda on Sunday. Monday when I got to the office Effie and the staff had it decorated in celebration. In just a few weeks I had orders to detach in June and report to the Surgeon General's staff in a position that would be abolished three months after I arrived! I also received a tasking from the SG to sit on a "Blue Ribbon Commission" looking at the National Naval Medical Center. Things had not been going well there, and many of the staff were complaining to their patients, who were senior officers or members of Congress, about the facility's being underfunded and poorly run.

Every year after all the Flag Boards have reported out, the CNO hosts a one-week course for the new Flag selectees and their spouses in Washington. This is a must attend-event and is humorously referred to as "Knife and Fork" School. It is anything but humorous; it is in fact a quite serious event where

The replacement facility for the Navy Hospital San Diego was commissioned in January 1988. From left to right are former commanding officers Earl Warden, Herbert Stoecklein, Willard Arentzen, Earl Brown, William Cox, Paul Rucci, me, and the commander at the time, Carl Weslowski (courtesy U.S. Navy).

we are told what is going to be expected of us as a Flag officer and Flag officer's spouse. All the selectees are congratulated but it is pointed out that promotion to Rear Admiral (Lower Half) will be the last promotion for about half of us. With a gentleman's agreement, we will be expected to retire if not selected for promotion to Upper Half three years from our date of promotion to Lower Half. Of those selected for promotion to Upper Half, only about 10 percent will be selected for promotion to Vice Admiral, and it is unlikely that more than one of us will make four-star rank. In other words, our careers will most likely end in the next three to six years.

There was much discussion about what is expected of our personal conduct during our Flag careers, and examples of what can get us in trouble are given. Nearly all Admirals who get in trouble do so over one of two things—extramarital affairs or money—and the vast majority is due to the former not the latter. The CNO made it quite clear that if any of us were involved in an extramarital affair at the present time he wanted to know about it now, not read about it in the papers. The money problems usually have to do with misuse of government funds. Spouses are told the same things. Guidance is provided about how to deal with Congress, the administration, and the press. There are social events where the attendees get to know each other. There are no presentations on etiquette, as it is assumed we already know how to eat with utensils and speak correctly.

An issue began during my HSETC tenure that would follow me through the rest of my career. The draft had ended a decade earlier and the last of the physicians who had come in during it had left. Dick Ridenour had come to HSETC from San Diego at the same time I had. He and another Navy doctor, Rob Harris, head of neurosurgery at Bethesda, and I had begun some informal conversations about retention of doctors in the Navy. Our impression was that retention of fully trained doctors beyond their obligated service was decreasing and that interest in the Navy's Health Professions Scholarship Program (HPSP) was down. We had historical data about applicants for HPSP for the years after the draft ended, and a significant decline was obvious. We had reached a point where there were barely enough applicants to fill all the available scholarships. This did not auger well for Navy Medicine's future. We didn't have data on overall Navy physician manning, but our sense was that there were a lot of "gapped" billets, meaning there was no one in them. Access to this information would become available to me in my next assignment. Physician retention became a big part of the rest of my career.

One memorable event from HSETC just before I was to detach was a visit with a senior medical student at Uniformed Services University of the Health Sciences (USUHS), Ensign Steve Schallhorn. He was graduating near the top of his class and wanted to go into ophthalmology right after doing an internship. This was unheard of in Navy Medicine. Medical Corps officers who wanted to do an ophthalmology residency always did a utilization tour first, usually as a flight surgeon. He asked if he could be exempted from that requirement because he had gone into the Navy in 1977 after graduating from college and had become a naval aviator, flying F-14s. He had excelled at this and was a Top Gun instructor, receiving many awards along the way. He had also been deep selected for promotion to CDR just before going to USUHS and had become an Ensign, again. It made sense to me that he should be exempted from a utilization tour, so I became his champion and using my newly found influence as a Flag select got him into an ophthalmology residency directly from internship.

The time to plan for the change of command was upon me. Admiral Zimble had asked me to represent him at the USUHS Board of Regents quarterly meetings. Everett Alvarez, from Salinas and the first American pilot shot down in the Vietnam, was now the chair of the Board of Regents. I reminded him my father was his high school math teacher and he remembered him—and even remembered me as a little kid who came to all the home football and basketball games with my Dad! I asked him if he would speak at my change of command. He accepted and we had a nice ceremony. My mother, now 81, came all the way from Salinas for the event. She got to meet Everett and talk with him about my dad. Everett was quite a celebrity in Salinas by this time, with a new high school in the community named after him.

9

Naval Medical
Command, Washington

OPNAV-933: 1 July–1 October 1988

Though it would be another fifteen months before I would officially be promoted, wear the rank of Admiral, and get the additional pay, I was moved into a Flag Officer position as head of OPNAV-933 immediately. I reported to my new—and what would be very short—assignment in July a few days after my change of command at HSETC. I relieved RADM Don Hagen, who had already been promoted from one-star to two-star rank. OPNAV-933 was to go out of existence with the start of the government's new fiscal year on October 1. Where I was to go after that was unknown.

OPNAV is an abbreviation—and is pronounced just the way it is spelled. It means Office of the Chief of Naval Operations. OPNAV-93 was the Navy Surgeon General. OPNAV-933, as indicated by the first 3, meant I was in the SG's 3rd Division. The second 3 was used in the Navy to designate "operations." So, 933 was responsible for developing operational policy for Navy Medicine. Once my office had it developed, we would pass it to the Surgeon General, and if he approved he would sign it and send it to COMNNAVMEDCOM for execution. If this all has you confused, don't worry. It all was to go away three months after I got there. That was because the program designed to separate policy development and execution designed by Secretary of the Navy Lehman and Vice Admiral Bill Cox in the early years of the first Reagan administration was being done away with after just six years—during the second Reagan administration!

We were going back to the old way of doing business. The Bureau of Medicine and Surgery would be resurrected, and policy development and execution would all take place there, with new signage being put up. One of the most senior secretaries at COMNAVMEDCOM/BUMED, Bonnie Schneider, announced that she wouldn't even have to order new letterhead stationery.

She had a whole locker full of it. She said she knew that new-fangled idea back in the early 1980s wasn't going to work, so she had saved it for the day we went back to just being BUMED. She should have received an award for that.

My time at OPNAV-933 was not all wasted. There was a really good Medical Service Corps officer, Captain Ron Turco, and a Nurse Corps officer, Captain Judy Dault, who had been there several years and knew the policy development business cold. I got a crash course in this—for what I had no idea, since I had no idea where I was going come October 1.

While in OPNAV-933 I continued serving on the Chief of Naval Operations Blue Ribbon Panel looking at the problems at the National Naval Medical Center, Bethesda. I could read the tea leaves; some heads were soon going to roll.

Running Short of Doctors?

I began to get some precise figures on the size and makeup of the Medical Corps. What I learned was not pretty. There were about 4,000 authorized Medical Corps billets, but there were only about 3,600 doctors. That meant we were about 10 percent short. About half of all the doctors in the Navy were in training—as interns, residents, or fellows. All the training billets were filled. That meant since we were short 400 doctors, they were all staff physicians—and about 400 of our "staff" physicians were general medical officers, flight surgeons, or other operational medical officers. None of the doctors in the latter group of 400 had done a residency in a recognized medical specialty. I did the math on this and figured we had about 1,200 fully trained board-eligible or board-certified doctors in the Navy. No one had figured this out before, or if they had they were sure keeping the information close-hold. I explained this to Admiral Zimble, the Surgeon General. He quickly became interested in what Dick Ridenour, Rob Harris, and I had discovered—that the Navy had a significant Medical Corps officer retention problem. The Navy had just taken delivery of the two hospital ships and fourteen fleet hospitals. Each of these "platforms" had manning requirements—including fully trained Medical Corps officers. No way did we have the trained staff to man them when "The Flag Goes Up." That's Navy talk for going to war.

Headquarters Shakeup

On October 1 I arrived and OPNAV-933 had gone away. Admiral Zimble told me to come to the Pentagon, where his office was located, and "hang out." He'd find a place for me to hang my hat and something for me to do. He invited me to attend all the briefings he was receiving—so that was interesting. Rear Admiral Paul Caudill, his deputy, took me under his wing, and together they kept me occupied. On Thursday of my first week there Paul said to me, "Tomorrow why don't you and I go to the Flag Mess for lunch?" I did not know there was such a thing and asked if I could go if I was just a Flag select? He said, "Tomorrow you will be my guest."

At noon Friday I had my introduction to one of the many privileges of Flag rank. Indeed, there is a Navy Flag Mess in the Pentagon, as well as an Army and Air Force one. The Marines had one at Headquarters Marine Corps, a half-mile away. Service in them was like in a high-end hotel dining room, Waiters were all decked out in fancy uniforms and you ate with Navy silver and on fine china. The menu had many choices but no prices; the waiter just took your name and at the end of the month you'd get a bill, and it wasn't very big. Over the next several years I ate in the Navy Flag Mess about once a month. As we left the mess Paul told me to be in the SG's office at 1600 (4:00 p.m.). He said, "It's going to hit the fan."

All he could tell me was the Chief of Naval Operations and the Navy Secretary had received the report from the Blue Ribbon Panel on Bethesda that I had been a member of and indeed heads were going to roll. The head of the National Capital Region was going to be relieved, as was the hospital commanding officer. Negotiations were ongoing between the SG and CNO over who would be relieving them. He said I could count on the fact that my name was in play, and I would no longer be without a job.

At 1600 I showed up in the SG's office. Only Admirals were allowed in. In addition to the SG there was Paul Caudill; Jim Sears, who was COMNAV-MEDCOM (he would be there until the following spring); and Don Hagen, who was the deputy for Medical Operations at COMNAVMEDCOM. The latter three were two-star Admirals. Then there was me, the one-star select. The SG told us the National Capital Region was being disestablished and the new CO at Bethesda would be one of us, but he wouldn't say who yet. He said the current head of the National Capital Region was being reassigned to the Uniformed Services University of the Health Sciences Surgery Department to get enough time in to be able to retire as a RDML, and the CO of the hospital was being reassigned to BUMED until he could make retirement plans.

Then Admiral Zimble pulled his rubber chicken out from under his desk—really. He kept it there for occasions like this. He would swirl it over his head holding its feet and then throw it at the person who was getting a new assignment. Around and around it went, everyone looking at me. He released it and it hit Don Hagen in the face. He told Don, "You're it. Report Monday morning—clean out your office this weekend." I had dodged the chicken! Then Jim Zimble, having retrieved the chicken, threw it at me and said, "You're relieving Don. Report Monday."

Don cleaned out his office on Saturday, and Monday morning I walked into it, my car parked just outside the door with the trunk loaded with all my personal gear for the office. The secretary, Joanie Jackson, and the aide, LCDR Paul Quinn, saw me enter and asked, "What brings you to Admiral Hagen's office so early on a Monday morning?"

I replied, "It's mine now."

10

Bureau of Medicine
and Surgery, Washington

BUMED-03: October 1988–June 1990

BUMED is in an area of Washington known as Foggy Bottom, which got that name because it's close to the Potomac River and often foggy there. It is a couple of hundred yards north of the Lincoln Memorial. The buildings were originally constructed to serve as the Naval Observatory. The frequent fog led to the construction of a replacement observatory complex, out in what was then the country, on Massachusetts Avenue. The old observatory became the headquarters of Navy Medicine and the location of the Navy Hospital, Washington.

Learning to Work at Navy Medicine's Highest Levels

This was an educational tour for me, as I had been a clinician for so many years. I had highly qualified people working with me, the best administrators in Navy Medicine. This was my first headquarters tour, and I learned how it operated.

Admiral Zimble moved back to BUMED from the Pentagon in the spring of 1989. He had a major impact on my career, some of it initially circumstantial but later on intentional. He sent me on many trips as his personal representative, as he said the travel was too hard for him. On each trip I learned a lot.

He sent me to Great Lakes to do an investigation of the commanding officer of the Naval Hospital there. She was the Captain Nurse Corps officer who had been the director of Nursing Services at Portsmouth when I was Executive Officer there. The command climate at Great Lakes had deteriorated during her tenure. She decided not to be interviewed by me during the investigation, the final conclusion of which was that she had to be relieved as commanding officer. This was done, and she was given an administrative assignment in Washington while she made preparations for retirement.

Another trip was a one-day trip from Washington to Orlando and return. The reason was to accompany the congressman from the area, Bill McCollum, on a site visit to the Naval Hospital. There was a rumor that the Naval Training Center in Orlando would be on the next Base Realignment and Closure (BRAC) list, and McCollum thought that if that came to pass he might be able to convert the Navy Hospital into a VA facility.

I met McCollum at the Navy flight terminal at Andrews Air Force Base and we made the 2-hour flight to Orlando in a small Navy jet. This was a fascinating trip because that morning Richard Nixon had made his first visit back to Washington since resigning as president and had met that morning with Republican congressmen. Nixon was an expert on foreign affairs (recall that he was the president who reestablished diplomatic relations with China). He told the congressmen the Soviet Union was no longer the major threat to the United States and world peace. He said the Soviet Union would soon collapse and the new threat would be radical Muslim fundamentalism. Nixon said there were more than a billion Muslims, and if anyone could ever get the two major factions, Sunnis and Shia, together they would be a formidable threat. That was incredible insight and the first time I had ever heard that.

McCollum and I toured the hospital. McCollum said it was too small for what he had in mind for a veteran's hospital. He said there were a lot of veterans in the Orlando area, and to get a facility large enough to meet their needs would require all the land the hospital was now on plus the adjacent land, which was the back nine holes of the base golf course. We said goodbye and I flew back to Andrews.

When I landed, there was a car waiting for me, not to take me back to BUMED but to the Pentagon. Secretary of the Navy Henry L. (Hank) Garrett III, wanted to see me! I went straight to his office and was ushered right in. Garrett asked, "What does McCollum want?" I told him he wanted the hospital and the back nine of the golf course. The Secretary said, "No way in Hell. The only thing I get more complaints about from retirees than appointments in Navy hospitals is tee times on Navy golf courses." The battle lines were drawn.

Admiral Zimble asked me to represent him at a Tri-Service military medical education meeting in Japan and deliver headquarters remarks for him. It was also a chance for me to give a presentation on our efforts to improve medical special pays. I was able to visit with my old friend Hidahiko Haruna, who was now the Japan Maritime Self-Defense Force (JMSDF) Surgeon General.

Harvard

Back at BUMED Admiral Zimble told me he wanted me to go to Harvard for a week to take a test presentation of a course they were developing on managed care. The course was a joint effort of the Business School and the School of Public Health. Only forty people were allowed to attend. The course was led by the Dean of the School of Public Health, Dr. Diana Barrett who was married to Bob Vila—the host of a popular TV home improvement show, *This Old House*. The course was very informative, but a memorable part of the trip for me was a reception at one of the faculty clubs the night before the course ended. Dean Barrett brought her husband over and introduced us. We talked through the entire cocktail hour. His parents were Cubans and he badly wanted to get to visit Cuba. I told him I would see if I could at least get him an invite to Guantanamo Bay. Eventually I did, but on the dates available he couldn't make it because of his commitments to make some TV commercials for Sears and Craftsman tools.

The Kennedy School

A few months later Admiral Zimble told me there was an intensive two-week course at Harvard in July at the Kennedy School. No officer from the Medical Department had ever been to it, but Vice Admiral Mike Boorda, the chief of Navy Personnel, said he would like me to go.

There were many really smart people in attendance—Military and Coast Guard generals and admirals and State Department ambassadors. The Dean of the Kennedy School of Government taught the course. I learned a lot about foreign policy. Every day we had a catered lunch in the school's main dining room followed by a speaker. One day there was a piano alongside the podium. I figured there was going to be a concert later on. The Dean introduced the speaker, telling us we wouldn't recognize the speaker's name, but we would probably hear a lot about her in the future. She was the nation's leading expert on the Soviet Union and a great pianist. If we pleaded hard enough, she might play a piece or two for us after she spoke. She was a faculty member from the "Harvard of the West," Stanford University. A petite African-American woman came out, and she was introduced as Condoleezza Rice. After her talk she answered questions and played two selections for us. A takeaway lesson from her talk and the course overall was similar to what Nixon had told the Republican congressmen earlier that year, that the Soviet Union was soon going to collapse. A few months later the Berlin Wall opened and a year and a half later the Soviet Union ceased to exist.

I flew back to Washington and on the way home we stopped at BUMED to check my mail. Admiral Zimble's chief of staff saw me enter and said, "Go down to the boss's office. He needs to talk to you." The Admiral asked about the course and then he told me Admiral Boorda wanted me to go to Capstone in October. "There's never been a medical corps officer in this course before. You've already been nominated and have a billet," he told me. "The reason he is doing this is he wants you to go to London next summer to be the CINCUSNAVEUR surgeon. Though it hasn't been announced yet, Mike is going to get a fourth star and become CINCUSNAVEUR. He wants you to be his command surgeon."

Capstone

Capstone lasted six weeks. About half the time was in secure classrooms at the National Defense University at Fort McNair and the other half on travel with visits to installations both in the USA and abroad. I had to have my security clearance augmented, from Top Secret to SCI, which means Secure Compartmentalized Information. The reason for this higher clearance was that we were going to be exposed to a plethora of signals intelligence—intelligence gathered by satellites, spy planes, and ground-level signal intercepts and humans. Much of what I was exposed to is still classified.

There were thirty in the class, all newly selected admirals or generals, and one ambassador designated to go to a country where this sort of information would be needed. In CONUS I travelled as far west as Denver; some others traveled clear to the West Coast. Among the highlights for me on this travel was a visit to the Strategic Air Command outside Omaha, where I went several hundred feet underground to a secure facility capable of withstanding a direct nuclear hit. While there I took a ride in a C5-A Galaxy and sat in the jump seat behind the pilot as we refueled from a KC-135.

I went to Tampa and MacDill Air Force Base to visit the Special Operations Command headquartered there. We travelled on to Fort Bragg and I watched an airborne artillery unit do low-altitude jumps from C-130s then set up and fire their artillery pieces at a target. The first unit to hit the target won a prize, a couple extra hours of liberty. Later we watched a Marine air-ground attack demonstration at Camp Lejeune. Then we flew out to the USS *George Washington* (CVN-73), where we watched night carrier operations.

I was to travel to Europe for ten days with nine others—an escort officer and a retired Air Force four-star. The four-star was with us to help out with protocol and access. Just before we left on this travel, the time for my official promotion to Admiral arrived. I slipped out of the National Defense University classroom for an hour and went to BUMED, where Admiral Zimble promoted me by administering the oath. Deena and the then-Deputy SG and Chief of the Medical Corps, Bob Higgins, put the new shoulder boards on me. Then Admiral Zimble helped me put on my new blouse with the big fat stripe. I had one more thing to do. A hospital Corpsman who had worked with me at HSETC was due to be commissioned an Ensign in the Medical Service Corps, so as soon as I got on my new rank he came forward and I put his new rank on him.

Our travels in Europe started in Heidelberg, Germany, and we visited up to three different installations each day. We were transported primarily by helicopter to avoid the all-too-frequent traffic jams on the autobahns. We also visited Belgium, Holland, and Luxemburg. From Germany we went to Naples, Italy, where we visited NATO South and the U.S. 6th Fleet (the Mediterranean Fleet). On Saturday we flew from Naples to Berlin in an Air Force jet transport, traveling the last portion of the flight just above stall speed so we could observe the East German army tank training grounds between Berlin and the border with West Germany.

We landed at Templehof Airport, which Hitler had built before World War II. By 1989 it was essentially deserted; the air traffic controllers told us there was less than one landing a week. The airport had been maintained in

My promotion to Rear Admiral, Lower Half, October 1988, with Deena and Rear Admiral Robert Higgins doing the honors (courtesy U.S. Navy).

the condition it was in twenty years earlier when the last commercial flights departed. Those flights were still listed on the schedule boards in the terminal. One other interesting anecdote was that when the airport was constructed it had several basements. When the Soviet army was bombarding Berlin with artillery at the war's end, German civilians headed to the airport and sought shelter in these basements. Hitler ordered the basements flooded. Several hundred thousand civilians are thought to have lost their lives there. When the allies entered and discovered this, they sealed the basements with cement.

Sunday was devoted to a tour of the Eastern sector. We had a U.S. Army Captain who was stationed in Berlin and was fluent in German as our escort officer. We went to Checkpoint Charlie in a U.S. Army van, all of us in full uniform, without passports. The quadripartite agreement between the allied powers required that within Berlin, military personnel in uniform could travel between sectors with only their military ID—and free, by the way, on public transportation. We were warned by our escort officer that the East German border guards would stall, have dogs sniff down the van inside and out, look under it with mirrors, and be a general pain in the neck, but they would let us through. When we got to the checkpoint the guards just waved us through. We never stopped. Our escort officer told us he had never seen that before, and when we returned that evening we could expect to get the "full-treatment."

The weather was mild for early November but there were few people out and about. The mayor of East Berlin and many other officials had resigned during the preceding week. There were many East German police on the streets. We visited an East German army base and a Russian base and even went to their commissary and bought some canned fish to take back for show and tell in Washington. Pickings in their commissary were really slim. We visited the Pergamon Museum, famous for its collection of classical antiquities, the ancient Near East, and its collection of Islamic art. We also visited a military museum that showed us the Soviet version of the end of World War II—a lot more graphic than anything I had ever seen in the West. We stayed for dinner in an East German hotel and had a private dining room with a single waiter. The meal was so-so, but the beer was great. We could take alcohol with us on our plane, so we asked the waiter if we could buy a couple of six-packs. He had no idea what we meant, so we just asked if he would put some in a box for us. He came out with about twenty bottles. We asked him how much? He settled for U.S. $5.00.

We drove back to Checkpoint Charlie and again the East German border guards just waved us through. Our escort officer had been going back and forth through the checkpoint for a few years and had never seen it like this. Back in my hotel room I turned on the TV. There were several German language stations. After being in Germany for several days my familiarity with German was coming back to me. The evening news was showing people on crowded trains, hanging out the windows. They were showing people from East Germany who had gone to Prague for the weekend, which they had been able to do all along since it was behind the Iron Curtain. But now the Czech border guards had stopped turning back East Germans at the border with West Germany! East Germans were pouring into the West by the trainload, and West Germans were welcoming them. Things were changing fast!

On Monday we visited some military installations that dealt with SCI material. Monday evening we flew to Oslo, Norway. The next day we saw some of their NATO installations. One thing that impressed me was their secure headquarters, a deep hole in the ground that was reached by a long elevator ride. It was like a huge office building, deep in the earth. That afternoon we flew to London. Here I spilt from the rest of the group because in eight months I would be coming here for duty. The rest of them went off to see more airplanes.

This was my first time ever in London. I was dropped off at a hotel, where I checked in and placed a call to Rear Admiral Joe Smyth to see if we could get together for dinner. He said for me to be in front of the hotel at a certain time and told me I should be in civilian clothes since the Queen did not allow military uniforms to be worn in London. I was told this was because the Brits did not want their subjects to know how many American military people were really there.

I went to the front of the hotel at the appointed time and within seconds a Brit approached me and said, "Admiral Koenig, I'm here to take you to your dinner with Admiral Smyth." I asked him how he knew who I was. He said, "We have our ways." I had dinner with Joe and his wife and they told me a lot about what to expect in the job. The next day I spent visiting all the principals in CINCUSNAVEUR Headquarters at 7 North Audley Street, Eisenhower's HQ during World War II. Thursday, I flew back to Washington, and while I was in the air the Berlin Wall opened. So I had been in Berlin just three days before that happened. Now that assignment to CINCUSNAVEUR was going to be a lot different. Europe was safer and our involvement in the region was going to rapidly decline.

A few weeks after Capstone ended, and less than two weeks before Christmas, Admiral Zimble sent me back to Germany for another NATO meeting. The meeting was held in Garmisch-Partenkirchen, a mountain resort town in Bavaria, which since World War II has been used as a recreation area for the U.S. Military stationed in Europe. This meeting was to begin discussions about ramping down of the U.S. forces in Europe after the opening of the Berlin wall. The world was already beginning to change fast.

On the way back I stopped in London overnight and stayed in the guest quarters at CINCUSNAVEUR—Ike's apartment during World War II.

Preparing to Move to London

Because Deena and I were going to England and there wasn't military housing in the city, the Navy gave me a week's time for us to go there and house-hunt. Before going I contacted CINCUSNAVEUR headquarters about getting hotel reservations and an estate agent to show us around. I thought they'd put us up in a hotel. Instead they connected me to the chief of staff, Captain Hank Dalton, father of my late patient Megan, who had died from a liver tumor. He and his wife, Penny, were planning to come to the States in early March for their son's wedding. They suggested we plan to come during that week and stay in their house. We did! We found a lovely house with an English garden that was being refurbished. The Navy executed the lease on it. The location was ideal for me, just two tube (subway) stops from where I would work.

As spring of 1990 arrived we prepared for our move. We put our house on the market, made arrangements to sell our reliable 1971 Mercedes diesel and found a neighbor who was willing to take our cat. Since the Queen didn't allow us to wear uniforms in London, my orders included a civilian clothing allowance of $1,500. I was told I would need three suits and a tuxedo, plus civilian shoes. I got all this, but it came closer to double that amount, so I covered the rest out of pocket.

Japan, Again

In May Admiral Zimble asked me to represent him again at the military medical education meeting in Japan. Off I went and this time Hidahiko took me to the Tsukiji Market, perhaps the largest fish market in the world. The market opened around 2:00 in the morning. After a couple of hours of seeing and smelling fish of just about every variety imaginable we left for another Japanese tradition following a fish market visit—breakfast sushi. We went to a very high-end restaurant nearby and his aide held the beaded entry curtain aside for me so I could enter first. When I entered, the maître d' raised his arms over his head, crossed them, and said directly to me, "No Gaigin." In English this means "no foreigner."

Hidahiko's aide was on him in a flash. The poor fellow went to his knees with his forehead on the floor. I don't know what the aide said, but it worked. We were escorted to a private booth, served the best sushi I have ever had.

and when we were ready to leave there was no bill, even though Hidahiko's aide tried to pay.

One Last Trip Before Detaching

When I got back to BUMED Admiral Zimble said he had another trip for me before I detached—to Norway for a Northern NATO medical conference. This was near the latter part of May. It would only take four or five days, but he said it was really important that I go because all my counterparts from the Northern NATO countries would be there.

A few days before I left for Norway a Public Health Service Rear Admiral, Ed Martin, came to my office on a courtesy call, a scheduled fifteen-minute visit. He had been the chief of staff to C. Everett Koop when he was the Public Health Service Surgeon General during the Reagan administration. Ed had been reassigned to the Pentagon to the office of the Assistant Secretary of Defense (Health Affairs). The fifteen-minute visit wound up lasting a couple of hours. We found a lot of common ground to discuss.

The next day I got a call asking me to come to Health Affairs in the Pentagon to meet the new Assistant Secretary of Defense (Health Affairs), Dr. Enrique Mendez. Dr. Mendez was a retired army Major General who had commanded Walter Reed. Ed Martin had suggested that he and I meet before I left for Norway. We had a cordial visit, rehashing a lot of the issues I had discussed with Ed Martin the day before. Among them was my growing concern for retention of trained physicians. I told the Secretary that retention was declining and one of the big drivers was the growing pay disparity between what doctors could make in the military and what they could make as civilians. My impression was that manning of the medical departments was more or less based on what was available and not well aligned with what was needed to man the deployable platforms in support of the nation's war plans. I said we were not doing a good job in serving the eligible population, especially the retired members. These are the people we really needed to support our training programs and we were driving them out of the system. My impression was that CHAMPUS was an archaic insurance program unresponsive to the needs of much of the beneficiary population—especially the retired members and their dependents. We really needed to start correcting these problems or we'd lose the all-volunteer force and have to return to the draft. That would not be popular. What I had learned at Harvard and Capstone had sunk in. Dr. Mendez listened intently.

The next day I flew to Norway for the Northern NATO medical meeting. I went to Oslo, spent the night, and the next morning was picked up by a Norwegian Military Staff car and taken to the airport, where I boarded a

Norwegian Air Force C-130 for the flight to Trondheim. They flew us through valleys at treetop level most of the way. This was a radar-evading technique they had developed to avoid detection if war broke out with the Soviets. C-130s aren't like civilian airliners with windows and passenger seats. There's just a web bench on which to sit along the bulkhead, with safety harnesses. To look out we had to go to a window, either up front or at one of the doors. We stood up, hanging on for dear life in a plane that was careening along twisting and turning.

While sitting in the conference room the second day of the meetings with the Norwegians, Brits, Germans, and several others, heroically fighting jet lag, a Colonel tapped me on the shoulder, and said, "There is an Admiral Boorda holding on the telephone for you." I picked up the receiver and Admiral Boorda said, "Harold, you may as well come back home. Your orders to London have been cancelled. You're going to be a Deputy Assistant Secretary of Defense in Health Affairs." I asked if there was any way I could get out of this. He said I could call the guy who signed the memo approving my orders. I asked who that was. He replied, "Dick Cheney."

What had happened was that the new Assistant Secretary of Defense (Health Affairs), Enrique Mendez, instructed each of the services to nominate a Flag officer physician for this position, so Admiral Zimble had offered my name but he hadn't bothered to tell me. Dr. Mendez had listened to Ed Martin about his meeting with me and then had me come over to check me out. That was my interview for the job in Health Affairs. Dr. Mendez had told Dick Cheney, "That's the guy I want." Cheney approved. I asked Admiral Boorda when I should report. He said, "You couldn't make it home by tomorrow morning, so Monday."

At home we had to undo a lot that was underway. The house had not sold, so that was easy to stop, as was giving the cat away. I had already delivered the car to the buyer, so there was no getting that back. I also had $3,000 in clothes, $1,500 of which had been paid for by the Navy. Within hours of my new orders being issued a Navy JAG Corps officer called me and told me to return the $1,500 right away. I called the Navy two-star JAG and told him what had just happened. He told the JAG officer to write it off. Fortunately the Navy had signed the house lease in London, so I had no problem there.

As for my office at BUMED, my administrative assistant, LCDR Paul Quinn, had packed up everything and taken it to my new office in the Pentagon, Room 3E336.

11
The Pentagon

Deputy Assistant Secretary of Defense, Health Affairs:
June 1990–June 1994

DRINKING FROM A FIRE HOSE

On Monday morning I went to the Pentagon and found my new office, Room 3E336. I met with Dr. Mendez, his interim Principal Deputy Assistant Secretary of Defense (PDASD), Dave Newhall, a holdover from the Reagan administration, and Ed Martin. They went over what my beginning responsibilities would be but warned me they would soon expand. Much of this was new to me. I started with military medical construction including all hospitals, clinics, and medical research units worldwide—Army, Navy, Air Force, and Marine Corps. I would have to review and sign off on all of the contracts for replacement or renovation of these facilities. Some of the contracts were over the hundred million dollar mark. The position was highly political since these projects created jobs in congressional districts and that fact helped get those in Congress reelected.

Another area dealt with analyzing workload data for the Military Health System down to individual facilities. This was a crucial effort because it would influence and justify future decisions about construction, budgets, and the Base Realignment and Closure process. This was under the direction of a positively brilliant Army Medical Service Corps officer, Lieutenant Colonel Stuart Baker.

We had to respond to all letters of complaint congressional offices received from constituents and sent to us for investigation. My staff would investigate and draft the response for the member to sign. There were several of these every day, and a short turnaround was always demanded. Our office was way behind in responding to these.

I was asked to continue what I had started regarding physician pay reform. It was now accepted that the disparity between what doctors made

90

in the military compared to civilian practice was a major contributor to retention. Serious discussions had begun with Congress. It involved a lot of money and the possibility that if improvements were not made the all-volunteer force would fail. When the draft had ended in 1975, a new draft law was written that included a provision allowing for drafting physicians should the military run short. It was referred to as "the doctor draft." Congress had correctly anticipated that doctors would be the weakest link in the all-volunteer force.

I was told I needed to select a deputy. I interviewed a number of outstanding candidates and selected Patty Watson. She had previously worked on the Senate Armed Services Committee and had a good understanding of how the legislative branch worked. Much of what I would be doing involved working with Congress. Patty guided me through that. She also said we needed a secretary, and she had someone in mind, Mimi Brooks, whom she had worked with before. We hired Mimi and she was with us my entire time at Health Affairs.

Two months after I arrived, Dr. Mendez fired the Senior Executive Service (SES) officer who was in charge of CHCS (Composite Health Care System). At that point CHCS had been deployed to two alpha and twelve beta test and evaluation sites. It was falling behind schedule and not getting good reviews. The SES officer was spending lots of money on travel and hosting an annual conference that was the most costly in all of DoD, held in the dead of winter, of course, in Florida. It was quite popular and very well attended. One of my first actions was to cancel that conference.

Dr. Mendez told me he was assigning CHCS to me, and whether it failed or succeeded would be up to me. He said with this changeover half the personnel assigned to Health Affairs would be working for me. At this point I hardly knew what CHCS was. My job was to get it to the point that the Defense Chief Information Officer (CIO) and the Government Accounting Office (GAO) would sign off on it so we could deploy it worldwide.

War

Early in the morning of August 2, 1990, I was called to the office of the Vice Chief of Naval Operations. He told me we had a huge problem that at this moment was classified at a level that did not permit its being discussed over regular phone lines. Saddam Hussein had sent 100,000 soldiers and 700 tanks into the Gulf State of Kuwait. He had threatened to turn Kuwait City into a "graveyard" if any country dared to challenge his "take-over by force." The vice chief told me, "We are going to war."

I returned to Health Affairs, told Dr. Mendez, and he called in the other Deputy Assistant Secretary of Defense (DASD) and the PDASD. We would be very busy until this was over. Planning for the medical force to support the invasion to push Saddam's forces out of Kuwait took precedence over all our other activities but not to their exclusion—we just worked longer and harder. Expectations were that casualties would be high, perhaps as high as one in three who deployed. We were planning to send a force of a half million to the theater, so in absolute numbers, we anticipated casualties that would overwhelm the capacity of the existing military medical infrastructure and the VA. During the previous decade Saddam had been involved in an eight-year war with Iran in which there were over one million casualties. Both sides had used chemical weapons on each other and their civilian populations.

We sent both of our hospital ships to the Persian Gulf and two of the Navy's 500-bed fleet hospitals. The Navy had to provide the medical support for all the Marine Corps units in the area. The Navy nearly emptied its CONUS medical facilities of its active-duty medical personnel. Reservists were called to active duty to replace them. The Army also sent deployable hospitals to the area, but manned them with reserve personnel, leaving their active component in place in their CONUS facilities. The Air Force was responsible for the air-evacuation program to return casualties to a dozen hub airfields in CONUS from where they would be sent to military or VA hospitals nearby.

The United States has a program known as CRAF, Civilian Reserve Air Fleet, that allows the military to take over up to 80 percent of all civilian commercial aircraft. In a matter of hours civilian airliners can be reconfigured to carry personnel or cargo or both. We activated what was called first-level CRAF, taking over 15 percent of all civilian airliners or commercial cargo aircraft. Many civilian pilots are members of the Air Force Reserve or Guard; there were plenty of people to operate the planes. The planes would fly to the theater with their loads and then could be reconfigured in a few hours to transport casualties back. The medical personnel to accompany and care for the casualties also came primarily from the Air Force Reserve or Guard.

We had to call up nearly all our reserve medical personnel. Though the numbers existed on paper, there were many problems. Many reservists had not kept up with their training and tried to use this as an excuse not to be called up. Several actually said, "I only joined the reserves for the extra money. I didn't think I would ever have to deploy." Others were eager to report and fulfill their obligation; but to do so their communities would lose the services of critically needed medical providers, and some small communities would lose all of them. These situations quickly became political hot potatoes. None of this went unnoticed by me, and it would become fodder for my arguments supporting physician pay increases after the war's end.

Proper equipment and supplies were a huge problem. The nation had been saving money since the end of the Vietnam War by slowing investment in military equipment and supplies, which had not been replaced after passing their expiration dates. Medical personnel in-theater found when they opened their supply modules the equipment and supplies dated from the time of the Vietnam War. Much of it was useless. We had to put enormous pressure on the nation's medical manufacturers to gear up production to provide enough to even get started. At one point I was informed there was less than a week's supply of X-ray film and IV fluids available in the entire nation. We had not maintained the industrial base.

Blood was a problem. We had plenty stored, but it is hard to transport. It is bulky and has very strict temperature requirements at which it has to be maintained to remain viable. In the liquid state it has to be kept at 4 degrees Centigrade and is viable for about six weeks. To get to the war zone it had to go by air—displacing such things as personnel, equipment, and supplies. We also had huge stores of frozen blood stored in classified locations around the world. But frozen blood has to be kept at minus 80 degrees Centigrade. This requires special and expensive industrial freezers and reliable electrical power. Reconstituting frozen blood is a process that requires specialized equipment and highly trained personnel. Once reconstituted it has to be used within a few hours or discarded.

A big concern for us with this conflict was that Saddam would make good his threats to use chemical and germ warfare on our troops. In particular we were concerned he would use nerve agents, most likely Sarin gas. We knew he had a lot of it because he had used it in his war with Iran. Nerve agents work by causing muscular paralysis, and they are lethal because the muscles supporting respiration become paralyzed. The victim dies a horrible death, similar to strangulation. We had an agent that we knew could block the action of Saddam's nerve agents, pyridostigmine bromide. We have used this agent effectively for decades in people with myasthenia gravis; it works and has minimal side effects. But it had never been used prophylactically in the numbers of people we would be giving it to in this conflict. To be effective it has to be taken prior to exposure. That meant all our troops in theater would have to take it daily. That was one of the most difficult decisions of the entire war for us. Dr. Mendez had to make that decision. Ed Martin, Peter Collis, and I were his DASDs who were physicians. Dr. Mendez called us together in a closed meeting and we discussed it. We knew there would be pushback and follow-on consequences, but not using it could have been far worse. Dr. Mendez, a devout Catholic, led us in a prayer asking for divine support and signed the order. The manufacturer had to massively ramp up production. Our troops in theater took it. After the war some developed an obscure set of symptoms that came to be known as Gulf War Syndrome or Persian Gulf Illness—and many tried to blame it on the pyridostigmine bromide they were forced to take. The debate about the etiology of this obscure condition continues to this day.

We also had to prepare for the possibility there would be many deaths in this conflict. A massive expansion of the Dover Air Force Base mortuary was made. Just before we invaded Kuwait, Dr. Mendez, Dr. Collis, and I flew by helicopter from the Pentagon to Dover, Delaware, to do a final walkthrough of the facility, which had more than doubled in size since Saddam invaded. We had 10,000 caskets stored in one warehouse. Inside the mortuary we had the latest equipment to aid in the identification of body parts using DNA analysis. CT scanners were installed to check for weapons and explosives as every body bag entered the facility, similar to how luggage is now screened at airports. There were uniforms for every branch of service, supplies of all medals, and rank identifiers, and seamstresses to appropriately prepare every uniform for the deceased member. Every deceased member would be buried or go to cremation with a complete uniform, no matter how much or how little of that soldier's remains were available. Finally, there was an American flag to cover each casket.

On February 24, 1991, the coalition forces led by the United States began the liberation of Kuwait. Five days later the war was over. Saddam's forces surrendered, ran, or died. Between 20,000 and 35,000 Iraqi soldiers died; 150,000 became POWs. Coalition losses were 1,155 dead and 70 POWs. About 70 Americans lost their lives. Soon after the Persian Gulf War ended our troops came home. There were victory parades and celebrations all around the country, including a huge one in Washington, D.C. Dr. Mendez asked me to represent him in a meeting with five other assistant secretaries. I was the only military person and physician present; all the others were political appointees. The group were high-fiving each other and were especially exuberant about how little this war had cost compared to Vietnam, Korea, and World War II. I told them they hadn't even begun to pay for this war, that the big price tag was yet to come. Soon came Persian Gulf Illness, or Gulf War Syndrome, and all the compensation the VA would wind up paying for illnesses related to service in the conflict. At this point I hadn't yet heard about the ammunition storage facility demolition in 1991 and the possible exposure of our troops to chemical agents. Not until 1997 did letters go out to 99,000 of our troops telling them of their possible exposure. In 2001 another 101,000 were similarly informed. War isn't cheap, even for the victors.

Work in all the other areas went on as well. The letters forwarded to my office from congressional offices seemed to fit into patterns. Most were complaints about access to care and were easily dispensed with. We simply quoted the law back to the member and the beneficiary. If they were retired, we encouraged them to get a supplemental policy or if they were over 65 to make sure they had Medicare Part B. We also took the opportunity to inform the congressional member that if access was to be improved it was the benefit that needed to be improved, and it was up to Congress to do that. Letters complaining about quality of care required a lot more research and almost invariably we would send a letter back to the Congress member telling them what we knew but also that we were in the process of gathering more information and would get back to them as soon as we had it. In a couple of months we were able to get current on these responses. This improved relations with many members' offices.

Changes with Quick and Big Payoffs

We tackled a couple of favorite issues of mine that I had dealt with earlier at Naval Hospital San Diego: smoking and the pharmacy. Dr. Mendez was opposed to smoking in the workplace, so he agreed with me about getting it reduced, if not eliminated, in the Pentagon. We felt that if we did that at headquarters it would make it easier to do throughout the rest of the system. He was able to convince the other leaders that this effort was worthwhile, and so half of the restrooms were designated as smoking areas. In all other areas in the Pentagon smoking was not allowed, including individual offices. Smoking reduction spread throughout the military, including in buildings, ships, subs, planes, and operational vehicles. The price of tobacco products was raised so it was comparable to prices on the local civilian market. Tobacco use dropped by more than 50 percent.

Pharmacy was the other area we tackled. Dr. Mendez agreed with what I had done in San Diego in increasing the maximum supply dispensed at one time from 30 days to 90 days for most prescriptions. We changed the entire DoD policy to allow a 90-day supply. Another pharmacy change came when I met a very sharp pharmacist at a small Army hospital. He had discovered and implemented a new system for refilling prescriptions using automation facilitated through the use of digital telephones. This technology would automate a phone-in system where patients would have to recite their name, their Social Security number (SNN), and their prescription number to a tape recording and then wait for a call back that their prescription was ready for pick-up. We estimated that throughout the military health system there were about 5,000 people employed listening to these tape-recorded messages, typing out the prescription labels, and calling the patients to let them know their prescription was ready to pick up. With the new system, patients used the push buttons on their phone to type in the last four digits of their sponsor's SSN and their prescription number. A recording would tell them when their prescription would be ready for pick-up. I convinced Dr. Mendez we should install this system-wide. It would be worth it many times over, not just in costs but also in accuracy and patient satisfaction. We were actually able to pull this off without asking "mother-may-I" of a higher authority. We eliminated the 5,000 positions filled by people listening to the audiotapes and typing labels and rehired them all in new jobs in the system. Patient satisfaction soared.

Now I had a chance to tackle the Military Medical Construction (Medical MilCon) budget that was a congressional "candy jar." This was where members could assure their reelection—getting a project for their district. This "candy jar" had about $300 million in it every year. We had to spread it around to cover as much of the department's needs as possible. Usually there was one really big project underway at a time, as the Naval Hospital San Diego had been while I was commanding officer there.

Gordon Dowery was the head of the Medical MilCon office. Gordon was in tight with the staff and members of the congressional subcommittee that dealt with Medical MilCon. He wasn't accustomed to having someone in Health Affairs looking over his shoulder and asking hard questions. As long as he stayed inside the $300 million target and the congressional members were happy, he basically got his way.

One of the first big projects I had some questions about was a new 200-bed facility for Whiteman Air Force Base in Missouri. This was not a big base; it certainly didn't have the population surrounding it to require that size facility. I asked him for the justification, and he said that Whiteman was going to be the home base for all 200 of the new B-2 bombers the nation was about to build and it would grow accordingly. I told Gordon that wasn't going to happen, that the Cold War was over. No way in the post–Cold War era were we going to build 200 new bombers at an estimated price of $1 billion per plane. I did some asking around in the DoD Comptroller's office, and they confirmed my suspicion. In he end we built only 21 B-2 bombers. We also built a new clinic at Whiteman with a few holding beds.

Another project I spotted was for the Navy, and dealing with it convinced me this DASD assignment would be the end of my Navy career. It was a replacement hospital for Portsmouth. This was a big one, with a price tag well over $300 million. Before I could sign a contract for construction we had to do a final review justifying the size, scope, and cost of the project. Stu Baker and his crew crunched the numbers on the workload from the hospital for the previous several years. They found the facility was sized at least 100 beds larger than could be justified. Stu and his staff had discovered that for several years Portsmouth had been inflating their number of admissions by double-counting women who were having babies. They did this by admitting women on paper when they came in for their routine mid-term ultrasounds to make sure all was going well with their pregnancies—with the bonus that the babies' genders could be determined. Done efficiently this can take all of

30 minutes; it certainly does not warrant admission. When we factored out these "admissions" the required number of beds dropped by over 100, which meant we should take an entire floor out of the planned facility.

We informed the Navy, telling them of our findings and offering them a chance to rebut. The Navy SG and Assistant Secretary responsible for facility oversight immediately went political without understanding our findings and how we arrived at them. They fired up the four Tidewater Virginia region congressmen and both Virginia senators. I had presented our findings to Dr. Mendez and he agreed with our analysis. He asked that I offer to do the presentation to BUMED. Stu and I went to BUMED anticipating there might be five or six at the meeting, but there were more than a hundred, a standing room only crowd in BUMED's Medal of Honor hall, including both the SG and the Navy Assistant Secretary. I gave the presentation, answered questions, and left.

Calls from congressmen and senators came in to Secretary of Defense Dick Cheney's office. Cheney wouldn't deal with "small stuff" like this. His threshold was $1 billion; below that he passed the problem to his deputy, Don Atwood. I was called to Atwood's office and I told him what had happened and how we had developed this information. He was thrilled with what we had done—really! He called the Navy secretary and told him to have a letter on Admiral Harold Koenig's desk by 0800 the next day accepting the resized facility or the project would be cancelled. When I got to my office the next morning the letter was there.

Later there was some redemption of my reputation with the Navy when Stu Baker and I did much the same thing to the replacement facility for Womack Army Hospital at Fort Bragg. The military services and Congress learned there was a new sheriff in Health Affairs. Two more major projects got this treatment. The first was the Air Force's request to build a new monster hospital at Lakenheath, England. What they wanted to do was make Lakenheath the major evacuation hospital for future conflicts in Europe, Southwest Asia, and North Africa. They wanted to displace Landstuhl Army Medical Center adjacent to Ramstein Air Base in Germany as the major evacuation hospital. Their request was for more than $300 million.

Stu Baker again crunched the numbers, and we spotted a huge problem in their workload reporting. Some simple math showed that they had about fifty births a month, but all of their newborns stayed in the nursery for a week or more. I went to Lakenheath and met with the hospital commander. We had provided him a copy of Stu's study—but he had not bothered to look at it. I asked him why babies were kept in their nursery for seven days. He said they weren't, they stayed for two days, which was our national standard then. I told him that was not what his workload data suggested. He said the data must be wrong. I reminded him that his staff submitted the data. We went on a tour of the hospital. When we got to the nursery I saw there were about fifteen babies there. I asked the Air Force nurse in charge why there were so many babies. She said this was normal. I asked her how long they kept babies. She replied it was a minimum of seven days. I asked why, and she said because it was command policy. The replacement hospital was never built.

The last situation I will mention involved a request for a replacement hospital for Fitzsimmons Army Medical Center (Fitz) in Aurora, Colorado, a suburb of Denver. Pat Schroeder was the congresswoman from the district. She wanted a replacement facility built that would cost a half billion dollars. We were already planning to ask that Fitz be listed for closure on the next BRAC list. She knew it, and she saw getting a replacement facility underway as a way to prevent that. We had crunched a lot of numbers and found that there were only about 1,500 active duty military personnel in the fifty-mile catchment area of Fitz and most of those were hospital staff. The way they kept their patient numbers up was through the Air Force medevac system. In that system, if a patient needs care beyond the capability of the facility nearest them, they can be medevaced to another facility that can provide that care. When we took a look at medevacs to Fitz, we learned that one out of every four individuals who boarded a medevac flight anywhere in the world wound up at Fitz. They came from Europe and the Far East, overflying several hospitals along the way that could provide the needed care. The Army was using the very expensive medevac system as a limousine service to bring patients to Fitz. Fitz was put on the next BRAC list and closed. At that point, after twelve terms in Congress, Pat Schroeder chose not to run for reelection. I've been told that during a community meeting with constituents she blamed the loss of the Fitz replacement program and its subsequent placement on the BRAC list on "those two Goddamn admirals in the Pentagon." Ed and I are both very proud of that.

Travel, MilCon and CHCS

Travel was a big part of my job and was primarily for the Medical MilCon and CHCS programs. I had made one trip to Hawaii and one trip to Europe before the war. The Hawaii trip was to look at both the Medical MilCon and CHCS programs. Tripler Army Medical Center on Oahu is the major facility there and was under the watchful eye of Senator Daniel Inouye. It was essential that I maintain good relations with him because he was chairman of the Subcommittee on Defense of the Senate Appropriations Committee—the committee that put the money in our budgets. The senator always had some projects going on at the medical facilities in Hawaii. He explained to me that this was essential to the state's economy. If he stopped channeling money to Hawaii, in a decade it would be back to little grass shacks. In the earlier days of transpacific transport most ships would make a call in Hawaii on their trips between the Far East and North America. With faster and larger ships this was no longer the case. Hawaii's economy was now dependent on the military and tourism.

Tripler was one of our two alpha test sites for CHCS. The other was at Fort Knox, Kentucky, which was much smaller. We'd introduce software changes at Fort Knox. If they worked there for a week or so, we'd then install them at Tripler. It was a much larger facility, and with a lot more program users we could stress the system and find bugs that might not become evident at Fort Knox. Using this approach, CHCS was progressing nicely.

I toured all the clinics on Oahu. They all had one problem in common: Being close to the ocean the salt air takes a toll on them much more rapidly than in areas farther from the sea. Consequently, there was a lot of maintenance and repair that had to be factored in for them, and this all came out of the Medical MilCon program. One other thing I learned from Senator Inouye was that he sponsored the $5 million a year brown tree snakes program. This was in the Medical MilCon budget because, he said, he couldn't find another budget to hide it in. It paid for airport personnel to examine the wheel wells of all planes that landed in Hawaii coming from other islands in the South Pacific. Many of these islands have brown tree snakes. The dietary staple of these snakes is small birds. Hawaii has no snakes of any kind, but it has lots of small birds and this program was designed to keep things that way.

Before the war broke out I had made one trip to Europe, which had been to Germany, where I visited all eleven military hospitals there plus several contingency hospitals. The latter were buildings that were ready to be activated should war break out with the Soviet Union. The hospitals could be ready to commence operations on just a few days' notice. It was from these facilities that we got a lot of the supplies we needed to replace the out-of-date supplies that had been shipped to support our forces in the Persian Gulf. We also sent many Army personnel from the facilities in Germany to support the Persian Gulf War effort. When the war ended, instead of being returned to Germany most were rotated back to CONUS and we began closing military hospitals in Germany.

I went to Italy, Sicily, and Sardinia to visit our medical facilities there. I met with a Naval Academy classmate, Vice Admiral Bill Owens, who at that time was in command of the U.S. 6th Fleet, with his headquarters in Gaeta, Italy. Bill had a special request: he needed help getting a new headquarters built. The Italians had offered to lease us a single building currently used as a warehouse on a hilltop overlooking the bay. He could identify all of the money needed except that needed for renovation of the medical clinic portion—that was my responsibility. I toured the existing clinic in Gaeta, and found it was a mess. I scraped together the needed money from leftovers in our Medical MilCon budget and funded it. Years later I got to tour the facility, and it was superb.

There were other facilities south of the Alps that I visited both for Medical MilCon and CHCS purposes, including Naples, where we were in the early stages of preparing to build a new hospital; our old, and later our new, hospital in Sigonella; and the Air Force and Army facilities in northeastern Italy at Aviano and Vicenza. We had CHCS operational throughout Europe and the ability to move data between facilities there before the SGs stopped quibbling about it in CONUS.

We had a new hospital under construction in Incerlik, Turkey, near Tarsus, the home of Paul of Tarsus, now better known as St. Paul. This was one of those hospitals built with six floors below ground, so it was an expensive one. We were having a problem getting computers into the hospital for CHCS. The Turks wanted to charge us a stiff tax for bringing them in. We eventually solved that problem by sneaking them into the country on a night flight during a local holiday. Our Army hospital at Vicenza was one where the Army planned to stop inpatient care. There were existing plans for a replacement hospital, but the Italians had been delaying the start of construction for over a decade. They have a good medical system that the Army planned to use. This was quite contentious among the dependents, but we eventually got it done.

An Interruption

One day in the middle of 1991 I went to the head (restroom) and noticed that my urine was brown. I thought that was strange, and I had no explanation for it. A couple of hours later I went again and it was still brown. I called my doctor at Bethesda, Captain John Eisold, who told me to get out there right away. John took me to urology, where the chief of service, Captain Kevin O'Connell, took me to the urology radiologic suite, where they first did an IVP, which was normal, then came at me with a rigid cystoscope, a procedure all male medical students agree is the last one they would ever want to have. That revealed the problem. I had a bladder tumor. I was taken to the operating room. I was lucky, as the tumor was not invasive, but I would require a course of six infusions of chemotherapy into my bladder at biweekly intervals, then a repeat cystoscopy every three months for two years, then every six months for the next year and annually from then on. After the procedure they made me stay home for two weeks, then for the next month they put me on shortened work hours. I couldn't arrive at work before 8:00 a.m. and had to leave by 3:00 p.m. During that time, I went through the chemo infusions in my bladder, which were quite uncomfortable. At 3:00 p.m. every day Dr. Mendez would come into my office and tell me it was time to leave.

Once the chemo was completed, my bladder was free of any tumors and so in September I went back to my regular routine.

Return to Full Duty and CHCS Certification

We had been using Europe as a separate test area for CHCS and had one hospital in Germany where we were trying something new. There were eleven outlying clinics around the hospital. These clinics did not have their own labs but instead sent all their specimens to the hospital's main lab for studies. We hooked all the clinics into the hospital's CHCS. Now instead of the printed report having to be transported back to the clinic, a process that routinely added a day to the doctors' getting the results, reports were ready as soon as they were entered into CHCS.

This success in Europe set me to thinking: If we could do this in Europe, why couldn't we do it in CONUS? The plan for CONUS was for each facility to have its own computer hardware setup. That meant a lot of computer rooms, disk drives, and assorted paraphernalia. Why not set up regional computer centers and just move the data back and forth? We could save a lot of money in hardware acquisition and personnel costs since we wouldn't have so many people running the hardware.

I talked with Al Andreoni, the SES directly in charge of CHCS. He agreed but told me this would not go over well with the three services. The SGs not only did not want the other services looking at their data, they also didn't even want their own facilities looking at each other's data. I said that was a bunch of crap and brought this up with Dr. Mendez, who agreed we needed to economize. He called in the SGs, had Ed Martin and me at the meeting, and told them what we were going to do. There were a lot of fists pounded on the table and threats made, but when the cursing ended they really couldn't come up with reasons, other than their traditional parochialism, not to do this. And so it was. We completely remapped how we were going to do the CHCS hardware and communications and saved multiple millions of dollars.

There would be many more trips to Hawaii, Europe, and throughout the continental United States to problem-solve and move CHCS adoption along. There were multiple meetings with Science Applications International Corporation (SAIC), the contractor for CHCS, the DoD chief information officer and the services. GAO, then known as the General Accounting Office and now known as the Government Accountability Office, was the final hurdle we had to clear before permission would be given for deployment beyond the two alpha and twelve beta test sites. The GAO is known as the "Congressional Watchdog" and investigates and reviews how the federal government spends taxpayer dollars. We received permission from the GAO to begin deployment of CHCS to all the military treatment facilities worldwide. But they weren't through with us yet. It took us a couple more years to complete deployment within the $2 billion budget—and the GAO watched us every step of the way. The GAO in its final report stated CHCS was the most successful information system program development and deployment they had ever observed.

CHCS served the Military Health System for several years, significant additions and enhancements being made to it. The name of the system has changed as enhancements have been made and different administrations have come and gone, but CHCS remains the core part of military medicine's electronic medical information system.

A Day Trip to Denver

On Tuesday, November 26, 1991, Dr. Mendez told me he needed me to go with him and Marty Kapert, the DASD who oversaw CHAMPUS, to Denver on a special mission the next day, the day before Thanksgiving. He said we'd have breakfast on the plane and lunch on the plane on the way back and would be able to eat dinner with our families at home that evening. He said he couldn't tell me the reason for the trip until we were in the air, but it was pretty obvious he didn't plan to be there long.

We flew on a Gulfstream, Mach 0.9 at 49,000 feet to Buckley Air Force Base outside Denver. We were whisked off to a meeting with the head of the CHAMPUS program, which had been in Denver for many years for political reasons. Dr. Mendez opened the meeting by firing the head of the CHAMPUS program, then he closed the meeting and we left. I think he brought me along for moral support. He must have had been given orders to fire this person by a higher-up, which could only mean Secretary Dick Cheney or Deputy Secretary Don Atwood. The date and time had been carefully chosen, the day before Thanksgiving, with the next four days among the slowest news days of the year. We were airborne and on our way back home after being on the ground for less than one hour.

A Trip Through PACOM

In January 1992 Dr. Mendez decided he wanted to tour our medical facilities in the Far East. He planned a trip that would take us to Alaska, Japan,

Korea, Okinawa, Guam, Hawaii, and Washington State, where we would attend the commissioning of the replacement facility for Madigan Army Hospital. This was to be a seventeen-day trip, all of the transportation being provided by the 89th Airlift Wing. The 89th provides global Special Air Mission (SAM) airlift, logistics, aerial port, and communications for the president and other senior leaders. This is the Air Wing that flies Air Force One. Dr. Mendez wanted me to go along and also Dr. Peter Collis, the DASD for readiness; Dr. Mendez's aide, Major Roberto Gonzales; and Surgeon General of the Army Lieutenant General Frank Ledford. We picked up Rear Admiral Bill McDaniel, PACOM surgeon, in Japan and he stayed with us until Hawaii.

We left in mid–February from Andrews Air Force Base (AFB) and stopped at Minot AFB in North Dakota to top off our fuel for the flight against the winter jet-stream winds en route to Anchorage. In Minot we got a tour of the B-1 bomber inside a warm hanger. In Anchorage we visited the Air Force hospital that had been damaged in a recent earthquake and for which we would have to quickly develop plans for a replacement facility. We flew on to Fairbanks, where we toured the Army hospital, for which Senator Stevens was lobbying hard for replacement. He wanted to make it into the major evacuation hospital for a war in the Far East, like the Air Force was trying to do with Lakenheath in England. We visited a new Air Force Clinic at Eielson AFB, about 25 miles south of Fairbanks, one of the nicest clinics I have ever seen. The base is the home of the 354th Fighter Wing. What they do there is chase the Russians away when they come too close to Alaskan air space.

From Fairbanks we flew to Shemya Island in the North Pacific, again to load up with fuel because of the winter winds but also to see the U.S. airborne intelligence platforms there that flew tracking flights of Russian intercontinental ballistic missiles. This is one of the most inhospitable and remote places I have ever visited. From Shemya we flew on to Yokota AFB outside Tokyo. On this leg the other passengers all fell asleep. One of the pilots invited me to come up front and I spent an hour with them. I could clearly see the curvature of the earth and one other thing that was really impressive. The pilots showed me two commercial 747s heading in the same direction as us but 10,000 feet below us. We went by them like they were standing still.

At Yokota AFB we visited the hospital. I had one of Stu Baker's books on this facility, as I had for every medical facility I ever visited. Dr. Mendez relied on me to do the Q&A with the commands after he did the "grip-and-grins." For this command I had several questions about their workload. After hearing the commander's report I asked questions about their health care utilization, because if it was accurate they had the highest in the entire military health system. According to their reports, the average beneficiary was being seen in their system more than twenty-five times a year. It turns out that they were counting patients multiple times when they came in. If the patients saw a doctor that was a visit. If they had an immunization that was another visit. If they attended a group counseling session, that was another. If they were weighed and had their vital signs checked, that was another, and so on. Yokota personnel were trying to increase their workload numbers to maintain budget and staffing levels. Uncovering this and confronting the command with these discoveries set the stage for some major changes later that year. We also visited the Army and Navy facilities in the Tokyo area where we didn't see this sort of thing.

We went on to Korea and visited another of the secure hospitals, one of those with five floors underground, the dental clinic being the only above-ground portion. This hospital's average daily inpatient census was four, and the three most common diagnoses accounted for over 75 percent of admissions and occupied bed days. The three diagnoses were wisdom tooth extraction, vasectomy, and adult male circumcision. The average length of stay for each of these procedures was a week. These are routinely done on an outpatient basis in the Navy and the civilian world. Dr. Mendez asked the hospital commander why he did this, and the commander replied that he had a goal to sterilize and circumcise every enlisted member on the base. He was relieved of command on the spot.

The next visit was to the Army's large hospital in Seoul, commanded by Colonel Hal Timboe, a West Point graduate who would go on to become a general and a good friend to me. We traveled to Panmunjom in the Demilitarized Zone and went to the hut where the allies and North Koreans (NKs) meet to settle issues that arise. While we were inside the hut the NKs were outside looking in and snapping pictures of us. We all had removed our nametags from our uniforms to make it difficult for the NKs to identify us. Inside the hut we could move across the white line painted across the floor and down the middle of the table, so we could say we had been in North Korea. An interesting observation was that there were UN, American, South Korean, and North Korean miniature flags on the table, with the North Korean flags on small poles an inch or so higher than the others.

Outside the hut was a different matter. Both sides had armed guards who would stand at their end of the building with a hand on their weapon at all times. The NKs had the biggest guys they could find for this duty. Their Southern cousins retaliated with guys of about the same size, but none were a match for the Americans, none of whom were less than 6 feet 4 inches tall. This was the most heavily fortified and ugly place I have ever visited. It is hard to believe this has been the state of affairs since the shooting stopped in July 1953. Technically we are still at war there.

Being in Korea over the three-day weekend of President's Day curtailed our ability to visit bases during this time. One day was given over to sightseeing and shopping in Seoul. After the holiday weekend Peter Collis, Bill

McDaniel, and I toured South Korea from top to bottom by helicopter. We went to so many bases and storage depots I have forgotten most of them. Dr. Mendez and General Ledford stayed in Seoul enjoying the fine hotel. We flew back to Tokyo, got briefings from the U.S. ambassador, the Commander U.S. Forces, Japan, and the individual service commanders. We toured Yokosuka Naval Base and our fine Navy hospital there. At Camp Zama we saw the facility where in 1967 and 1968, as a GMO, I had brought burn victims. The last night I was there I hosted my friend Hidahiko Haruna for dinner, this time at the New Sanno Hotel in downtown Tokyo.

From Tokyo we went to Okinawa and toured the hospital there that the Navy had taken over a few years earlier from the Army. There was little Navy presence on Okinawa, but there were a lot of Marines, so the Navy ran the hospital. The Air Force had a large presence on Okinawa and a clinic at Kadena AFB, which was only a few miles from the Navy hospital. The Air Force clinic was staffed with several family practice (FP) physicians. A bone of contention between the Air Force and the Navy was that FPs are supposed to do routine obstetrical deliveries, but for years the Air Force FPs on Okinawa had refused to do so. We had two obstetricians at the hospital that shared night and weekend call with a couple of Navy FPs. The Air Force FPs were living the good life while the Navy obstetricians and FPs were busting their humps. I called a joint meeting of both groups, including the Navy and Air Force facility commanders. I told them about the physician special pay program I had been working on for several years and that it would become effective with the beginning of the next fiscal year—that October. I told them I was disgusted with FPs who would not do routine obstetrical deliveries, something they were all trained to do as required by their specialty board. I told them that if they wouldn't do deliveries where facilities were available, I was going to require that they be eligible only for the much lower GMO special pay rates rather than the FP rates. The Air Force FPs rapidly polished up their OB credentials and started doing deliveries.

From Okinawa we made the turn toward home—first stop Guam. I had never been there, but my father had spent most of 1945 there and loved it. I had a thorough tour of the island, both Anderson AFB and the Navy facilities that are near the main population center of the island, Agana. The island native Chamorros account for about 37 percent of the population and are American citizens. Filipinos make up about 26 percent of the population; the rest are a mix of Caucasians and people from other South Pacific islands and East Asia. Total population in the mid-1990s was estimated at about 155,000. The economy is supported by two industries, tourism and the U.S. military, primarily the latter. Tourism caters mainly to the Japanese, since it's only 1,560 miles from Tokyo to Guam. The Japanese come to Guam to get warm in the winter, play golf, and shop at the local Wal-Mart.

We landed in mid-day, and the control tower noticed smoke coming from our left landing gear. An examination of it revealed damage that would require complete replacement of that unit, so our travel to Hawaii was going to have to be by commercial airliner. Dr. Mendez, General Ledford, Peter Collis and Bill McDaniel relaxed at the BOQ while I toured the Air Force clinic at Anderson AFB and the Navy Hospital. Anderson AFB had become a contingency base, so there was hardly anything going on there, just a small force to maintain the base for future needs. There were no planes on the base. It had been in this condition since just after our involvement in Vietnam ended, when it housed large numbers of Vietnamese refugees in transit to CONUS.

The Navy hospital was constructed right after the end of World War II. It was huge, much larger than currently needed. It was about fifty years old and, though made of concrete, its constant exposure to the salt air, heat, humidity, and a couple of typhoons each year made it structurally unsound. Getting funding to replace this building was a challenge, because Guam has only a single representative in Congress, who can lobby but not vote. Nonetheless, we kept asking for funds and eventually, some years after I retired, the funds were provided.

Our Navy doctors really were *the* medical presence for Guam. There was a civilian hospital there, but it had only a small staff and not many specialists. Many of our Navy doctors moonlighted at Guam Memorial Hospital. This was mutually beneficial, since there wasn't enough work to keep them busy at the Navy hospital. Pediatrics and obstetrics were an exception to this generality. If a patient needed care beyond the capability of the Navy hospital, they had to be medically evacuated to Tripler Army Medical Center in Honolulu, Hawaii, some 3,958 miles distant.

Continental was the only airline serving the route between Guam and Hawaii. There was one flight a day, and it was a night flight. Roberto Gonzales managed to get us seats—in coach, quite a step down in comfort from our Gulfstream. We got to Hawaii the day before we left Guam because we crossed the International Date Line. The good news when we arrived in Hawaii was that the 89th Air Wing was sending another Gulfstream to Hawaii to take us on the rest of our journey.

In Hawaii I again toured the clinics and went to Tripler to deal with CHCS issues. The most interesting part of the trip was a meeting we had with the PACOM Commander, Admiral Charles Larson, who had been my Plebe summer company officer at the Naval Academy and remembered me. He gave us a presentation about his command, which covered half the surface of the planet. I gave a presentation on our medical capabilities throughout the region.

I also made a visit to the Central Identification Lab, Hawaii (CIL-HI).

This was similar to the mortuary I had visited in Dover, Delaware, but with a different mission emphasis. Remains of Americans lost in World War II, Korea, and Vietnam were still being found. They were brought to CIL-HI, where there was a group of professionals who included forensic pathologists, anthropologists, and many technicians. They had the latest science available and had identified every set of American remains brought there. In the Tomb of the Unknown at Arlington, there once were some remains from an unknown from Vietnam, but they are there no longer. CIL-HI identified those remains. They were reburied where his next of kin desired. This is what is done with all identified remains. Even if just a few bones are available the remains are given a full uniform with all medals, a casket, an American flag, a military burial, and a headstone.

There were evening social engagements that in Hawaii are always fun—luaus and barbecues—and then it was off to McCord Air Force Base in Washington State for the dedication of the replacement Madigan Army Medical Center. (The plane crew had learned it was my birthday, and they had a birthday cake, candles, and ice cream for me at 49,000 feet.) I had been to Madigan during the final phase of construction to check on their needs for CHCS. While there I learned some interesting things about the project. The footprint of the hospital had been rotated 90 degrees from the original site plan to provide a better view for the patients. From one side they could see the Cascade Mountains and from the other Mount Rainier. Another thing I had learned was that digital radiology was installed throughout the hospital. It was the first installation of this technology in a hospital in the USA. There would be no X-ray films to store, so a huge room designed to serve as the X-ray storage room was converted to other uses.

After our stopover in Washington it was just a short four-hour trip to Andrews AFB. When we arrived home we had been gone seventeen days and had covered over 17,000 miles.

The Defense Health Program (DHP)

I was assigned to a board to suggest ways to revise how the individual services' healthcare budgets were managed. Historically, each of the three services had its own health care budget, and, historically, every year each would run short of money toward the end of the fiscal year. During the year the services would use the money in the health care accounts to pay other bills. The services would postpone paying the CHAMPUS bill during the year, leaving civilian health care providers unpaid and, in turn, those providers would refuse to see CHAMPUS patients. Congress had tried all sorts of tricks to prevent this, such as requiring healthcare providers who accepted

Medicare patients to take CHAMPUS as well. The result was that providers would also stop taking Medicare patients. The services would also short hospitals' and clinics' budgets, creating situations where there would not be enough money to purchase pharmaceuticals for outpatient dispensing. Patients would then have to take their prescriptions to civilian pharmacies, where they would have to pay a 20–25 percent co-pay to have them filled. The services were using both CHAMPUS and the direct care system budgets as piggy banks to pay for their own operational activities. This had become a habit, especially for the Navy. In July, just before Congress was ready to take off on August recess, the military services would ask Congress for emergency supplemental funding so they could pay their medical bills. Congress wanted this practice to end.

This board consisted of ten members plus a chairman who were to make recommendations for revisions to health care budgeting. The Army, Navy, Air Force, Joint Chiefs of Staff, and Health Affairs each had two members on the board. The chairman was the Health Affairs PDASD, Jack Lanier. I was one of the two representatives from Health Affairs; the other was Katherine Ladd, the DASD for program budgeting. The individual services all sent one senior person from their medical department and one from their comptroller's office. We were given a month to come up with recommendations. We met several times and of course were not able to come up with a unanimous recommendation. The services were hard over on retaining control of the money; Health Affairs and the Joint Chiefs wanted more centralized control. The results of the deliberations were sent to Secretary Cheney, and in short order the decision came back: Funding for all care in the military treatment facilities and all purchased care (primarily CHAMPUS) would come under Health Affairs in what would now be known as the Defense Health Program, or DHP. The services would retain the money for their operational health care needs, things like troop clinics, shipboard medicine and manning deployable medical systems and contingency hospitals. This was all to take effect at the beginning of the new fiscal year, less than six months away.

The next several meetings got pretty bloody. The services did not want to open their books to show how much they had historically spent. The work that Stu Baker had done on health care utilization—especially length of inpatient stays and admissions for diagnoses not normally requiring hospitalization in our efforts to properly size replacement hospitals—took on a new role. It became apparent that both the Army and the Air Force were padding their workload statistics across their entire system by putting people in the hospital who did not need to be there and keeping people in the hospital far longer than necessary. Budgets came under threat.

Once the temper tantrums and breath-holding spells ended, we got down to figuring out just how much money each service really needed to provide care for the beneficiary population it served. Allocations were made and—surprise—they made it. We didn't have to go back and beg Congress for more money the next year.

Physician Special Pays

My efforts to make Defense leadership and Congress aware of the declining retention of physicians were paying off. Dr. Mendez had worked this issue with the higher-ups in the department. We had several meetings with the staff of the cognizant congressional committees, in particular Karen Heath of the House Armed Services Committee, Subcommittee on Manpower. They all understood the problem; pay differentials were the one thing they could do something about to possibly prevent having to start a physician draft. They knew this was not going to come cheap; the first year's tab would exceed $100 million.

A civilian expert on physician compensation, Jim Rodeghero, was brought in as a consultant. After we brought Jim up to speed on the problem and the present design of physicians' pay in the military, he proposed that we develop a multifaceted special pay program that would recognize both achievement and commitment. There were five elements to his proposal:

Variable Special Pay—a monthly pay for medical officers on duty for more than one year that increased based on the number of years they had been a military physician;

Additional Special Pay—entitled to it after they completed internship or initial residency training and agreed to stay on active duty at least one year;

Multi Year Special Pay—a bonus if they agreed to serve for an additional 2, 3, or 4 years;

Board Certification Pay—for officers' board certified in their specialty;

Incentive Special Pay—paid to specialists, by medical specialty, not in internship or residency if they agreed to remain on active duty for at least one more year.

Jim and I traveled to the four largest facilities of each of the three services and gave presentations to the medical staffs. In addition I spoke about it on my travels to other facilities both in CONUS and abroad. We published articles on the subject in several military publications, so there was an abundance of information available on it. Doctors began to sign contracts for these pays. When we entered the new fiscal year the doctor hemorrhage began to slow as numbers stabilized and began to rise. In a few years, service physician manpower had reached authorized end strength, even though the mix of specialists was not precisely what the manpower tables called for. This physicians' special pay program has now existed for over twenty-five years. The amounts are adjusted yearly to account for inflation and change pays depending on specialty manning.

In the summer of 1992 it came time for my promotion to Rear Admiral, Upper Half. Dr. Mendez did the honors this time, in his office. I figured this would be my last promotion.

A Political Tsunami

The presidential campaign was underway. A former governor of Arkansas I had never heard of was challenging the incumbent, George Herbert Walker Bush. I thought this "kid" from Arkansas had no chance. I went to lunch one day with my deputy, Patty Watson, and Diana Tabler. Both of them were career government employees and well plugged-in to the D.C. rumor mills. They told me this Clinton fellow was going to pull off a big upset— and on November 3, 1992, he did.

With a new president from the other major party scheduled to be sworn in on January 20, I was able to witness a rapid exit of civilian political appointees. They started bailing out as soon as they found another job. Dr. Mendez stayed on the job until noon on Election Day, and then he picked up his attaché case and left the building. By Inauguration Day the Pentagon was like a mausoleum. When I walked down the halls my footfalls echoed through the corridors. About three-quarters of the people who work there are civilians, and many of them are political appointees. Unless they are asked to stay on by the incoming administration, their paychecks end at noon on Inauguration Day. Ed Martin, a rear admiral in the Public Health Service, stayed on in HA as the Acting ASD. Marty Kapert was a career SES, and he stayed on as DASD running CHAMPUS. I stayed on as DASD for Operations. Together we were the corporate memory for Health Affairs. Clinton appointees did not begin to show up for a long time. We would run the show for the next fourteen months.

When the Clinton administration took over there was a skeleton crew of civilian leadership in the Pentagon. Les Aspin, a long-time liberal congressman who had not been a friend of the Pentagon unless it involved political pork for his district, was named Secretary of Defense. I met him a few times, and he was really a fun guy to talk with. In the Pentagon he was a fish out of water. He stayed on the job for a year then retired. His deputy, Bill Perry, a former math professor who had significant previous national security experience, replaced him. He turned out to be one of the best Defense Secretaries in some time.

A New Health Benefit

Pressure was coming from the military coalition to improve the Defense Department's health benefit for dependents and retirees. CHAMPUS—the health care benefit that covered care provided in the private sector when care was unavailable from the direct-care system or patients had tired of trying to gain access—was the beneficiaries' option, except for retirees over 65 who had only Medicare. CHAMPUS was really an outdated form of indemnity insurance. It had up-front deductibles that patients had to pay before it would pay anything. The amounts CHAMPUS would pay varied for active-duty dependents and retired. Once the deductible was met ($100 for active-duty dependents, $300 for retired), CHAMPUS would cost-share, picking up 80 percent of allowable costs for active-duty dependents and 75 percent for retired. There was a $3,000 annual out-of-pocket cap per family, after which CHAMPUS would pay the entire remaining bill. Three thousand dollars was a lot of money for most active-duty or retired families. Many opted to buy a supplemental policy offered by some military organizations. This protected them from catastrophic medical bills but was still costly. For retirees on Medicare the situation was even worse. Contrary to popular belief, Medicare does not cover all costs; in fact it barely covers 80 percent of costs. Older people need a lot more health care than do younger people, so their bills can become catastrophic.

The military coalition wanted active-duty dependents, retirees, and members of their families to be eligible for FEHBP, an insurance program for many federal government employees. FEHBP had an annual "open season" in the fall during which employees could sign up for any of a large number of insurance programs to suit their and their families' needs. Premiums were taken out of the employees' paychecks and that money was not taxed. This seemed very attractive, but there were a couple of major problems that would result if FEHBP became the benefit for other than active-duty military health care beneficiaries. For one thing, the youngest members of the military aren't sophisticated enough to make these sorts of choices—most of them had been covered by their parents' policies, if they had any coverage at all, before entering the military. To suddenly expect them to make wise choices about coverage was not realistic. They would almost invariably opt for the cheapest coverage, and should a significant medical situation arise they would not have adequate coverage. Another issue was that people would seek care from both the military system and private providers, which had been a problem with CHAMPUS coverage; people would get care from both sectors with little or no communication between them. A third problem was that the military health system needed a large beneficiary population to acquire and maintain skills. If patients didn't come to the military facilities, providers would not have the patient volume and variety they needed. If this occurred, we would have to go back to the draft—something no one wanted to do. There were many other issues associated with the FEHBP approach, but these were the main ones and enough to convince the Joint Chiefs of Staff and the cognizant congressional committees that FEHBP was a nonstarter.

The challenge to us remaining in Health Affairs was to come up with an acceptable alternative. A number of demonstration projects had been conducted over the preceding decade testing a variety of managed care approaches. We worked with Karen Heath of the House Armed Services Manpower Subcommittee and her equivalent in the Senate, the Joint Chiefs, the Service Secretaries, and the Service Chiefs of Staff to come up with an alternative, all the time keeping the military coalition leaders informed.

The coordination between all of these offices was a major challenge, and we were at the hub of it. In the end we came up with what became known as TRICARE. We chose the name for a couple of reasons. First, it involved all three services and second, it offered three choices. We would split the country up into geographic regions, have commercial contractors bid to build provider networks in each region and then manage the care within that region. Originally there were twelve defined geographic regions—twelve because that was the number of major military Medical Teaching Facilities (MTF) and each SG wanted his teaching hospitals to have their own well-defined catchment area. Having their own catchment area meant that people who lived within it would have to get their care from them. This was fine if a facility was the only MTF in the area, but that was not the case in the National Capital and San Antonio regions, where there was more than one MTF involved in multispecialty Graduate Medical Education (GME). There were some real knockdown, drag-out fights between the three services' SGs over this. For a bit I thought it might stop the whole effort. Finally, I told Ed Martin the way to deal with it was to tell the SGs to grow up, stop fighting, and get along. We also told them it was time to start thinking about merging the GME programs in these overlapping catchment areas, and that became the next thing on our agenda. They had seen Ed and me operate long enough now that they knew we meant it. We began the process of merging GME programs in these areas. It took a long time, longer than either of us were around, but it is now complete.

That took care of the three services part of the TRICARE name. Now we had to deal with the three choices part of TRICARE. The military coalition had insisted there needed to be choices for beneficiaries, so we gave them three. We had Prime, Extra, and Standard. Here's how they differed:

Prime: An active-duty family or retiree signed up for a year to use only the MTF or the provider network set up by the contractor for their region. All active-duty were automatically in Prime. Those enrolled in Prime were given preferential access to care from the MTF. There was no charge for signing up for Prime and no co-pays or deductibles as long as they used network providers. Contractors were required to have adequate numbers of providers in all specialties to meet beneficiary needs. After a year families could switch to another option.

Extra: Beneficiaries did not have to sign up for this. If they used the contractor's network providers there were no co-pays or deductibles. If they used out of network providers they paid the CHAMPUS co-pays and deductibles.

Standard: They did not have to sign up for this either. It was like the original CHAMPUS with its co-pays and deductibles.

TRICARE was made law and we were off and running. Though there were originally twelve regions to satisfy the SGs' parochialism, by the time the contracts were let we had reduced the regions to seven, with only four contractors, some covering more than one region. The contracts were re-competed at about three-year intervals and reduced to only three, with three regions. (In 2018 it was reduced to two.) The prefix TRI took on more meaning. Now with more than twenty years of operation, TRICARE is a very popular program. The Extra part of the program has now been eliminated, which makes sense to me, as it should have been eliminated a long time ago. Either beneficiaries sign up for Prime or they go outside for care on Standard.

After a few years of operation a new benefit was added, TRICARE-FOR-LIFE (TFL). TFL extended the TRICARE benefit to those eligible for Medicare, if they opted to enroll in Medicare B. There are multiple parts to Medicare. Payroll deductions are used to finance Medicare A, which pays hospital bills. Medicare B is an optional program that pays 80 percent of doctor bills and is financed through deductions from Social Security pensions. TFL is a supplemental insurance that pays any medical bills that aren't covered by Medicare but are a TRICARE benefit. In addition, TFL provides an essentially no-cost pharmacy benefit option for beneficiaries.

Filling in for the ASD-HA

In February 1994, Dr. Steve Joseph had been nominated to become the new Assistant Secretary of Defense for Health Affairs (ASD-HA) but was not yet confirmed by the Senate. He had reported to the Pentagon, was in his office, and was allowed to attend meetings and participate in discussions but not allowed to make any decisions or sign off on any directives. Ed Martin still had to make decisions and sign off in his role as the Acting Assistant Secretary. For several years during the Cold War the U.S. Army Medical Command, Europe (AKA 7th MedCom), held a large continuing health education conference in Germany every March. Attendance was Army and Air Force medical department personnel. Most doctors and many nurses from these facilities attended with only a small staff remaining home to keep services open. This was going to be the last of these very large conferences. Plans for the drawdown of forces from Germany were now well underway. They asked Steve Joseph to address the conference, but he had to decline since he was not confirmed. Attending this conference fell to me. This would work out well because I already had a trip scheduled just after this conference to our bases south of the Alps in Italy and Sicily to check on CHCS and some medical construction issues. The conference was held in a winter resort area a two-hour drive north of Frankfurt. It would last four days and end on a Friday. That left Saturday for me to entertain myself. Sunday I would travel to Italy.

This was going to be interesting—a Navy Medical Corps admiral delivering the keynote address at the Army Medical Department's "grand finale" in Europe. Almost all of these Army and Air Force facilities would close soon, some of them in less than a year. (All but the hospital at Landstuhl, adjacent to Ramstein Air Force Base and now designated a Regional Medical Center, and the Air Force facility at Lakenheath, England, are now closed.) I did not let interservice rivalry enter into my presentation and gave a talk lauding all that the Army and Air Force had accomplished there since the end of World War II.

BRAC

We dealt with more in Health Affairs during this time than just designing TRICARE and the drawdown in Europe. The year 1993 was an odd-numbered one and thus not a federal election year. Congress had carefully crafted the Base Realignment and Closure process so that all the dirty work and voting occurred during these nonelection years. This was the BRAC round where a lot of decisions were going to be made about the future of several military hospitals. Developing and implementing TRICARE fit nicely with this because we had a safety net, of sorts, for areas that were losing their military hospitals. The Navy alone wound up with three hospitals on the list—Charleston, Oakland, and Orlando.

The Navy had three Basic Training Centers (boot camps) and said they needed only one. San Diego was one the Navy wanted to close and there was little local opposition to this. Great Lakes and Orlando were the other two.

The Navy preferred to keep Great Lakes, but Congressman Bill McCollum was fighting hard to have Great Lakes put on the list instead and to keep Orlando open. Among the arguments he offered to the BRAC Commission in support of keeping Orlando was that there was much better weather (Great Lakes had to move much of the basic training indoors during the winter), the facilities were much newer and in better shape, and there was a much larger dependent and retiree population in the Orlando area who were using the Navy hospital there as their source of care. That's where I was brought into the process. I was tasked to do an analysis of Great Lakes and Orlando's beneficiary populations, their health care utilization, and the costs to the government should the facility be closed and the beneficiaries had to get their care on TRICARE and Medicare. I was asked to keep our findings close-hold and present them at a meeting of the eleven-member BRAC Commission.

On the scheduled day, my deputy, Patty Watson, and I went to the hearing, which was in a large room in one of the House office buildings. I was scheduled to be before the commission for 10 minutes. The first thing I noticed upon taking my seat was there were a lot of TV cameras facing directly at me. I quickly summarized our findings and recommendations which showed that the costs to the government for medical care would be far less if Orlando was retained and Great Lakes closed. A number of members of the commission had been primed with questions from interested parties from other congressional districts where medical facilities were also being closed. Beverly Byron (D-MD), in seeking her eighth term, had been defeated in the 1992 general election. President Clinton had named her as one of the eleven members of the commission. She and I had worked closely on a number of issues while she was a member of the House Armed Services Committee. She served me some "softball" questions—questions she knew my answers to. She gave me the opportunity to discuss how the closure of the military medical facilities would have a negative financial impact on beneficiaries, especially the retired over age 65. I pointed out that right down the street in another federal building the Health Security Act was being discussed with a goal of providing universal health care for all Americans. The BRAC process was doing the exact opposite! Before the chairperson dismissed me I had been before the commission for 45 minutes.

Patty and I stepped into the hall outside the hearing room and were greeted by a corridor full of video cameras and reporters who had been alerted by others that something really interesting was happening in the BRAC hearing. They were shoving microphones at me and shouting questions. Patty said, "Let's get out of here." We ran for the nearest exit. There was supposed to be a DoD pool vehicle waiting for us, but since we were late it had left. Patty spotted a cab, and we ran for it. As we slid into the backseat, microphones were shoved through the still-open door and questions were shouted. The cabbie took off and we left the reporters in the dust. The video cameras in the hearing room were the ones used to record and televise important congressional hearings on C-SPAN. Recordings of that hearing were shown repeatedly for the next month on C-SPAN and excerpts shown on network and cable-TV news broadcasts.

Educating Congress

I now had more notoriety. That afternoon I got a call asking if I would come see a congressman from Texas who had Carswell Air Force Base in his district. Carswell and its 400-bed hospital had been put on the closure list in 1991. It hadn't closed yet, but the day for closure was fast approaching. Now he had found someone who knew something about the impact of hospital closures and what would happen to beneficiaries.

I spent an hour with him explaining how TRICARE and worked. TRICARE was pretty easy for him to understand, but Medicare flummoxed him. We got through Medicare A okay, but when I got to Medicare B he'd never even heard of it. He didn't know that a military retiree could decline Medicare B, which paid the doctor bills, and get a bigger monthly retirement check. At that time the Medicare B premium was about $90/month per beneficiary, so for a married couple that meant their retirement check would be docked $180 each month if they both elected Medicare B coverage. Many people who retired from the military had decided to stay near a military base with a hospital, decline Medicare B, and have $180/month more to spend. They hadn't anticipated that someday the bases and their hospitals might close, leaving them only with Medicare A and a lot more out-of-pocket expenses. He asked what could be done. I told him Congress had unintentionally created a hole in the safety net with BRAC. They needed to pass legislation to fix that hole.

Then I had to explain that if a retiree declined Medicare B but later decided to take it, there was a 10 percent penalty for every year they had been on Medicare without Medicare B. For example, for someone who had waited until age 75 to decide to take Medicare B their monthly premium would be double what it would be if they had taken Medicare B at age 65. I went on to tell him that a lot of servicemen had done this and not told their wives, assuming the military hospital would always be there for them. I also told him that most servicemen predeceased their wives, leaving the widow with little health care coverage.

He was shocked. He had just gotten a tutorial on Medicare that he had never imagined. He asked me if I thought many of his colleagues who had military hospitals in their districts were aware of this. I said, "Of course not." He asked if I could return the next day and have the same discussion with some of them, as a group. I said, "Your wish is my command." The next day, I returned to his office and he took me to a conference room where more than 40 members were waiting. After a brief introduction I launched into my pitch and watched the color of the members' faces go beet red and then blanch snow white. They asked what could be done. I said they needed to give relief to military retirees who had not taken Medicare B and had used military medical facilities as their main source of health care. Some thought they could do this because of their membership on the House Armed Services Committee. I pointed out that Medicare was under the control of the Ways and Means Committee, and they'd have to convince some of their colleagues on that committee to do this. Eventually this was done and a disaster was averted.

A final point on this is that the BRAC Commission voted to close Orlando and keep Great Lakes. There were a lot of other things that entered into this decision, among them the overall cost to replace a lot of the infrastructure in place at Great Lakes that was not present in Orlando. Great Lakes had a lot of advanced enlisted specialty schools with one-of-a-kind training venues, whereas Orlando was strictly basic training. I don't think the health care costs for dependents and retirees was a drop in the bucket compared to this and they didn't need me to make the presentation I had, but it really did pay off in getting the Medicare B fix in.

American Expatriates

There was more fallout from my BRAC Commission presentation and the follow-on C-SPAN and newscast coverage. There was a lot of blowback both at home and from Europe. We were closing bases with medical facilities and the Secretary of Defense and Congress were hearing from a lot of disgruntled military families, especially retirees. The noise level from Germany was especially high. In the half-century we had operated bases there many military men (recall there were few women in the military during these years) had married local girls, had families, and upon retirement elected to stay in communities adjacent to the bases. Many had taken civilian positions on these bases, often doing similar jobs to what they had done while on active duty. As retirees they were eligible to use base facilities such as hospitals and clinics, commissaries, exchanges, and recreational facilities. American enclaves had sprung up in many of these areas. The local German economy had become dependent on the American presence. Our rapid drawdown was hurting German and American people alike. Dr. Ed Martin, the Acting ASD (HA), was asked to personally visit several of these areas and report back on his observations. Ed made a ten-day trip to Germany and Vicenza, Italy.

Every afternoon (evening in Europe) I, along with Diana Tabler, Patty Watson, and a few others would gather in a conference room and get a debriefing from Ed and his entourage about their observations. There were no surprises for me. I could have written the script, but it was good to have a second opinion to what I had previously seen and reported. This visit and report did nothing to either slow the drawdown or placate the retirees living in Europe. CHAMPUS eligible retirees had a health benefit called TRICARE-Europe that would help with their health care coverage. But Medicare-eligible retirees were no longer eligible for TRICARE, and Medicare does not provide coverage outside the USA. Later, when TRICARE-FOR-LIFE became a benefit, they would have coverage, but that was still a few years away. As for commissary, exchange, and recreation benefits, they were out of luck. They had to turn to the local economy or come home to the USA.

Change on the Horizon

There was turmoil at the CNO level that involved Senator Barbara Boxer (D-CA), who wanted the CNO, Admiral Frank Kelso, reduced in rank from full Admiral (four-star) to Rear Admiral Upper Half (two-star) upon retirement because she did not agree with his handling of an investigation. By law, retirement of all flag or general officers at the three- and four-star rank had to be approved by the Senate. Senator Boxer's attempt failed to force his early retirement and reduction in rank. As a compromise, Kelso retired a few months earlier than his expected retirement date. The new CNO was Mike Boorda. He asked Don Hagen to stay on for a fourth year so he wouldn't have to deal with replacing an SG so early in his tenure. Don asked me if I would come to BUMED and serve as the Deputy SG for a year, until he retired. He told me if I did that he and Admiral Boorda had decided I would be their recommendation to be the next Navy SG. All of a sudden my transgressions as a DASD had been forgiven. I left Health Affairs on June 30, 1994, four years after I had reported.

Admiral Mike Boorda had been sworn in as CNO on April 23, 1994. A grand reception was held in the Navy Museum at the historic Navy Yard in Washington. Deena and I attended and I remember what Admiral Boorda said to me as I went through the receiving line: "It looks like things are working out very well. You have done a great job as a DASD and I am glad you are coming back to the Navy. I look forward to working with you for several more years."

12

Deputy Surgeon General

July 1, 1994–June 29, 1995

When I became the Deputy SG, BUPERS swung into action. I got a call from the head of medical department detailing, offering up a couple of names to serve as my aide. I chose Commander David Maloney. He had an impressive career history, starting out as a Surface Warfare line officer after coming out of an NROTC program. After a few years in this role he completed the requirements for a master's degree in healthcare administration, was transferred to the Medical Service Corps, and proved his talents in some earlier jobs. He had the reputation of being a very hard worker—loyal and dependable—just what I was looking for. We hit it off immediately. He worked diligently and never let anything slip between the cracks.

I had set a personal goal for myself. I was going to take the very challenging certifying exam of the American College of Healthcare Executives, but I hadn't told anyone. The reasons I wanted to take it were:

1. I had learned a lot about health care administration during my four years in Health Affairs.
2. The Medical Service Corps officers of the three military services had been saying they were more qualified than Medical Corps officers to command hospitals.
3. I was pretty sure I could pass the exam.
4. No Medical Corps officer from any military service had ever taken this exam.

David Maloney had done so. In fact, it was just about impossible for a Medical Service Corps officer in health care administration to be promoted to Commander without passing this exam. Most who passed it had a master's degree in health care administration—a two-year educational process for most. About one-third who took it failed on their first attempt. I told David I wanted to take this exam. He said he would get a bunch of his Medical Service Corps buddies together to provide me with the reading material I needed to digest and to coach me. There was both a written and an oral part of the exam; together they took up the most of a day. I took the test in August. I passed. Later that year I attended the American College of Healthcare Executives annual meeting in Chicago, where I was recognized as the government senior medical executive of the year.

A second area where I changed the game was in an ancillary assignment, as Chief of the Medical Corps. There had always been a Chief of the Nurse Corps, Dental Corps, and Medical Service Corps. In fact, for one of the Admirals in each of these corps, this was the primary title, and they had a staff of officers, enlisted, and civilians to assist them. There had been no equivalent for the Medical Corps until I started pointing out while I was the CO of HSETC that the numbers of Medical Corps officers were in decline, the retention of physicians we had trained was in decline, and medical students were not taking the HPSP scholarships. Jim Zimble established a Medical Corps Office at BUMED, manned part-time by a handful of physicians, the senior officer being a captain about to retire. When Don Hagen became SG he made this an ancillary responsibility of the Deputy SG.

Most of the medical specialty groups in the Navy had a meeting where they got together for a few days, often with their colleagues from the other services or with their national medical specialty groups. I made it a point to attend every one of these meetings and address the groups on a broad array of issues of importance to them, among them pay, retention, and continuing and graduate medical education. I invited them to contact our Medical Corps office at BUMED with questions, and if they couldn't come up with an answer they could bring the question to me and I would get the answer. I also told them that in the post–Cold War environment Navy Medicine would not be left alone. We would be changing also. A part of that change would be that promotion opportunity would not be what it was in the past, when it was pretty automatic from the time of entry to Captain and all you had to do was stay out of trouble and you'd be promoted. I told them that to get promoted beyond lieutenant commander they would have to be more than just a good doctor, they would have to be a good Navy officer as well. This meant that they wouldn't be promoted if they just hung around practicing medicine in a single geographic location. To get promoted to these higher ranks they were going to have to serve with the operating forces. I told them I was not making these rules. It was the way things were going to be. I told them that to get command and certainly to make Flag they were going to have to be both a good doctor and a Navy officer, with the credentials to prove it. I told them that any of them who aspired to either or both of these positions needed to come see me personally and we would do some career planning.

My day-to-day job was to work with Don Hagen, the current SG, and run BUMED when he was away. Don had told me coming in that he had done little traveling during his first three years and felt he needed to at least get to some of our facilities in Europe and Hawaii. All of Europe was too much for him, as was East Asia. He did manage to get to Northern Europe, Italy. and Hawaii.

During the Christmas Holiday Season our three sons managed to make it home. We decided we should take this opportunity to get a family photo of all of us in uniform. Though I was pretty sure at this point I would be around for a few more years, I wasn't sure yet, and I sure couldn't be sure the boys would all be able to gather together. So we had one done.

Koenig family portrait, December 1984. Back Row: Ensign Scott Koenig, Midshipman Grant Koenig, and Lieutenant Steve Koenig. Front Row: Deena and me.

At BUMED we had a weekly meeting with all of the Code Directors that lasted about 90 minutes, plus there were three meetings in the Pentagon that either the SG or Deputy SG had to attend. There were meetings with the media, foreign officials, and congressional staff and periodic congressional hearings. We were never short of things to do. One "pop-up" meeting I attended during a time Don Hagen was away deserves special mention. I was told to be in the White House in 55 minutes—in my service dress blues and with my passport for identification. I kept a set of blues in the office for occasions like this. The reason was for the promotion of Commander Connie Mariano, MC, USN, to the rank of Captain. Connie was one of the five physicians assigned to the White House Clinic during the Bush administration. Bill Clinton had been president for more than eighteen months when it was discovered that the law said someone has to be appointed physician to the president and if that person is a military physician he or she must be at least an O-6, a Navy Captain, or a Colonel from the other service branches. Connie was eligible for consideration for promotion by the next selection board, but the Commander-in-Chief also could promote her.

I went to the White House, about six blocks away, and was escorted to the Oval Office. Only a few others came in: John Dalton, the Secretary of the Navy, Connie's husband and their two sons, and six of the Navy petty officers assigned to the White House who serve as the president's personal valets. The president then came in, having been briefed that the occasion was to promote Connie. He said he had never promoted a military person before. He was handed a 3" × 5" card with the oath on it, the same oath he had taken when he became president. Connie told him to read it a few words at a time and she would repeat them. He did and the deed was done. Then Connie asked if she could make a few comments and he said, "Sure." She proceeded to say how she was the youngest of seven children, the only one born in the USA, all the others being born in the Philippines. Her father had joined the U.S. Navy and had taken his family here. The goal of her parents and her siblings was to get the "baby" through college. None of her siblings had that opportunity. Not only had she made it through college but medical school as well, at the University of California, San Diego, with the financial help of the Navy Health Professions Scholarship Program. She had trained in Internal Medicine at the Navy Hospital, San Diego, while I was its commanding officer. This was quite a personal story. I looked at the president and noticed he had tears running down his cheeks. He said, "Only in America do people have opportunities like this." Afterward the president shook hands and made small talk with each of us in attendance. A few years later I would meet with him again. When I did I was sure he would not remember me. I was wrong.

A program that I had heard about while I was a DASD was Navy Medicine's THCSRR (pronounced "thick-sir"). The acronym stood for Total Health Care Support Readiness Requirement. Besides being a tongue twister it could be a brainteaser as well. This was an effort that Don Hagen had started. It was an attempt to quantify how many personnel of each type were needed to meet the full deployment requirements for the Navy Medical Department. This meant doctors, nurses, corpsmen, ancillary providers, and other support personnel like cooks, mechanics, Seabees, and so on. Full deployment meant having to man all of our deployable assets including the hospital ships, all fleet hospitals, the Marine Corps medical billets, and, of course, the hospitals and clinics worldwide. Nothing like this had ever been tried before, by the Navy or any other service branch. This was an elegant work effort carried out over a couple of years by some superb Medical Service Corps officers. Not surprisingly, the study revealed that since the end of the draft the services really had no plan for medical manning; they just took what they could get. Prior to the end of the draft, the services, at least for physicians, drafted basically the entire male output of the nation's medical schools, requiring all male doctors to serve at least two years. With the THC-SRR for the first time, we found out how short (or "fat") we were. As could have been expected, we found we were way short of general surgeons, orthopedists, neurosurgeons, emergency medicine, intensive care, and other "cutters," and had way more obstetricians/gynecologists (Ob/Gyns), pediatricians, and others. One area where we had nearly ten times as many as the THCSRR justified was pharmacists. This information sent shock waves through the Navy Bureau of Personnel, the Joint Chiefs of Staff, the Office of the Secretary of Defense, and some in Congress. Once the numbers were out, we began to look at "specialty substitutions." We decided that OB/GYNs could substitute for some of the surgeons, and pediatricians could work as emergency physicians and intensive care physicians. This didn't cover all the deficiencies but it was a start. It also started us looking at what we were doing in graduate medical education and led us to determine that our efforts were way short in some areas and way over in others.

Don Hagen asked me to go to Puerto Rico with a side trip to Guantanamo Bay and a second trip to Zagreb, Croatia, where we had a fleet hospital deployed in support of the war in the Balkans, and then on to Naples and Sigonella, Italy, and Rota, Spain. Along with my EA, Commander Dave Maloney, I made these trips. I had been to Rosie Roads (Roosevelt Roads Naval Station in Puerto Rico) while I was a DASD, so this was not new to me. But the command had not had a Navy Medical HQ visit in several years, so this was a big deal for them. They were great hosts. I toured the facility, had Admiral's call with the staff and attended a barbecue. I took a side trip to the island of Vieques, eight miles east of Puerto Rico. It had served as a U.S. Navy bombing and artillery range for decades. Naturalists, environmentalists and antimilitary groups had been protesting the Navy's use of the island for these purposes for several years. Pressure was mounting for the Navy to leave, but the folks at Roosevelt Roads knew if Vieques closed they wouldn't be far behind. I handled questions on this but could not provide definitive answers, though I suspected closure was close on the horizon for this base. Sure enough, by 2003 the Navy had had enough and pulled out of Vieques and Roosevelt Roads lock, stock, and barrel, leaving a lot of Puerto Ricans unemployed.

The Navy flew me to Guantanamo in a fixed-wing aircraft over the much larger island of Hispaniola. This was my first trip to Guantanamo. Near the southeast corner of Cuba, not far from Santiago, it's a pretty desolate place. My visit there was before the now notorious prison was erected. At this time it was providing temporary housing and shelter for 30,000 Cubans who had fled the Castro regime and 5,000 Haitians who had fled their homeland by sea. We kept them in tent villages on different parts of our base, not allowing them to intermix because they hated each other and would fight. We had a program to teach the men (~90 percent were men) basic English and how to pass the Florida driver's license test. Eventually we would move all of them off the island, about 90 percent of them to the USA and virtually all of those winding up in the Miami area. The others were distributed to other nations of the Caribbean Basin. This was a very impressive operation few Americans knew about and fewer remember. It was an effort our nation should be proud of. I flew back to Puerto Rico, spent another night, and then flew back to Washington.

The second trip was to attend the change of command ceremony at the fleet hospital in Zagreb, Croatia. The Navy was the military branch that had operated the hospital for the past six months, under Captain Jim Johnson. The Air Force was taking over, the three services each having a six-month rotation. The Navy had operated it through the winter, and the weather had been vicious. They hadn't seen much trauma but they were seeing a lot of very sick Croatian children, so many that they had asked for more pediatricians. We sent three more. There had been a measles epidemic, a disease rarely seen anymore in the Western Hemisphere but rampant in this war-torn region.

The senior officer present for the ceremony was Admiral Leighton Smith, who had just taken over as CINCUSNAVEUR from Admiral Boorda. He became the senior officer primarily responsible for conducting the NATO operations in the war in the Balkans. I knew Admiral Smith from my year at the Naval Academy; we were classmates and had been in the same Plebe Summer Company. When we met he said he knew my next stop was Naples, and he wanted me to come to his quarters for dinner the next evening. After finishing my day's work in Naples I was taken to his quarters overlooking the bay. We had a great time, alone except for the steward who prepared our meal. We spent three hours on a veranda overlooking the bay, catching up on the thirty years that had passed since we were together at the Naval Academy. Within a few minutes, all those years had telescoped in and we were back to calling each other "Snuffy" and" Hal," names we went by back then. We would see each other many times in the next few years. He retired two years before I did, and upon retirement Queen Elizabeth knighted him.

On Thursday morning we went by military air to Sigonella, Sicily, where we visited the Navy hospital and its blood depot. The hospital is built into the side of a mountain, with the dental clinic the only area at ground level. From the dental clinic the hospital descends several floors into the ground. The hospital portion of the facility can be totally sealed off from the dental clinic. The hospital is supposed to be able to withstand a nearby nuclear bomb attack. Like the others, this facility is a repository for tens of thousands of units of frozen red blood cells, mostly type O, Rh-negative blood, a universal donor that can be transfused into anyone without danger of reaction. Thousands of units are stored in dozens of massive freezers that maintain a constant temperature of minus 80 degrees Centigrade. We don't know how long blood can safely be stored this way, but the oldest units stored over three decades ago are still viable. It takes an hour to thaw frozen blood and have it ready for transfusion, but it can't be done by taking it out of a freezer and putting it on a shelf at room temperature. There is a lot more to it than that. Once thawed, it has to be used promptly or discarded. We then flew to Rota and had Admiral's call with the hospital staff and whoever else wanted to join in. The next morning we caught a local flight from Cadiz to Madrid, from where we would fly home.

We did all of this in seven days.

One other thing I did during this year as Deputy SG was to become acquainted with the BUMED Comptroller, a member of the Senior Executive Service (SES), John Cuddy. I told him that office automation at BUMED needed to be upgraded and that we needed to build into our budget the funding necessary for that. He agreed, so his office got busy and figured out what it would take to put a new computer on every desk at BUMED and install a Local Area Network (LAN) so that we could end the days of our staff using outdated software and hand-carrying 7¼" disks around with every paper document generated. That was wasting a lot of time, paper, and 7¼" disks. He and his staff did it.

The year was flying by. Admiral Boorda had conducted interviews of all the Medical Corps two-star Admirals in a search for Don Hagen's relief, but he told me I was going to get the nomination, both he and the Secretary of the Navy agreed on that. Of course, the nomination would have to wind its way through the Pentagon, be blessed by the Secretary of Defense, make it to the president's desk, and from there to the Senate Armed Services Committee, where I would be vetted and, it was hoped, confirmed by a vote of the Senate. They anticipated no problems with this, but until the Senate vote occurred nothing was to be said.

Senate confirmations don't necessarily stand alone but are lumped in with others for Senate approval. Usually these votes are by acclimation, meaning the Senators are asked for all in favor to say aye and all opposed, no. If any one Senator has a reason to oppose a person for confirmation that is known ahead of the vote the person's name is removed from the list until such time the reason for opposition is worked out or the candidate's name is withdrawn. I was confirmed unanimously. Don Hagen had decided he wanted to make the announcement of his successor at the annual Navy Medical Corps Birthday Ball, which was to be held the end of March at the Ritz-Carlton Hotel in Arlington, Virginia. He asked the two Senate staffers who had interviewed me not to publish the announcement of my confirmation in the *Congressional Record* until the Monday following the ball, which was on a Friday night. They agreed to this. Don also wanted the unveiling of his life-size oil portrait, which he had been sitting for over the past few months, to happen at the ball. It would be hung along with portraits of the other SGs in the National Naval Medical Center, Bethesda.

We were set for the ball. Deena and I had earlier decided at such events we were not going to sit at a table with other Flag officers and their spouses but instead we would sit with junior officers to get to know them. This did cause some eyes to roll, but we had done it for as long as I had been an admiral and saw no reason to change now. I purchased a table of eight and asked the Uniformed University of the Health Sciences to find three senior medical students and their spouses or significant others to be our guests.

There were a couple more items of business to attend to before the ball, because Don Hagen had warned me that once the announcement was made, things would happen fast. Among them would be people soliciting for assignments, especially on my personnel staff. David Maloney and I put our heads together and came up with a slate. First, I needed to select an aide. This would be an officer who would look after my schedule and travel with me wherever I went. In recent years this had always been a male Medical Service Corps officer, usually a LCDR or CDR. I had gotten to know a lot of officers over the course of my career. One officer I had seen over the past year that I felt had attributes I wanted was LCDR Tracy Malone, NC, USNR. The reasons I thought so highly of her was that she was very bright, had very polished manners, and really knew her way around Capitol Hill. She had spent the last two years in BUMED's Legislative Affairs Division, but before that she had served as a White House nurse. There were three problems though:

1. She was a single woman.
2. She was Nurse Corps, not Medical Service Corps.
3. She was a Reserve Officer, not a regular officer.

There was only one male admiral I knew who had a female aide. That was Admiral Chuck Larson, who had been recalled from retirement to serve a second tour as Superintendent of the Naval Academy. Having known Admiral Larson since my Plebe Summer at the Naval Academy, I called him and asked his advice. Admiral Larson told me that if I felt Tracy was the best person for the job to select her and ignore any comments about gender or corps. As for her Reserve commission, he said to ask her to submit an application to be augmented to a Regular commission. As long as that was in place BUPERS would not be able to release her from active duty.

I asked David to call Tracy and ask her to come see me, and a few minutes later she arrived. I asked David to close the door and for both of them to have a seat. I told Tracy that I had been confirmed by the Senate as the next Surgeon General, but the announcement would not be made until the Medical Corps Ball this Friday. I asked her not to breath a word of this and told her the reason she was in my office was I wanted her to be my aide. She responded that she would have to think about it, there were things in her personal life she had to consider (she had a boyfriend). She also brought up her being Nurse Corps and not Medical Service Corps, which I dispensed with as "no problem." She mentioned being a Reservist. I told her to put in her request for augmentation for a regular commission, and I would take care of the rest. She asked if she could get back to me the following morning. I said, "Sure." Before lunch she was back to tell me she accepted.

The other position I needed to solidify quickly was my chief of staff. Having recently sat on a selection board for one-star admiral, Medical Service Corps, I had a good view of the talent pool. One person who really stood out was David Fisher, whose career I had been following for some years. He was trained as a comptroller, just what I was looking for to be able to keep the BUMED comptroller in line. David was currently the commanding officer of the Naval Medical Information Command (NMIMC, pronounced nim-ick). I asked David Maloney to call him and ask if I could stop by on my way home that afternoon and visit him. No problem. I dropped in, told him the same thing I had told Tracy that morning, and said I wanted him to be my chief of staff. Without hesitation, he said yes. David Maloney would move with me as the Deputy Chief of Staff and we would keep LCDR Joan Queen, who had been an executive assistant for Don Hagen. Joan was a LCDR MSC. She was a superb officer and would provide needed continuity through the transition.

We were all set. No one leaked a word before the Medical Corps Ball.

Deena and I showed up at our table with the three USUHS seniors and their partners. (Two of the students were Don Crain and Kim Davis. Several years later both became my doctors. Kim was a glaucoma specialist and Don a urologist.) After dinner Don Hagen took the floor and announced we would unveil his portrait. He asked me to do so and everyone applauded. Then he said the other thing we had all come for was to find out who the next SG would be, and, he said, "He's standing right here next to me." More applause and then people surrounded me with congratulations and best wishes. Don Hagen had said to me earlier in the day, "People who were trying to stick a knife in your back this morning will be trying to kiss your behind tonight." How true.

On the Monday following the announcement BUMED was buzzing with rumors. I got a call from Milt Benson at BUPERS, who wanted to review a list of candidates to be my chief of staff, deputy chief of staff, and aide. I told him I had already decided who they would be. He had real heartburn with my choice of a single, female, Reserve Nurse Corps officer as my aide and went over the reasons, including that this was usually a Medical Service Corps officer. I told him I had already thought of all of these objections and had plans to deal with them. He suggested that I go over this with the chief of the Nurse Corps, and I told him she was due in my office later that morning for that discussion. When Joan Engel came to my office I told her Tracy was going to be my aide. She was thrilled because she saw her as very highly qualified and believed that my choice of a woman and a Nurse Corps officer would send a lot of positive messages. She was concerned about Tracy's Reserve rather than Regular commission. I told her Tracy had agreed to apply for a Regular commission. Joan knew the people in the Nurse Corps well and said she knew if only one of the applicants for augmentation was selected Tracy would be the one. She also knew that Tracy would be in zone for selection for promotion to commander soon after augmentation and this would not sit well with some in the Nurse Corps who had served longer with a Regular commission. I said that was too bad, and they'd have to live with it. This all came to pass, right on schedule.

My personal staff was set. There were a couple of civil service secretaries, Bonnie Schneider and Linda McFadden, who would stay on. I had to choose someone to replace me as deputy and selected Todd Fisher, a Medical Service Corps Rear Admiral who had been in my old job of Med-03. Todd was the first non-physician to become Deputy SG. I had to replace him, and chose Rear Admiral (Select) Ed Phillips, who had been Don Hagen's chief of staff. With the others they provided more front office continuity.

One other item had to be taken care of before I took over. There had to be an "official" Navy photograph of me that could be posted in all Navy Medical facilities worldwide and a lot of extra copies had to be made to give to people or agencies that requested them. Also, Deena and I moved the two miles from our home in Rockville to the Surgeon General's quarters on the grounds of the National Naval Medical Center, Bethesda.

The change of command was scheduled for Thursday, June 29. My mother and other family members began showing up a couple of days early. On Tuesday, June 27, Admiral Boorda had offered to promote me to Vice Admiral in his office in the Pentagon. Both Admiral Boorda and the Secretary of the Navy would be there. We were told how many guests we could bring, so besides me there was Deena, two of our sons, my mother, Don Hagen and his wife, Dave Fisher, Dave Maloney, and Tracy Malone. That filled our contingent and the room.

The photograph of me that was posted in every U.S. Navy medical facility worldwide (courtesy U.S. Navy).

June 29 dawned a beautiful sunny day. The change of command ceremony began at 10:00 in front of the iconic Building One at Bethesda. There would be around 1,000 people there including the Navy Secretary, the chief of staff of the Marine Corps and the chief of Naval Operations, plus many Flag and General officers, even some members of Congress. Don Hagen and I and the others on the dais prepared to go out to our places for the ceremony. Don went out just before me and was announced as "Surgeon General of the Navy, arriving." Eight bells were bonged and three Ruffles and Flourishes were played by the Navy band. I thought of how many times I had passed through these doors, but this time it was really different, as a lot of responsibility would be riding on my shoulders when I passed back through them at the ceremony's conclusion.

As I ascended the dais the announcement was, "Vice Admiral, Medical Corps, United States Navy, arriving." For the first time I got eight bells and three Ruffles and Flourishes. I saluted and took my seat. We went briskly thorough the ceremony. Don made his retirement remarks and I made my acceptance remarks. Then it was time to depart. This time I went before Don, and as I left, I was announced as "Surgeon General of the Navy, departing." The ceremony was followed by a reception at the base officer's club. In the receiving line Don and his wife were first, then Deena and me. Lots of people

On June 30, 1995, I had the honor of relieving Don Hagen as Surgeon General. From left to right appear Admiral Jeremy Boorda, Chief of Naval Operations; General Carl Mundy, Jr., Commandant of the Marine Corps; Vice Admiral Don Hagen, me and a pastor from Vice Admiral Hagen's church (courtesy U.S. Navy).

I knew passed through. Steve Lewis had come all the way from Oakland and Kevin Shannon from the University of California, San Francisco, colleagues from my days at Oak Knoll. Equally memorable was Dr. Howard Pearson, my mentor who really got me kick-started in pediatric hematology. He was now not just the chairman of Pediatrics at Yale, he was also the president of the American Academy of Pediatrics. What an honor.

13

Surgeon General

My Four Goals

I became the Navy's 32nd Surgeon General on June 27, 1995. From my office I could see the Lincoln Memorial, the Mall, the Washington Monument, the Capitol, Arlington Cemetery, the Kennedy Center, and the City of Arlington. I was responsible for the total Navy Medicine budget of about $5 billion per year. There were 27 hospitals with operating beds, 9 of them outside the continental United States, and over 100 medical clinics. We provided the medical care on all of the Navy's ships, submarines, aviation squadrons, and shore stations, and all Marine Corps units and bases. Along with the Army and Air Force we shared responsibility for the care of all active duty, retirees, and their eligible dependents. There were 11,000 officers, 30,000 enlisted personnel, and 10,000 civilians working in the Navy Medical Department.

I had been in the job only a couple of days when Lewis H. Seaton, the 29th Navy SG, died suddenly and unexpectedly in Jacksonville, Florida. His wife had his remains cremated that day and a memorial service planned at 1000 the following morning at the Jacksonville Naval Air Station Base Chapel. The command wanted me to present the flag to his widow. Tracy and I would be the only ones going. There went our plans that the two of us would never travel without a third party along to "chaperone." We arrived late that night and went to the BOQ for a few hours of sleep before we were to be picked up at 0500 for breakfast, a tour of the hospital, and an Admiral's call with the hospital staff. When we left the BOQ Tracy asked me what I had done with the welcome basket of fruit in my room. I asked, "What basket of fruit?" She said there was a basket of fruit in her room, so there must have been one in mine. Turns out we had slept in each other's rooms. Good thing her boyfriend hadn't called to say good night.

A few days later Tracy and I, along with my Public Affairs Officer (PAO), CDR Sheila Graham, and the Force Master Chief, Mike Stewart, flew by Navy

Air from Andrews Air Force Base to Norfolk Naval Air Station to attend the groundbreaking for the new Navy Hospital at Portsmouth, Virginia. I turned over a spade full of dirt along with several members of Congress and other dignitaries. On the trip back to Andrews I talked about my goals for my tenure. I laid out what I thought were the most important things I wanted to achieve, and by the time we landed Sheila Graham (the PAO) had them condensed into the following:

1. Take Health Care to the Deck Plates.
2. Move information, not people.
3. Improve business practices.
4. Make Tricare work.

Those four goals were part of every formal presentation I made throughout my tenure. I knew from experience you must have a simple message from the beginning that can be understood by all. Below is a little amplification:

TAKE HEALTH CARE TO THE DECK PLATES

Take care of our Sailors and Marines as close to where they work as possible. Don't bring them to the hospital for every little thing that ails them. Consulting physicians should focus on helping unit corpsman and doctors to take care of their patients at or near their command.

MOVE INFORMATION, NOT PEOPLE

This followed naturally on the first point. If you were a deck-plates provider, try to send the pertinent information you have about your patient to the consultant and see if you can get management advice on how to take care of them without moving them.

IMPROVE BUSINESS PRACTICES

Look at all the steps in processing patients through your system and eliminate non–value-added steps.

MAKE TRICARE WORK

Tricare was just getting started, and like anything new in a large bureaucracy there was resistance. I emphasized that there were three choices for dependents and retirees to deal with: Tricare Prime, Tricare Extra, and Tricare Standard. It really wasn't hard to understand. For active duty it was really simple: they had no choice, only Prime.

SITREPS

My PAO, CDR Sheila Graham, had an idea about how to share ideas by sending out a SITREP (situation report) every other week. In it we wrote about what was going on at BUMED, Health Affairs, the CNO level, Congress, and the Administration that would affect them and us. The SITREP itself was a change in business practices for all of us, and I made sure all the commands knew that. Prior to this, communications from BUMED went only to what we called the second echelon commands. It was their responsibility to get the word down to the third and fourth echelons. Now the commands, even the smallest, were getting it straight from the top and right away.

The second week, Tracy told me two leading researchers at the Naval Medical Research Institute, Bethesda—Captains Carl June and Dave Harlan—wanted a meeting with me to present their research. Carl was a Naval Academy graduate, top of his class, and went directly from the academy to Oxford as a Rhodes scholar, where he received a master's degree. He returned to the USA, went to medical school, and then trained in hematology-oncology and immunology. At Bethesda Carl and Dave were doing research on T-lymphocytes—memory cells in the bone marrow, blood, and tissues. Dave was at the meeting, but Carl was absent. Dave gave me a wonderful presentation on their work, and when he finished he told me the reason Carl was absent was that his wife had just been found to have inoperable cancer. With the best care available her life expectancy at best was one year.

Carl had an idea. He wanted to give his wife a massive dose of chemotherapy, to kill the tumor, but for sure this would wipe out her bone marrow and all of her T-lymphocytes. Then he would try to restore her bone marrow and T-lymphocytes with some of her own stem cells that he had obtained from her bone marrow before treatment began and he had preserved and stimulated to expand exponentially in vitro. This was very advanced science at that time; no one had tried it before. Georgetown University Hospital had a bone marrow transplant program and they said they would provide the in-hospital support for him to treat his wife for $150,000.

I told Dave to tell Carl I would pay for it. Back at BUMED I called in my comptroller and told him, "Write Georgetown University Hospital a check for $150,000." He said I couldn't do that. I said I could. Within an hour I had a call from the Assistant Secretary of Defense for Health Affairs, who also told me I couldn't do this. Again I said I could, and I had already done it. I was correct. This story went in our next SITREP. It showed all the echelons of Navy Medicine that headquarters was taking the lead on innovation.

From time to time we sent out progress reports on Carl's wife. After the procedure she was out of the hospital in about eight weeks. She lived for nine more years and raised her two sons, getting to see one graduate from college.

Carl retired from the Navy after 22 years and went to the University of Pennsylvania, where today he is a full professor and one of the world's foremost researchers in this field. I convinced the ASD (HA) that bone marrow transplants, though cutting edge and available in only a limited number of centers, could no longer be considered experimental. He ordered the CHAMPUS office to start paying for them.

This was a great start for SITREPS.

While Don Hagen was SG we had begun having telemedicine discussions with the command staff of our fleet hospital in Zagreb, Croatia. We'd also begun taking pictures of mothers holding their newborn babies and then we sent digital copies to the fathers' ships. These were great morale boosters. We wrote about this in a SITREP and someone suggested that we try to set up a link between ships and hospitals and let dads see their wives holding their new babies and allow the parents to have a conversation. We did it, starting with aircraft carriers, which had the most advanced technology. This practice spread rapidly. Then someone suggested we try doing some medical consults with ships this way. Dermatology lent itself to this naturally; dermatologists take a lot of pictures and share them with colleagues, securing additional opinions and guidance. Soon we had general medical officers or corpsmen on ships sending pictures to dermatologists ashore who assisted them in managing skin conditions. Ship to shore consultations became routine.

Our process for handling X-rays at sea was laborious and inefficient. We had the logistical problems all hospitals had: keeping an adequate inventory of unexposed film and developing fluid available and proper recycling of used developing fluid (it contains a lot of silver). In addition, we had no radiologists at sea. Ships kept all their X-rays onboard until they returned to their homeport, then the corpsmen would load up the accumulated X-rays taken during deployment and deliver them to the local Navy hospital, where radiologists would have to read them before they were filed. Some of the films would be several months old, and sometimes things would be spotted on them that had been missed. I thought about the potential for teleradiology at sea. If we put digital radiology on ships, we could send X-rays via satellite links to stateside hospitals where radiologists could read them and send the reports back to the ship. I put this idea into one of my SITREPS and Rear Admiral Dick Ridenour, commanding officer of the National Naval Medical Center, responded that he had two officers who were interested. Both were USUHS graduates, one a CDR nuclear medicine physician, Rich Bakalar, and the other a LCDR pediatrician, Forrest Faison, with advanced training in neurodevelopmental pediatrics. I met with the two and outlined my ideas.

In less than a year Rich and Forrest had teleradiology on a carrier. This technique rapidly spread to other carriers, large deck amphibious ships, and some remote shore stations, including Guantanamo Bay, Cuba, and our base in Antarctica. (A note about Rich Bakalar and Forrest Faison: Rich retired as a Captain and is now Managing Director of Clinical Informatics and Tele-health/Telemedicine at KPMG in Denver. He is also a past president of the American Telemedicine Association. Forrest Faison is now the Navy Surgeon General.)

The Vice Chief of Naval Operations (VCNO), Joe Prueher, asked me if there wasn't something we could do about the ugly glasses Sailors and Marines were given to correct their visual acuity problems. He was referring to our "Government Issue" glasses with black frames. Sailors referred to them as BCGs (Birth Control Glasses). I talked with the commanding officer of the Naval Ophthalmic Support and Training Activity (NOSTRA), an optometrist, and came up with the idea of doing a test and evaluation of alternative frames on board the USS *George Washington*, one of our aircraft carriers. He selected a couple of dozen different frames, took them to the ship, and let every sailor on board who wore glasses pick the frame he liked, then made a pair of glasses with it. After a few weeks the sailors were asked for their opinions. From this a dozen of the most popular frames were selected. We computed what it would cost to outfit every sailor in the Navy who wore glasses with a pair of what we called "Frames of Choice," paid for this by moving a little money around in our budget.

I introduced this program to Navy leadership at the CNO's 0700 weekly meeting with the senior local Admirals. I opened an attaché case and dumped a bunch of glasses on the conference table showing alternative frames to BCGs. Several people picked up frames and tried them on. All agreed they looked much better than BCGs. One Admiral said it was the quickest sell to the CNO in memory. In the next SITREP we announced the Frames of Choice program was going fleet-wide. I got the expected pushback from Health Affairs telling me I couldn't do this, and I told them (again) that yes, I could. It was front-page news in the next week's edition of *Navy Times*. CNN did a several-minute segment on it that ran repeatedly. Congress became interested and after a few months of feedback ordered the other two services to follow the Navy's lead.

Admiral Prueher, Vice Chief of Naval Operations (VCNO), approached me soon after we had replaced all of BUMED's old computers and IBM Selectric typewriters and installed our Local Area Network (LAN). We had stored all the old equipment on the ground floor of a remote building on the compound. He wanted to know if he could have them and send them directly to the Bureau of Navy Personnel—where they were working with even older typewriters and photocopy machines and where there were very few computers—rather than sending them through the Navy's recycle program. I said sure. He had a working party and truck pick them up before noon.

We had to fill any valid prescription for any beneficiary whether a military provider or a civilian wrote it, as long as it was on our formulary. Prescription medications were free, so people drove long distances to get them filled. If they brought a new prescription to our pharmacy, no matter where it was written, if it was on our formulary we had to fill it. Our pharmacy waiting rooms were overflowing. Many people were waiting just to pick up refills. In several of our larger hospitals waiting times had gone back to several hours. This caused parking problems because our parking garages and lots were always filled.

Captain Dan Horan, the head of the pharmacy at Bethesda, came up with a novel solution. He suggested we establish a drive-through satellite pharmacy dispensing location remote from the hospital, much like a fast food franchise drive through. To use it patients had to use the automated telephone refill system we had installed throughout the military medical system while I was in Health Affairs and select the Bethesda satellite pharmacy as their pick-up location. They received a message telling them what day their prescription would be available for pick-up, usually the next working day.

Soon Bethesda's parking garage was no longer congested. The idea of drive-through pharmacies and remote facility dispensing locations quickly took root and other military hospitals implemented this. Many satellite-dispensing locations were established on military bases adjacent to other facilities like the Military Exchanges and Commissaries. Today this method of delivering prescriptions, along with mail refill, is the rule rather than the exception. There were many people who contributed to this, but it was Dan Horan who first came up with the idea and Dick Ridenour who implemented it.

The chief of Navy Personnel, Vice Admiral Frank Bowman, and I were chatting outside the Navy Operations Center when the CNO, Admiral Boorda, saw us and asked us to come into his office. Admiral Boorda had recently been the subject of an article in *Reader's Digest*, highlighting his rise from Enlisted Seaman to Admiral. A lady in Wisconsin had read the article and written Admiral Boorda about her high school student son. He wanted to get into the Navy's guaranteed entry program. If he could qualify and maintain good grades, he could come into the Navy right after graduating from high school—no waiting and looking for a temporary job. His problem was his vision couldn't be corrected to 20/20 in one of his eyes. Admiral Boorda had a good question: "Aren't there some enlisted ratings in the Navy that you don't need vision correctable to 20/20 in both eyes to do your job?" Bowman and I said we'd look into it. We found some ratings in electronics fields that met this requirement. This young man had high scores in the required areas on his aptitude test, and right after high school he went to boot camp and then directly to electronics training. He got his electronic rating, made two deployments on aircraft carriers, completed his four-year enlistment and went off to college using the GI Bill. He graduated from college, got married, and produced grandkids for his mom.

The first innovation to come in through the SITREP process from the field came from Captain Mike Kilpatrick, Commanding Officer at the Navy Hospital, Millington, Tennessee, who had developed a simple way to measure patient satisfaction. Every patient was given a uniquely colored-coded poker chip for the area where they had received service. When they left the facility there were three buckets, one with a happy face, one with a sad face, and one with a neutral face. The patient put the poker chip into whatever bucket best fit the experience. The command had immediate feedback and could take prompt action on areas that started accumulating poker chips in the sad face bucket.

Meetings

I wasn't overburdened with meetings at BUMED. We had a 90-minute meeting every Wednesday attended by all the division heads, at which one of them gave a briefing on activities in that specific area. Then we'd ask each division head to report on anything new or of general interest. Once a month we'd have an awards ceremony. We had several hundred people working at BUMED, which was locally referred to as "Navy Hill." Many of them were civilians. They'd get longevity awards every five years, so there were plenty of those to hand out. There were also civilian of the quarter or year and similar sailor of the quarter or year awards. Promotions were the most fun. We'd try to have family there to be part of it. We'd do the promotion by putting on the person's new shoulder boards or collar devices, depending on the uniform of the day. I'd usually put one on and a spouse, parent, or colleague the other. The most interesting promotion I did was for an old friend, Bonnie Potter. Bonnie was a LCDR internist when I went to Oakland in 1980. She served at Portsmouth during my time there. She was Commanding Officer at Camp Pendleton when she was selected for promotion to Admiral. We had her promotion scheduled during one of our regular awards ceremonies. Bonnie was the first woman selected for Admiral in the Navy Medical Corps. Attendance for this was huge; people were packed in, spilling into the halls and the parking lot. We got through the ceremony before the fire marshal could shut us down. We had a monthly meeting of code (or division) heads. These were all Admirals with the exception of our comptroller, John Cuddy, who was an SES. We held these meetings at the Navy Medical Information Management Center a three-minute walk from my quarters. These meetings weren't interrupted, because mobile phones didn't have e-mail, instant messaging, or photographic capability yet. Those few who had mobile phones turned them off during the meeting.

Another regularly scheduled meeting was called the Black Book meeting and was led by our JAG officer. This was not a fun meeting. Having about 50,000 people in the BUMED claimancy, we were bound to have some with problems. Here we kept track of all the cases that were not nonjudicial punishment. There were cases of the medical department personnel who had questions of malpractice brought up in investigations or any who had felony charges pending. We had an extensive process for reviewing providers whose ability to practice had been brought into question and a documentation and reporting system for those who were found lacking. We could, and did, limit and in a few cases remove providers' clinical privileges and report this to the National Practitioner Data Bank. Once reported, any facility where they applied for clinical privileges in the future would have access to this data. We also had some criminal cases that were being processed in civilian jurisdictions. We followed the progress of these and recorded the progress and final outcome. Drunk driving and drug convictions were included in this.

There were some cases that were being handled within the military judicial system. One was a LCDR MSC officer who had established a dummy corporation that was submitting fictitious charges to CHAMPUS for reimbursement. He had learned that CHAMPUS's baseline for auditing billings was $30,000 per month. So each month he would submit invoices to CHAMPUS for some amount just under $30,000. The payments were sent to a post office box near his home. He and his wife ran this scam for a couple of years. We found out about it when his wife learned he was having an affair and she decided to provide state's evidence in return for being held immune from prosecution. I sent this officer to a court-martial. He pled guilty and got five years of hard labor.

At the CNO's weekly meeting with the VCNO and the senior local Admirals we would discuss the hot issues. Sometimes there were uncomfortable questions for us. I'd be on the hot seat whenever there was an unexpected death in the Navy. It didn't happen often, but when it did it was tough to deal with. One I faced occurred when a recently promoted one-star Admiral in Hawaii dropped dead while doing the mile and a half run for his Personal Fitness Test. Another was when a female plebe at the Naval Academy was found dead in bed. It took a lot of medical sleuth work, but eventually we were able to find the cause of the untimely demise in both cases.

Right after the CNO's meeting there was a follow-on meeting in what is called the Navy Command Center. This was a secure conference room away from the outer walls of the Pentagon that was swept for listening devices prior to each meeting. There were armed Marines at the entrance. The Secretary, Under Secretary, and Assistant Secretaries of the Navy would also attend. Most of the content of this meeting was classified at the Secret or Top Secret level and dealt with where our assets were deployed at the moment and where they would be heading.

I attended weekly meetings in Health Affairs along with the Army and Air Force SGs, the ASD (HA), and his Principal Deputy (PD). When I first became SG Steve Joseph was the ASD and Ed Martin was the PD. Alcid (Cid) Lanoue and Edgar R. (Andy) Anderson were the Army and Air Force SGs respectively. During my tenure as Navy SG all of these folks would move on and be replaced. The weekly meetings at this time were nearly totally consumed with making Tricare work and dealing with the budget, which was now nearly totally in the hands of the ASD since the Defense Health Program (DHP) had been implemented in the waning days of the Bush 41 administration. Later on Ron Blanck became the Army SG and Chip Roadman the Air Force SG. The three of us worked together to make sure Tricare was working. At one high-level tri-service event the three of us donned sombreros, called

This photograph has always been known as "The 3 Amigos," from left to right: Me, Navy Surgeon General; Lieutenant General Ron Blanck, Army Surgeon General; and Lieutenant General Chip Roadman, Air Force Surgeon General.

ourselves the Three Amigos, and made a pitch about the necessity of making Tricare work.

There was a lot of initial resistance to Tricare from patients, providers, and the military services. The services were particularly incensed because their control of personnel and assets had been significantly eroded. Quarterly the three SGs and the two principals from the office of the ASD and a select few senior staff would have a two-day off-site meeting where we would sort through the Tricare issues. We moved the location of these meetings to different sites in Maryland and Virginia and kept quiet on their location so the press and beneficiary groups looking to lobby wouldn't interrupt us. Our next meeting was May 16–17, 1996, in suburban Maryland at a small hotel.

On May 15, the day before this meeting, I spent an hour with the CNO, Admiral Mike Boorda. He had asked me to talk about suicide in the Navy because recently a psychiatry patient at Bethesda had jumped off the sixth floor of a building and also a young Marine standing guard duty outside the Navy Command Center in the Pentagon shot herself in the head with her 45. He was particularly interested in how we investigated suicides, so I explained the process of a psychiatric autopsy. The next day, about an hour into the off-site Tricare meeting my chief of staff, Captain David Fisher, entered the room and said he needed to see me outside right away. He then told me the CNO, Admiral Mike Boorda, had been shot and was dead, and it looked like suicide. He said I needed to get back to the office right away. I went back in the meeting room, told the others what I knew, and departed.

The Secretary of the Navy called a meeting the following morning of the senior Flag officers and told us that the Vice Chief, Admiral Jay Johnson, would be acting CNO until a new CNO was nominated and confirmed. Johnson had become VCNO after Joe Prueher had departed to become Commander in Chief, Pacific Command (CINCPAC). Johnson had been VCNO long enough to know what it entailed but was the antithesis of Admiral Boorda, who had risen from Seaman to Admiral and had been a surface warfare officer. In contrast, Johnson was a Naval Academy graduate, tall, thin, athletic, and a fighter pilot from the Top Gun mold. During his tenure as Vice Chief the contrast between the two had been obvious and it was common knowledge that they did not get along.

It took the Senate a few weeks to confirm Johnson as CNO. I had been a favorite of Boorda's and so I suspected I would not have the same relation with Johnson. Johnson had two areas he disagreed with Boorda on that I knew would impact our relationship. One was women at sea—he opposed this totally—and the other was the Defense Health Program, which had taken most of the medical budget from the services and placed it in Health Affairs. He had made it clear to me from our first meeting that he wanted the money back.

Johnson's feelings about women at sea were sharpened by the congressionally forced integration of women into increasing numbers of Navy communities. Historically, about the only place women had served in the Navy was in the medical department, initially only as nurses but gradually in every role. The last areas to face gender integration were the war-fighting communities of surface warfare, submarines, and aviation. The Navy was now being told to train pilots in all aspects of aviation, including the supersonic jet fighters—Johnson's community.

Johnson saw a final bulwark he thought would keep women off of ships. He wanted to impose a regulation that required any woman assigned to a ship to have a negative urine pregnancy test every month. If it was positive she would not be allowed on board. The Secretary was opposed to Johnson's position on this as was the Clinton administration and all women senators. Johnson tried to get me to agree that this was a necessary precaution to protect women's health. I checked with the American College of Obstetrics and Gynecology and they agreed with me that serving on ships posed no danger for the first twenty weeks of pregnancy as long as the woman was experiencing no complications. They also recommended that women not remain on board if the ship was going to be more than fifty miles from land so that if problems should develop she could be promptly returned to port. Most ships on local operations easily met this requirement. I drafted a regulation with these requirements in it and got it approved at the SECNAV level. This really upset Johnson. Over two decades later this regulation still applies.

The DHP was another tough nut. Every time he saw me, Johnson would ask, "When are we going to get our money back?" He knew I had been involved in establishing the DHP and so reasoned that if I came out against it that would provide leverage to get the money back. The reason he wanted it was that the Navy had historically used medical program money as a slush fund for most of each year, then as the end of the fiscal year approached and they were running out of funds they'd go back to Congress and say they needed supplemental funding or they wouldn't be able to pay the medical bills. That meant Sailors, Marines, and retirees would be left with huge medical bills for care provided through CHAMPUS and have their credit ratings damaged. (I know this sounds crazy, but that's the way it really was.) Congress had always come through but had figured out the Navy's game. The DHP had stopped this. I told Johnson he would not have my support. My relationship with him through the rest of my career was not good.

I had many meetings with members of Congress, both on the House and Senate side. One of the more pleasant was when I promoted Nancy Lescavage, a Nurse Corps officer, to Rear Admiral along with Senator Dan Inouye (D-HI). Nancy had worked with me in Health Affairs while I was a DASD. Following her tour in Health Affairs I helped her get a one-year congressional internship with the senator. Following that I got her the job as executive officer of Great Lakes Navy Hospital and then as commanding officer of the Corpus Christi Navy Hospital. The senator had thought quite highly of Nancy and agreed to assist in her promotion.

Another pleasant meeting with Congress was when I, along with the other two military SGs, Ron Blanck and Chip Roadman, made our annual appearance before the Senate Armed Services Committee. When the hearing was over we had been told to remain for a few minutes because Senator John Glenn wanted to personally thank each of us for all the work we had done to make Tricare work. John Glenn was one of my heroes. When he shook hands with me I reminded him that we had met before. He asked if that was in Ohio, the state he represented. I told him no, it was in Methodist Hospital in Houston, where his wife was having elective surgery and he observed a kidney transplant being done by Dr. Michael DeBakey. He asked if I was the medical student who had escorted him to and from the operating room. I said yes. He told me that one of his sons had gone to medical school and was an anesthesiologist in private practice.

There were some meetings with Congress that were not pleasant. The worst followed a series of Pulitzer Prize-winning articles that appeared in the *Dayton Daily News* chronicling several catastrophic cases that had occurred in military hospitals over several years. The long time frame made no difference; the public and Congress were outraged. Most of the cases were in Army hospitals, some in the Air Force, and only a couple in the Navy.

The other discovery the reporters had come up with was that there were a number of foreign-trained doctors in our military with questionable state licenses. It made no difference to the reporters that until just a few years earlier doctors could come into the military with no state license. The reason a state license became mandatory was that as we were downsizing small military hospitals to clinics the patients wanted their military doctors to care for them in local civilian hospitals, if possible. Medical staffs of several local hospitals tried to block this, using the fact that the military doctors lacked a valid license to practice in their state. Congress passed a law preempting all state laws requiring military doctors to have a local state license; military doctors had to have only a valid license to practice in one state, as long as they were in the military. The law also required that all military doctors get a valid state license no later than when they completed their first year of graduate medical education. Virtually all U.S.-trained physicians had a valid state license. A lot of foreign-trained physicians didn't.

When this licensure requirement went into effect, some staff in the medical licensure office in Oklahoma started issuing licenses to foreign-trained physicians in the U.S. military without any examination. The cost was $500 renewable every six months. They kept the files on these physicians separate from all others. The *Dayton Daily News* reporters discovered this and the Military Health System got painted with the tar brush. We didn't have any of these doctors in the Navy, but that didn't matter.

Ed Martin was acting ASD (HA) at this time. The four of us—Ed, Chip, Ron, and I—went to work rebuilding confidence in our system. Instead of challenging the veracity and severity of the disclosures, we developed and presented a plan to Congress for correcting these deficiencies. We had a closed meeting with four members of the House of Representatives to review our proposed plan and discuss any further issues they might have. The word had gotten out about the meeting and the hall outside our meeting room was clogged with press. The chairman of the committee stood his ground with these people, said this was a closed meeting, and told them they might as well find something else to do. Most of them left, but a few hung around to see what they might learn when the meeting ended. They learned nothing but harassed us as we left.

I belabor this to complete one more story I've left dangling. I knew all of these House members. One of them was from San Diego, Randall "Duke" Cunningham, whom I mentioned in my section about when I was CO of Navy Hospital San Diego. To refresh your memory, we had a USO fund-raising Mexican dinner in the galley of the soon-to-be-opened replacement hospital. The "Duke," having recently retired from the Navy and a local hero because he had been a Vietnam War fighter ace, was preparing to run for the House of Representatives. "Duke" had tied one on during the dinner and afterwards I had to pull him down from running around on the tabletops swatting at the decorative piñata's with a broom. "Duke" had a reputation in D.C. for similar behavior. In this meeting, "Duke" was sitting directly across from me. I wondered if he remembered my chasing him out of the Navy Hospital galley? Apparently not. He passed out soon after the meeting began and slept all the way through it. When the meeting ended the chairman of the committee gave him a nudge and he got up and along with the others thanked us for our help and left. Fast forward to November 25, 2005. "Duke" resigned from the House after pleading guilty to accepting at least $2.4 million in bribes and under-reporting his taxes. He was sentenced to 8 years and 4 months (100 months) in prison and was ordered to pay $1.4 million in restitution.

I had one more big effort at improving business practices. Earlier I mentioned the THCSRR. We had learned from the THCSRR that our production of trained physicians, advanced training nurses, allied scientists, administrators, and specialized corpsman was not in line with THCSRR requirements. We had made corrections in all areas except physicians. GME was considered the "third rail"—touch it and you were dead. Yet it was clear that we were making far too many specialists in some areas and not near enough in others.

I called in the Corps Chiefs: Medical, Nursing, Dental, Medical Service, and Hospital. I told them I wanted them to make some recommendations for change. They spent months on this and came back with recommendations that we close several residencies at the National Naval Medical Center, Bethesda. I knew what was being planned for the National Capital Region in the future, but that was close-hold, so I said that if programs were to close they would have to be at Portsmouth. That did not go over well. There was such an uproar that the CNO ordered me not to make any further GME program changes. It became such a hot issue that the House and Senate subcommittees on military personnel asked the GAO to study the issue. They did and they issued a report in April 1998. As a result, no changes were made—for seven years—until BRAC 2005. Then closures and consolidations were mandated in law.

I had another meeting at the White House. Connie Mariano, the physician to the president, had Deena and me and a few of my senior staff to the White House every year during the Christmas holidays. We would have a lunch in a private dining room just off the Oval Office, served by the Navy Mess men. This was elegant. After lunch Connie took us on a tour of the White House, visiting rooms not on the normal public tour.

Invited to lunch at the White House, December 1987, from left to right: Ed and Mary Phillips, Deena and me, President Bill Clinton, Tracy Malone, and David Fisher (courtesy U.S. Navy).

Connie had asked me to stay after the tour because she wanted me to meet privately with the president. When I did, I discussed Connie's remaining with him as the physician to the president. He and she were both concerned that if she continued through his second term, it might negatively impact her future Navy career. I told him that as president he had the authority to promote her to Rear Admiral, that Ronald Reagan had done this with an Army officer who had served as his physician near the end of his term, so there was precedent. That set his mind at ease. As his second term came to a close he did this, and Connie retired as a Rear Admiral (Lower Half).

Social Events

Deena and I attended many receptions at foreign embassies, some of them spectacular. The most interesting to me was the British embassy. I attended a dinner there for active duty only that was incredible. We were told by the CNO's office that in addition to wearing our mess dress uniform with miniature medals, we would not be allowed to drive to the embassy. We had to come in a limousine, and the driver would have to pick us up at the evening's end and return us home. The reason was that we would drink so much there was no way we would be able to legally drive. This was true.

We attended the grand opening of a new German embassy that reportedly cost over $1 billion to build. It was stark and sterile, and even some of the Germans quietly complained of that. During the evening I talked for a while with a tall gentleman who turned out to be Associate Justice Anthony Kennedy of the Supreme Court. We attended a reception at a new Japanese embassy. In contrast to the German one it was elegant in its simplicity. Japanese food was served that was being prepared on the spot. I stayed close to the sushi table. The Chinese embassy occupied a run-down hotel building on Massachusetts Avenue near Rock Creek Park. The event was a dinner, all Chinese food, catered by a local restaurant. Typical of the Chinese, at dinner's end they gave us each a cardboard box for our leftovers.

I visited the Egyptian embassy, not for a reception but for a visit with the ambassador at his request. I was ushered into the ambassador's private office and offered a small cup of hot Egyptian coffee that was nearly syrup. The purpose of the visit was that the ambassador wanted to extend the Egyptian government's thanks for the care we had provided at the National Naval Medical Center, Bethesda, to the wife of the then-president of Egypt. This had been a delicate undertaking; the Egyptians did not want it known that she was ill. We did this in the Presidential Suite at Bethesda with both American and Egyptian Secret Service controlling entry to the unit at all times. A very limited number of highly screened hospital staff cared for her. I visited her every week during her multiple admissions. After extending the government's thanks, the ambassador asked if I would be attending the 50th anniversary celebration of the U.S. Navy's Infectious Disease Laboratory in Cairo in February. I told him I would and that my wife would be accompanying me. He told me the Egyptian government wanted to take us on a tour of the Egyptian antiquities that would involve a four-day cruise up the Nile River from Luxor to Aswan and then on to Abu Simbel. I told him that I was forbidden from accepting such gifts by Navy regulations. He told me the Secretary of the Navy had already granted an exception on this for me.

The Navy reciprocated for all these galas by hosting other countries with receptions for ambassadors and attachés in the State Department reception rooms, across E Street from BUMED. These rooms don't meet the standard of the inside of the British embassy, but they are the finest U.S. rooms I have seen in D.C.

We also entertained a lot. We took small groups out on the Potomac on what was called the CNO's barge and also had frequent events at our home. Sometimes these were large receptions, with up to 150 people attending. Other times they were dinners for a dozen people. For all of these events our Mess Specialist would do all the shopping and food preparation and round up staff from the Navy Medical Center's galley to aid in serving and cleaning up.

One year we were invited to a Naval Academy football pre-game reception at the superintendent's house. After the reception we walked to the stadium. I was in the uniform of the day, summer whites, the same as the Brigade of Midshipmen. As we approached the stadium entrance we saw the brigade outside the stadium waiting to march on. We spotted son Grant's company and I went down to say hello. Once I got to Grant's company a plan rapidly hatched in the mind of his Company Commander. "Why don't you march on with us, sir," he asked. "Why not?" I replied. After all, I'd spent a year at "Canoe U" and still knew how to march. They stuck me in the center of the company, surrounded by about 100 Midshipmen, and off we went. I didn't miss a step. The companies form up on the field and remain in place through the national anthem. When they are dismissed they bolt for their reserved section, where they stand for the entire game. As I approached the stands, there right in front of me were the CNO, Mike Boorda, and the Secretary of the Navy, John Dalton. They saw me and asked, "Did you really march on?" I said, "Yes, sir, with my son's company." They thought that was neat.

A few days later I got an e-mail from Grant. His company wanted to know if I would do a repeat performance with them at the Army-Navy Game in Philadelphia. Apparently word had spread about these hijinks and the fact that Navy had won the game made them believe this was a good omen. We rode the Army-Navy train to the game, along with a lot of other Generals and Admirals and senior civilians. One service had the front half of the train, the other the back half. Neutral ground was the center car of the train, appropriately the bar car. We were sitting with Doug and Sheila Johnson; Doug was a Navy Reserve two-star, MSC Admiral from Norfolk and also a fun-loving man. He asked if he could join me in the march on. I said, "Why not?"

When we got to Philly we gave our wives their tickets and headed to the brigade in one of the parking lots. We found Grant's company and off we went. As we approached the playing field there were a couple of junior officers watching to try to catch interlopers attempting to join in and sneak into the game. They spotted Doug and me and yelled, "Hey, there are two!" I told them we were for real and to back off. By the time they had recovered we were on the field, marching smartly into position.

This was the second Saturday of December, and it was really cold. We were wearing what was called bridge coats, heavy wool, navy blue overcoats that come down just below your knees. Shoulder boards are worn on bridge coats, so our solid gold ones stood out like sore thumbs, as did the double scoop of "scrambled eggs" on our hat visors.

CBS TV was on the field getting B-roll for use during the game. It didn't take them more than a few seconds to spot us and start shooting. Everything they were shooting was being shown simultaneously on the main stadium scoreboard, on monitors through out the stadium, including the two clubs, one for the Navy and the other for the Army dignitaries who had ridden the train up from Washington. A hot lunch was being served in these clubs along with all the booze anyone wanted to consume. After the Midshipmen had completed their part of the march on they broke for their seats and Doug and I found our way to the Navy reception. The Secretary and CNO were waiting for me, and when we entered a cheer went up. This was the 1996 Army-Navy game. Army won a close one, 28–24. Navy had last beaten Army in 1991. I had been to all five of those losses and even my marching on with the brigade did not break the jinx.

CONUS Medical Facility Visits

CONUS means Continental United States, the lower 48. It does not include Alaska or Hawaii or our territories of Puerto Rico and Guam. I visited all of our medical facilities in CONUS. The purpose of these visits was to emphasize my four points to the staff of each facility in person and to get feed-back from them. It was an opportunity for them to show off for the "boss," and they did—magnificently. Members of my staff who accompanied me on these visits included Rear Admiral Joan Engel, director of the Navy Nurse Corps, my PAO, Captain Sheila Graham, my Aide, Commander Tracy Malone, and Force Master, Chief Mike Stewart. These people did a lot of career counseling on these visits. Sometimes Deena would go along—at my expense. She was great at striking up conversations with shy or reserved people who had important observations to offer.

I can't go into detail on each facility I visited, but I will provide a few highlights. There were no longer any facilities with operating beds north of the National Capital Region. The Navy Medical Clinic on the Newport Naval Station served the Naval War College, the Naval Academy Prep School, and nearly fifty other local commands. During Don Hagen's tenure as SG, the hospital there became a clinic. All inpatient care was moved to the Newport Community Hospital and the Navy doctors became members of this hospital's medical staff and cared for the military beneficiaries hospitalized there. This was the first time such an arrangement had been done anywhere. It was also what led Congress to pass a law requiring that military doctors had to have only one valid state license to practice, including in a civilian hospital, as long as their practice was a part of their official duties. It didn't apply to moonlighting. There had been some pushback from some civilian members of Newport Community Hospital's medical staff initially and the licensure issue was used to try to prevent Navy doctors from becoming staff members. Congress changed that with the new law. A few years after this change, a Navy doctor was elected president of Newport Community Hospital's medical staff. This arrangement has served as a model for several other communities.

The National Naval Medical Center, Bethesda, Maryland, faces challenges no other hospital does, as there is hardly a day that it does not have a dignitary hospitalized there—members of Congress, other high government officials, and "special patients" from other nations we were directed to provide care for by either the State Department or the White House. Over 80 percent of Supreme Court justices, congressmen, or other officials requiring hospitalization went to Bethesda, not Walter Reed—a surprise to many.

Throughout Dick Ridenour's tenure at Bethesda he and I were in frequent contact with Rear Admiral John Eisold, attending physician at the United States Capitol. John would routinely try to direct VIPs needing specialized evaluation or hospitalization to Bethesda. He pointed out that these people needed access to secure communication technology for themselves and senior members of their staffs—beyond that available with POTS (Plain Old Telephone Service). Using existing resources and funds, Dick and his staff provided this, making these assets available to all who came to the hospital and needed them. Medical care at Bethesda was as good as you could get. I can speak from personal experience. I was hospitalized there twice while I was in Health Affairs and twice more when I was SG.

The clinic at Annapolis was established as a hospital in 1846 and converted to a clinic in 1979. We put Independent Duty Navy Hospital Corpsmen into Bancroft Hall to conduct daily sick call for the Midshipmen so they would learn how they would receive medical care once they graduated and went to the Fleet. This also provided valuable experience for the Corpsmen. I went to the academy every year to speak with the pre-med students. For the past several years the academy had sent up to 15 members of the graduating class directly to medical school.

Patuxent River is the home of the Naval Air Systems Command, where the Navy does its flight-testing. A 90-minute drive on state roads from Bethesda, it's located near the point of a peninsula surrounded by the Potomac River to the west, the Patuxent River to the east and the Chesapeake Bay to the south. There had been a Navy hospital there since 1968 and Don Hagen and I had both wanted to downsize it to a clinic. Higher authority in the Navy kept us from doing so. Their reasoning was that we needed a hospital in case there were any non-fatal accidents with aircraft being tested. There was a perfectly fine, much more capable hospital in the nearby community of St. Mary's. The next round of BRAC made it possible for us to get out of the inpatient business there.

A few miles south of Williamsburg is Yorktown, where General Cornwallis surrendered the king's troops to General George Washington, resulting in the United States gaining its independence. Near that historical battlefield is the Naval Weapons Station, Yorktown. It is a secure base; the public is not allowed on board because of the arsenal of weapons stored there. The Naval Ophthalmic, Support and Training Activity (NOSTRA), is located aboard the Naval Weapons Station. NOSTRA is the organization that stood up the Frames of Choice program, which provides eyewear to all the military services and fabricates as many as 75,000 sets of eyeglasses in a single month. They run a 6-month training course in both laboratory and dispensing/technician programs, the only optician school in the nation to have both programs fully accredited.

Naval Medical Center Portsmouth was our other East Coast multispecialty training hospital, one of the "Big Four." The original hospital had been built in the mid–1800s and had served both the Union and Confederate forces during the Civil War. An addition was made to the hospital in the 1950s, thus its design and construction were quite dated and it needed replacement. I participated in the groundbreaking ceremony for the new hospital, but construction was not completed until after I retired. There were several clinics in the area, one in Little Creek, where the SEALS trained. We had become aware that many SEALS were physically "burning out" at the 10–12-year career mark, so I assigned physical therapists there. The SEALS were doing a lot of exercises that the therapists modified to prevent permanent damage to their bodies. Physical therapists have been with the SEALS ever since.

Cherry Point is a Marine Corps Air Station located between Portsmouth and Navy Hospital Camp Lejeune, North Carolina. It is the second most physically isolated medical facility the Navy operates in CONUS, the most isolated being Key West, Florida. Cherry Point was a small hospital and had major problems with obstetrics. An unfortunate case that occurred there during my tenure became a disaster. A 16–year-old dependent daughter of a retired service member thought she was pregnant, so her Family Practice physician did an ultrasound and did not spot an early tubal pregnancy. A few days later the teen had severe abdominal pain and her parents rushed her to the hospital. The tubal pregnancy had ruptured. The patient hemorrhaged and died despite heroic efforts to save her. Extensive reviews of her ultrasound by experienced obstetricians who knew her history were able to spot the site where the tubal pregnancy had occurred. They agreed that this would have been easy to miss.

The girl's father sued, and he also threatened to kill the doctor, so we had to get the doctor out of there. The father continued to make threats, but eventually the local authorities were able to get him under control. This case was what I used to get the attention of the Marine Corps when I contended that we shouldn't be providing obstetrical care there or at other small facilities when there were other options. Now the facility operates only as an ambulatory clinic. Women with routine pregnancies are referred to hospitals in New Bern or Morehead City—each about an hour's drive in good weather. Complicated cases are sent to Camp Lejeune, where they remain during the last weeks of pregnancy until they deliver. Camp LeJeune's hospital is located on the base overlooking the New River. The present facility was completed in 1982 and had been steadily growing in size and complexity of care provided.

Captain Mike Cowan was the commanding officer during much of my SG tenure. Mike was selected for Flag while I was SG and served as the Navy Surgeon General from 2001 to 2004. While I was SG, there were no medical training programs at Camp Lejeune, but Don Hagen and I had both wanted to see a Family Practice program installed there. We worked toward that goal and during Mike Cowan's tenure as SG the program was started. It has become one of the Navy's best Family Practice programs.

While visiting the hospital I also visited the Marine Corps Combat Service Support Schools (MCCSSS). This is a satellite camp of the main base that houses the Field Medical Service School (FMSS) that trains Navy Corpsmen and religious program specialists for service with Marine Corps units. They are trained in combat survival, defensive techniques, and the treatment of combat injuries.

Fort Bragg is located west of Camp Lejeune, in the middle of North Carolina. This is the location of the Joint Special Operations Medical Training Center program that trains medics for the Army, Navy, and Air Force Special

Operations Forces (SOF). The shortest period of training for SOF medics is 6 months, much longer than the basic curriculum for Army and Air Force medics (8 weeks) or Navy Corpsmen (14 weeks). Each of the military services has additional training they provide for their medics before they deploy with operational units.

The Naval Hospital Charleston building was completed in 1973 during the Cold War military build-up, replacing a much older facility. Until the mid–1990s it was one of the busiest Navy Hospitals. A Family Practice residency was started when the new facility opened but BRAC 1993 resulted in a huge decrease in the Navy presence in the Charleston area. One year later the Family Practice residency had its final graduation. I visited the hospital soon after the residency had been disestablished and the hospital was in the process of rapidly downsizing operations. A few months after I retired the hospital closed its emergency room and stopped inpatient admissions. Since 2010 the Naval Health Clinic Charleston has operated in a newly constructed facility that it shares with the Veteran's Administration at the Naval Weapons Station Goose Creek.

Naval Hospital Beaufort is located in Port Royal, South Carolina, midway between the Marine Corps Air Station and Parris Island Marine Corps Recruit Depot. The hospital was constructed in 1949 and has a twin! The Peruvian Navy built an identical hospital in Lima, Peru, using the blueprints, construction plans, and policy and procedure manuals from this hospital. The U.S. Navy Medical Service Corps officer who served as the onsite consultant for the construction of the hospital in Beaufort served in the same capacity in Lima.

The Marine Corps Recruit Depot (MCRD) at Parris Island is one of our two MCRDs. The other is in San Diego. Parris Island trains the recruits from east of the Mississippi River and all the women recruits. MCRD San Diego trains the male recruits from west of the Mississippi.

In Beaufort I gave the address at the recruit graduation ceremony. Recruit graduation is a "big deal" there. Parents and family come from all over the East for graduation and the locals provide a great time, with barbecues, fish and clam fries, and plenty of beverages to wash everything down. Recruits go through 12-weeks of strenuous mental and physical conditioning. Teamwork is emphasized, and recruits learn to look out for each other. The final phase of recruit training is called the Crucible, a 54-hour period when recruits are challenged physically, mentally, and morally. It includes food and sleep deprivation and 45 miles of marching. The recruits face obstacles at teambuilding warrior stations, each station named for a Marine hero whose actions epitomize Marine Corps values. It is a rite of passage that finishes with a 9-mile hike ending at an Iwo Jima flag-raising statue, where each recruit receives a "Globe and Anchor." The recruits are called Marines for the first time here.

While I was SG a recruit became ill during the Crucible but his fellow recruits did not want him to fail. Despite his high fever and lethargy they dragged and carried him to the finish. He died a few hours later of meningitis. This unfortunate event led us to assign a Navy Corpsman graduate of the FMSS program to each recruit unit for their entire time of training to watch for signs of illness to, it is hoped, prevent any future such occurrences. This strengthens the bond between Marines and Hospital Corpsmen.

The Naval Hospital Jacksonville was one of our four Family Practice training hospitals. It had five branch clinics as part of the command. The King's Bay Branch Clinic is a primary care outpatient facility providing routine general and pediatric care. Several pediatric medical misadventures had occurred at this facility. The pediatrician there was a foreign medical graduate, and I played a role in his removal. King's Bay is the homeport for all East Coast-based Ohio Class Ballistic Missile Submarines. They are one leg of our nuclear Triad. I had never seen one of these so was taken on a tour. The "boat" was almost 600 feet long. Inside it had 16 ballistic missiles equipped with multiple individually targeted nuclear warheads.

The clinic in the port Mayport facility is located on the Atlantic Coast near the mouth of the St. John's River. When I visited, the aircraft carrier USS *John F. Kennedy* (*JFK*), was home ported there. Mayport had been a carrier homeport since the mid–1950s, but as the military drawdown progressed after the cold war ended so did the size of the Navy and the number of aircraft carriers. The *JFK* was the last conventionally powered carrier in the Navy. Due to budget constraints the Navy retired her. Mayport was not equipped to handle nuclear powered ships and there have been none there since.

Naval Hospital Jacksonville also has clinics at the Naval Air Station, Jacksonville, and aboard the Marine Corps Logistics Base in Albany, Georgia. Another clinic that comes under Jacksonville is quite a distance away in Key West, at the end of the Florida Keys. I flew from Jacksonville to Key West by Navy Air. The clinic supports active duty and their dependents at the Naval Air Station as well as permanent resident retirees. It had a couple of Family Practitioners. A Flight Surgeon was the senior medical officer. They weren't very busy. What they couldn't handle the local private doctors tried to assist with; if it was beyond their capability the patient was off to Miami.

I stayed in the VIP quarters on the beach on the southernmost point of Key West. Havana is just 100 miles away. I was given a "panic button" to push if Spanish-speaking people showed up around the quarters. Armed responders would come and take them away. I didn't have to use the button.

Pensacola may as well be in Alabama it is so very close to the state line that divides the East and Central time zones. The Florabama bar sits on that line and is open an hour later on the Alabama side than the Florida side. There were several things for me to do in Pensacola:

- Stay in the VIP guest house. This was an antebellum house similar to our quarters in Portsmouth. There was a guest book in the house with the signature of Marion Mitchell Morrison, who stayed there when he made movies about Naval and Marine Corps aviation. His stage name was John Wayne.
- Visit the hospital.
- Visit the Naval Aerospace Medical Institute (NAMI).
- Take a ride with the Blue Angels.
- Visit the Naval Branch Clinic in New Orleans.

The hospital had one of Navy Medicine's Family Practice residency-training programs. I toured the facility and addressed the staff. The hospital had a very light patient load compared to others where we had Family Practice residencies, and I questioned the viability of the program. The training program was closed in 2016.

Naval Aerospace Medical Institute (NAMI) annually trains over 400 U.S. and international students in aerospace fields including primary aerospace medicine, aerospace physiology, aviation experimental psychology, aviation optometry, and aviation physical examination technicians. It is the equivalent of a college specializing in all aspects of aerospace medicine.

My flight with the Blue Angels was in an F/A-18B, a two-seat aircraft. All the Blue Angels' aircraft had served in the fleet and reached their maximum service life. These planes were "rescued" from the bone yard and stripped of all their instrumentation except that which was absolutely essential for flight. There was a red light that meant "there's a problem," so either the aircraft had to land or the pilot and passenger had to "punch out." The plane was equipped with ejection seats. These aircraft all had a new shiny Royal Blue and Bright Yellow paint job. I donned an unpressurized flight suit, was told to do a Valsalva maneuver when we were pulling more than a couple of Gs to keep from passing out, and got a short tutorial about how to eject if the pilot told me to.

At takeoff the pilot ran up both engines, said "hang on," released the brakes, and we sped down the runway. After 15 seconds we lifted off, continued in level flight about 10 feet above the runway for several more seconds rapidly gaining speed, then the pilot put the plane on its tail and up we went nearly vertically to 15,000 feet. We flew out over the Gulf of Mexico, where we had a "box" in the sky that was all ours alone to "play" in for the next hour. We did all the maneuvers done in the air show, twice breaking the sound barrier. I endured everything the pilot could throw at me. No ride at any amusement park comes close to those aerobatics. All too soon we got low on fuel and headed back. On the way, the red light came on. The pilot notified the tower and we were cleared to land in the opposite direction planes normally land at Pensacola. There was no problem; the light came on because our fuel was low. As I climbed out Tracy, asked, "Did you puke?"

The Branch Clinic, New Orleans, was operating in what was once the Naval Hospital, New Orleans. The hospital was named after F. Edward Hebert, a local congressman who had pushed for its construction. The clinic had a very small staff. There were hardly any active duty in the area; most of the patients were reservists getting annual physicals and immunizations. New Orleans Naval Hospital had been authorized by Congress in 1971 and was constructed as a 250-bed facility opened for business in December 1976. During the next year it operated with an average daily inpatient census of 23, less than 10 percent of its built capacity. It became a national political football when a GAO report to Congress 18 months after it opened recommended both inpatient and outpatient care should be discontinued and the hospital be closed and either turned over to the state to fulfill other needs or leased to a private medical group.

A Catholic order leased the hospital except for a small area still used by the Navy for a clinic. The Navy was the landlord and was making money on the rent! When a new Navy clinic became available we sold the hospital to

Here I'm strapped in and ready to go on a demonstration flight with the Blue Angels, December 1987 (courtesy U.S. Navy).

the Catholic order, about twenty years after the hospital first opened, recovering some of the original construction costs.

The main mission of Naval Air Station, Corpus Christi, was advanced flight training for newly minted Navy pilots who went there or to nearby Kingsville (George H.W. Bush trained in Corpus Christi in 1943). When I went to Corpus Christi for "orientation" in 1967 the base was very busy. In addition to the Navy's advanced flight training there was a huge helicopter repair facility there. The hospital then was busy, even caring for some war-wounded who had returned to the area. But by the time I became Surgeon General the base and hospital had become a "sleepy" place. The hospital's average daily census for the last several years had dropped to four. I wanted to close the inpatient services and redesignate the facility a clinic. Local civilian hospitals were capable and willing to accept the Navy inpatient workload and to give the Navy doctors clinical privileges, similar to what we had done in Newport, Rhode Island. The main obstacle was the local Democratic congressman, Solomon P. Ortiz. I was finally able to cut a deal with him: we'd stop inpatient care but not call it a clinic, retaining the name hospital. Ortiz served in Congress beginning in 1983, until finally losing a close election in 2011. The facility was immediately renamed a clinic.

Naval Hospital, Memphis, was actually in the town of Millington, a suburb of Memphis. Historically it had been a problem command. For years there hadn't been much activity at the base, including a little-used single runway. Despite that, the state's congressional delegation worked to keep it open—it was all about civilian jobs. At one point the hospital commanding officer's secretary had Senator Al Gore's office number on her speed dial. If a position that became vacant was not immediately advertised the commanding officer could expect a call from the senator's office. BRAC 1995 redesignated the base as the Naval Support Activity Mid-South, and the airstrip became the Millington Jetport. The Bureau of Navy Personnel was transferred there in 1998 from its location in dilapidated World War II–era buildings in Arlington, Virginia. All inpatient activity was discontinued and the facility became a branch clinic of the Naval Hospital, Pensacola.

North Chicago, Illinois, is the location of Great Lakes Naval Training Center. When I became SG the Navy's other two basic training centers had been closed. Great Lakes had horrible winter weather, so cold that training had to be done indoors. The HVAC system in these buildings recirculated the air, so airborne contagious diseases spread rapidly among the nonimmune. Chickenpox was a problem every year, as only about 80 percent of recruits were immune and the nonimmune would almost surely get it if just one recruit came down with it. Most people think of chickenpox as a mild childhood disease, but it can be lethal in late adolescents and young adults who are under a lot of stress. Every few years a recruit died from chickenpox at Great Lakes.

I had been on a crusade since the 1970s to immunize all recruits against chickenpox. The Japanese had been using this vaccine for over two decades and had proven its safety and efficacy. It had been introduced in the USA and was proving equally effective here. The reason the Pentagon wouldn't use the vaccine on recruits came down to money: it wasn't cheap. Following another recruit death I was tasked with doing a JAG Manual investigation. Because of my report the Navy sprung for the money and added the chickenpox vaccine to the standard immunization program for all recruits. The other services followed suit.

The Navy hospital at Great Lakes had been built in 1960. During the Vietnam conflict it had been a very busy hospital, even conducting rotating internships for several years. After the conflict ended the inpatient census declined and the internship was terminated. The 1993 BRAC recommended significant realignment of the command. The VA had a medical facility on the grounds of Naval Station Great Lakes. After lengthy discussions, the Navy Hospital Great Lakes and the North Chicago VA together formed the Captain James A. Lovell Federal Health Care Center on the Great Lakes Base. The Navy closed its hospital and the new facility served both the Navy and veterans well, saving taxpayers hundreds of millions of dollars.

I never served in the Pacific Northwest but had visited it several times while I had been at BUMED-03 and while I was a DASD. I visited three nonmedical commands in the Bremerton area. The first was the USS *Nimitz*, CVN 68, and our second-oldest nuclear powered aircraft carrier. It was homeported at Puget Sound Naval Shipyard. My middle son, Scott, was assigned to the ship at the time. I visited Scott, the ship's commanding officer, and the medical department. Both of my other sons, Steve and Grant, also served on the *Nimitz* during their Naval careers.

The second was the Puget Sound Naval Shipyard in Bremerton, where I visited the base branch clinic. There I saw the process for nuclear submarine disassembly. This is a complex process and it takes more than a year to completely take a submarine apart. The third nonmedical command was the Strategic Weapons Facility Pacific in Bangor. I visited the branch clinic there and toured the base. This is where nuclear warheads and the missiles that deliver them are stored. The security at this facility is intense. Aircraft are not allowed to fly over it. The Bremerton Naval Hospital was one of the Navy's Family Practice Training Hospitals. I had been there several times. Captain Jim Johnson was the commanding officer at this time. Jim was soon selected for Flag and went on to be medical officer of the Marine Corps and then commanding officer of Naval Medical Center San Diego. The Naval Hospital, Oak Harbor, is on Whidbey Island, a few hours' drive north of Bremerton. The hospital is on the Naval Air Station but is called Oak Harbor after a nearby community. It is directly East of Victoria British Columbia across the Straits of Juan de Fuca.

Departing USS *Nimitz* in 1987 after an onboard visit with the commanding officer
and my son Scott, who was a crew member at that time, and a tour of the sick bay
(courtesy U.S. Navy).

While I was in BUMED-03 I had represented then-Surgeon General Jim
Zimble for the opening of an obstetrical addition to this facility. Whidbey
Island is quite isolated and in the winter inclement weather can make it difficult to get a patient to a civilian facility where they can safely deliver. So we
operated this hospital as a small five-bed, obstetrical facility. I was stationed
at the Naval Medical Center, Oakland, California from 1980 to 1984 and wrote
about that in an earlier section. In 1996 I returned there to close the facility,
locally known as Oak Knoll. It was one of the facilities on the 1993 BRAC
list. Its surrounding clinics at Treasure Island, Alameda Naval Air Station,
Moffett Field, and Mare Island had already been shuttered, as all other activities on those bases had ceased.

Nearly all of the Air Force and Army facilities in the Bay Area had been
closed as a result of BRAC decisions of 1988, 1991, and 1993. The decision to
do this was driven by the high cost of operating the facilities and the high
cost of living in the area. To the south, Fort Ord, the Army's huge basic training base between Monterey and Salinas, was closed in 1994 following a decision in the first round of BRAC in 1988. The Lester B. Hays Army Hospital
on Fort Ord that had served that region's eligible population had also closed.

Travis Air Force Base, about 50 miles east of Oakland, had the David
Grant Medical Center, an Air Force multispecialty teaching hospital on base.

With the post–Cold War drawdown all of its medical specialty training programs with the exception of Family Practice were discontinued. It was resized to support just the population in its immediate vicinity.

The Naval Medical Center, Oakland, closure ceremony took place on Tuesday, April 2, 1996. It was planned for the spacious lawn in front of the hospital with hopes for a bright sunny day, but the weatherman didn't cooperate. A heavy downpour forced the ceremony into the base gymnasium. An overflow crowd heard Captain David Snyder, the commanding officer through the hospital's final year, give a wonderful speech about the hospital's history from its opening in 1942. I followed with more remarks and then announced the facility closed. A fifteen-round cannon salute followed and the "Sick Call" flag was hauled down for the last time. The last cannon shell casing was folded inside the Sick Call flag and presented to me. I took it to BUMED to add it to other Navy Medicine memorabilia. At the conclusion of the ceremony there was a reception in the base officer's club. Many former commanding officers, staff and old friends from my years in Oakland came. I tried to greet as many as I could and share some memories with them. I was on a tight timeline and could only stay for an hour because I had to catch a late afternoon flight to get back to Washington at midnight so I could go to work the next morning. Tracy, my aide, was trying to lead me toward the car waiting to take us to the San Francisco Airport, but she said there was one more person I had to see. It was Admiral Walt Lonergan, who had been the commanding officer when I reported to Oak Knoll in 1980. He had been commanding officer here for five years. Now he had advanced Parkinson's disease and his wife, Rita, was pushing him around in a wheelchair. I shook hands with both of them and told him how nice it was to see them. He looked up at me with tears streaming down his cheeks and said, "This is the saddest day of my life." Walt died 5 months later, perhaps not from Parkinson's but a broken heart?

On one trip West I took a couple of hours to drive to Madera, where my father had been raised and Carmen, his only sibling, lived with her husband, Bud. I had not seen Carmen and Bud since I had been best man in their son Wayne's wedding in 1986. Bud had been a large, robust man all his life, a grain farmer. He was now confined to a wheelchair. Carmen, though ambulatory, wore nasal prongs connected to an enriched oxygen supply. I was on my way to Lemoore Naval Air Station, where we had a small hospital, so I arrived in uniform and this thrilled them. Their daughter Arlene came by, but Wayne was away. This turned out to be the last time I saw them. After saying good-bye I drove to Lemoore, a small hospital like Oak Harbor at Whidbey. Then it was many miles to a community with a large hospital and it could become impossible to get patients there when the intense and all-too-common Central Valley fog settled in.

One afternoon after the normal workday ended in Washington I flew to

29 Palms on one of the Navy's Gulfstream aircraft. Traveling at Mach 0.9 and at 49,000 feet we flew 10,000 feet above civil air traffic and in a straight line from Andrews Air Force base to 29 Palms. It took about 3½ hours. We landed on a Marston Mat runway in time to check into our quarters and go in to town for dinner. The only place open had a special, liver and onions. It was on special because they were out of everything else. My mother made me eat this as a child. I hated it, but with a beer or three I was able to get it down.

The 29 Palms Marine Corps Air Ground Combat Center is in the high Mojave Desert. It is almost as large as the state of Rhode Island. It is arid, with summer temperatures reaching 120°F and winter temperatures dipping to 15°F. Annual rainfall is about 4 inches. There are plenty of desert tortoises and rattlesnakes around. It's just the kind of place Marines love. The new hospital at 29 Palms had opened in 1993 and was modern and much more capable than the one it replaced. Trauma cases could be stabilized in it. But I had a problem with an overzealous orthopedist who had trained to do major joint replacement surgery in his residency and wanted to do it at 29 Palms. There was a retiree population in the area adjacent to the base and he had found a few patients in need of the procedures. This was just plain dangerous. Doing one of these cases every once in a while didn't provide the experience for skill maintenance, not to mention the skill development of the support staff and the budgetary needs necessary to support this surgery. I said no, not just there but throughout Navy Medicine, making it policy that joint replacement surgery should only be done at the hospitals where we had orthopedic residency programs. There was a Navy Reserve Rear Admiral orthopedic surgeon in Santa Barbara who did as many as twelve joint replacement surgeries a day. I asked him for his advice about doing infrequent joint replacement surgery at a hospital. He said this would be malpractice. Though my decision was not popular with some people, notch another policy win for me.

Naval Hospital Camp Pendleton was familiar territory for me. The years I was doing Pediatric Hematology-Oncology in San Diego I held a clinic there once a month. It's about an hour's drive from the hospital in San Diego to the one at Camp Pendleton. In 1975 I made several trips there to see patients at the relocation center for Vietnam refugees. They were housed in a tent city on the base and we provided their medical care. Our first challenge was to find those with communicable diseases. There was plenty of tuberculosis. As we examined the people we found four children with cancer. All of them became my patients until the families could be relocated then we'd find specialists in their new community to care for them

While at Camp Pendleton I took a helicopter out several miles off the coast where a combined Navy-Marine Corps exercise was underway. We landed on one of the large deck amphibs and went to the hangar deck where a medical evacuation unit and hospital were set up. Our large amphibs are set up to function as evacuation hospitals after they land the troops they are carrying. Some can have as many as 400 beds. Just about all Navy medical personnel are assigned to some kind of medical mobilization team. The people on this ship had come from Navy medical facilities all over the West. This was a great opportunity for them to learn what their job would be like if and when they had to be mobilized. After visiting the ship we took the helicopter back to the base. The next day I spoke to the staff and then officiated at the hospital change of command as Tom Burkhard relieved Bonnie Potter.

Naval Medical Center San Diego was operating better than any of the others in the new managed Tricare environment. Part of the reason for this was because San Diego had been a test area for the program that preceded Tricare, which was called the CRI (CHAMPUS Reform Initiative). The San Diego community was also one of the locations where managed care had been first introduced, so people were used to it. Dick Nelson had taken command in 1993 and was doing a great job. The local line Navy was pleased with his leadership. Don Hagen and I both agreed he should stay there until he retired or was selected to be SG.

San Diego had several branch clinics; the newest one was still under construction adjacent to the Naval Training Center, which was being closed under the most recent round of BRAC. Congress had put many millions of dollars into this new facility and it was a shame that we would lose it before it opened. Dick Nelson was able to work with the local community and the Navy to get this exempted from the turnover of the Training Center property to the city. The clinic continues to operate to this day as an excellent multi-specialty outpatient facility with clinics staffed by physicians from the hospital. Being away from the hospital makes it a great example of taking healthcare to the deck plates. The same applies to other clinics that are operated at Miramar Air Station, the Naval Station aboard the Marine Corps Recruit Depot and in El Centro and Yuma, Arizona.

I also visited a unique command in San Diego, the Naval Health Research Center on Point Loma. I had driven past it many times in the past but had never gone in. From the outside its not very impressive, a gaggle of two-story pink "temporary" buildings constructed during World War II. Made of redwood, which is virtually impervious to insects, it has lasted over 70 years. It is the premier deployment health research center performing research unique to the military environment. I spent the better part of a day there, on the advice of Steve Joseph, the ASD (HA) who had visited there earlier and was equally impressed.

Not all my trips were to visit our facilities. There were meetings I was expected to attend. In addition to the Navy and Health Affairs meetings, I attended the annual AMA Board of Governors meeting and the annual American College of Healthcare Executives meeting, both held in Chicago at different times of the year. There was also the Association of Military Surgeons of the United States meeting held in different cities each year. I attended and spoke at a variety of specialty meetings.

OCONUS Travel

EGYPT

While I was a DASD I traveled extensively outside the continental United States (ONUS) and have covered that travel in the chapter on Health Affairs.

The Egyptian ambassador to the U.S. had invited Deena and me to tour the Egyptian antiquities after I attended the 50th anniversary of the U.S. Naval Medical Research Unit (NAMRU-3) in Cairo. The lab was the oldest and largest of the U.S. overseas military medical research facilities, established in 1942, and after the war the Egyptian government invited the U.S. Navy to take over the lab. It remained in continuous operation even through the seven-year lapse in U.S.-Egyptian diplomatic relations (1967–1973). During that time the lab was the conduit for all communications between the Egyptian and U.S. governments. Unfortunately, operations at the lab were discontinued in 2016 because of the political unrest in Egypt.

The mission of the lab was to detect, monitor, and study emerging or reemerging disease threats of military and public health importance and to develop mitigation strategies against these threats in partnership with the nations of the region. It was one of three Navy Research labs in equatorial regions; there were also three run by the Army. Together they were the most important monitors of tropical diseases in the world and worked closely with the U.S. Centers for Disease Control and Prevention.

We visited the laboratory, a modern six-story building and one of only two level-3 biological containment labs in all of Africa. Our hosts took us on a tour of Cairo and then we took the tour up the Nile and on to Abu Simbel that I previously mentioned the Egyptian government had arranged.

CHINA

In early 1996 Steve Joseph, the Assistant Secretary of Defense for Health, was sent by the Secretary of Defense as a member of a U.S. delegation to China. When he came back he told the three Surgeons General that the Chinese would be hosting an international military medical conference in Beijing later that year and he wanted all of us to attend. The meeting would be in October 1996 and would last an entire week. There would be numerous scientific meetings but also a lot of social engagements and educational experiences to help us learn about China. My, aide, Commander Tracy Malone, had been to China a few years before when she was a White House nurse and accompanied President George H.W. Bush and his delegation there for a state visit. She wanted someone else to have the opportunity to visit China. My Chief of Staff, Captain David Fisher, volunteered to go. David and I decided to invite our wives, since there were going to be several special programs planned for them while we were in meetings.

When we landed we were picked up by U.S. Army personnel attached to our embassy and transported to our hotel, adjacent to the meeting site. On the way there they told us that the van we were in had just been swept for listening devices, so we could talk freely in it. But for the rest of the time we were in China we should assume that everything we said, no matter where, was being listened to by the Chinese. We should assume listening devices were in our hotel rooms. We were told that our notebook computer should not be left in the room. The Chinese would copy the hard disc, even if we stored it in the safe in the room.

The opening session of the meeting began with a concert by a huge People's Liberation Army (PLA) band. They played the national anthems of several countries including ours. There were speeches the delegates could follow using devices for simultaneous translation into their choice of several different languages. Once through the opening session there were many breakout sessions to choose from. One I recall was a presentation on the consequences of chemical warfare with presentations by Iraqi and Iranian military officers about their version of the recently concluded eight-year war. I was seated in the front row, in Service Dress Blues. An Iranian presenter sat on one side of me and an Iraqi presenter on the other, in their service dress uniforms. They each gave PowerPoint presentations that began with a slide that said, "Allah Akbar, " meaning "God is Great." They then followed with slides of piles of dead bodies, both military and civilian, and statistics as to how many were killed and what agents were used. They screamed accusations about atrocities at each other for a while and then it ended; they sat down again on either side of me and all was peaceful. There were many more sessions, many of them including tours, demonstrations, or exhibits. One was a session on traditional Chinese medicine that covered herbal medicine, acupuncture, massage, and exercise and dietary therapy.

We toured a PLA hospital in Beijing said to be their largest hospital. I remarked to our escort how clean the hospital was despite the high foot traffic. His comment was, "That's the result of 1,000 Chinese with toothbrushes cleaning every square inch of the hospital for the visitors." It was a training hospital with residencies in multiple specialties and departments of traditional Chinese medicine integrated right along with Western medicine. There were computers in the lab areas, most of them similar to our early personal computers. Many of them weren't even plugged in. In the medical library we learned that doctors could not go into the medical stacks. They had to request an article from a library technician who would find it, make a photocopy, and then notify the doctor the article was ready for pick-up.

The Chinese could hardly wait to show us their deployable medical facility. A Captain in the PLA-Navy escorted me. Their deployable medical facility was a knock-off of our deployable medical facilities. David had been the finance program manager for our deployable medical facilities previously. He found the level of detail the PLA had "mined" to copy the plans and concept of operations of the facility remarkable. It is often said the Japanese can copy something we make and make it better; the Chinese can copy something and make it worse. That was certainly the case with what we were shown. There was nothing secret about our deployable hospitals; we'd probably have sold them one if they wanted it.

The Chinese had a formal dinner for all the meeting attendees and their spouses in the State Banquet Hall of the Great Hall of the People in Tiananmen Square. David and I sat at a table with our wives; the other four people were Chinese military. David was acting as my aide and had to wear an aiguillette, a gold and blue ornamental braided cord with decorative metal tips worn on the left shoulder. The aiguillette that goes with the dress uniform is fancy, almost as snazzy as those worn by the chief bellman at the world's fanciest hotels. The Chinese thought David was the "top dog" because of the fancy device he wore around his left shoulder. They all wanted their picture taken with him and soon Chinese from other tables showed up wanting their photos taken with the American big shot. He tried his best to convince them that I was the senior officer and they should have their pictures taken with me. They did not believe him.

The meal, all Chinese food served promptly and hot, went on for several courses and lasted a few hours. The Chinese at our table spoke English and let us know what each course was. Most of it was very good. One course we were warned to avoid was the sea slugs. I had eaten these many years before in a Chinese restaurant in Japan and had learned my lesson. Even the Chinese at our table passed on the sea slugs.

One evening we attended a formal dinner hosted by senior Chinese military officials in a restaurant in the Summer Palace Gardens. There were probably two dozen or so in our group, at least two Chinese military senior officers for every one of us. Before departing for China we had been given a briefing from the CIA warning that there would be attempts to pump us for information and we should be on the alert for a beverage called Mao-tai, made from fermented sorghum. Assigned to sit right next to me was a U.S. Army Major, an African American who spoke Mandarin Chinese. A PLA General kept

David and Alberta Fisher, Deena and me. Dinner in the Great Hall of the People, Beijing, October 1996.

trying to get me to drink Mao-tai with him and I kept saying no. Finally the Major had enough. He pulled the Chinese General out of his chair, stuck his finger in the General's chest, and yelled things at him in Chinese that I didn't understand but the General did. The party ended on that note.

Another evening we went to a theme park on the history of China. The park was reserved for attendees at the medical conference and their guests. China has a recorded history of about 6,000 years, so there was a lot to cover. These weren't just static displays; there were actors, artists, and musicians performing. We looked and listened to some of this, but a Chinese opera presentation did us in. We exited the park, found a cab and gave the driver a business card for our hotel, and retired for an early evening. We knew the time we were away at these planned outings was when the PLA would go through our rooms. We hadn't followed the PLA's "plan" for this evening and the PLA complained to the U.S. embassy about our early return. On our trips outside the meeting place or our hotel a PLA officer accompanied us. We asked one of them what her job was and she responded, "I'm a military intelligence officer." When we asked her why she was assigned to the U.S. delegation, she responded, "To watch you."

The Beijing meeting concluded just before the Veterans Day weekend back home, so we took a flight to Hong Kong. The 99-year lease of the New Territories between China and the British would expire only a few months from then, and Hong Kong Island would return to Chinese sovereignty at the same time. The area would become a Special Administrative Region of China with a high degree of autonomy for the next fifty years. I wanted to see it again before it became a part of China.

We had a post-travel meeting with the CIA where we answered questions about our observations. The PLA had given me a sample of medications we were told prevented high-altitude sickness. This was a concern to the PLA for crossing high mountain terrain ostensibly between China and India. I gave the medications to the CIA.

Japan

I had been to Japan several times during my career. As SG I visited our bases on Honshu, Kyushu, and Okinawa. Topics of concern were discussed in the Admiral's calls I had at all of the facilities. As part of the Status of Forces Agreement, the Japanese government built a new hospital for our use at Yokosuka in 1981. This is one of the finest hospitals I have ever been in. The Japanese scrupulously maintain it for us. I visited three of this hospital's branch clinics: one nearby at Atsugi Naval Air Facility, one to the south at Marine Corps Air Station, Iwakuni, and one at Commander Fleet Activities Sasebo. On a subsequent trip I would visit the Naval Support Activity Diego Garcia.

In Yokosuka the Japanese hosted a dinner for nearly two-dozen people at a 400-year-old hotel just off base that had survived World War II. It had been in use since the Shogun era and there were pictures of many senior Japanese Imperial Navy officers who had dined there over the centuries. We sat on the floor, eating Japanese style.

I had read a translation of a book by a Japanese Imperial Navy physician who served during World War II. He wrote about his experiences taking care of casualties from battles in the jungles on islands in the South Pacific. Before leaving for Japan I had told my staff about the book. To my surprise, the author sat directly across from me at the dinner. He spoke no English and I spoke very little Japanese. Sitting next to him was his granddaughter, who had just completed five years of study at Oxford University and spoke impeccable English. We had a wonderful evening.

We flew to Okinawa to visit the hospital there and its clinics. It's the largest overseas Navy Hospital and serves as the referral facility for the entire Western Pacific. When I arrived at the hospital there was a greeting party waiting out front for me: the Commanding Officer, Executive Officer, Chief Nurse, and Command Master Chief. The Command Master Chief looked familiar. She was the Hospital Corpsman Apprentice (E-2) who had worked with me in the pediatric clinic in San Diego in the early 1970s. The Okinawa Hospital had been built in 1958 as a U.S. Army Hospital. Because the Marine Corps replaced almost all U.S. Army presence on Okinawa by the mid–1970s the hospital had been transferred to the Navy in 1977.

I visited the new Air Force primary care and flight medicine clinic at Kadena Air Force Base, which relied on the Navy Hospital for specialty care and all inpatient services. This is the Air Force clinic where, while I was a DASD, I had told the Family Physicians to start attending their normal deliveries at the hospital or lose their specialty pays. They were now doing this and the problem was solved. In addition to the main hospital, I visited the Navy medical clinics located at Camp Schwab, Camp Hansen, Camp Courtney, Camp Foster, MCAS Futema, and Camp Kinser.

From Okinawa we traveled to Sasebo. It had been 27 years since I had last been in Sasebo, and I hardly recognized it. Much of the main base had been returned to the Japanese in exchange for property in the Hario area, a 30-minute drive from the main base. In contrast to when I was stationed there and most Americans lived in off-base housing, nearly everyone now lived in base housing in the Hario area. There was no longer a hospital but instead two Family Practice clinics, one on the main base and one in the Hario housing area. Patients needing hospitalization went to a Japanese facility or were flown to Yokosuka. Women having babies now had a choice: they could travel to Yokosuka and subsist in a "Stork's Nest" there from the 36th gestational week on or deliver in a Japanese hospital in Sasebo.

The waterfront was the one area that appeared unchanged—except that now most of the ships were Japanese, not American. In the evening we attended a dinner in a Japanese restaurant along with some of the clinic staff and several Japanese doctors. Some of them had been there when I was stationed there! There were many sake and beer toasts followed by shouts of

"Kanpai!" As the evening progressed one of the Japanese doctors pulled out a guitar and started serenading in both English and Japanese. He had imbibed more than his share of sake and began singing love songs. It was at that point I decided it was time to say sayonara.

The next morning we traveled to Fukuoka on a local train that made the trip in one hour and 40 minutes. In the 1960s this trip took over three hours. In Fukuoka we boarded the Shinkansen that took us to Hiroshima. It is near our Marine Corps Air Station at Iwakuni. That trip took only a couple of hours. We operate a primary health care and flight medical clinic at Iwakuni. For emergencies patients are sent to local Japanese facilities. We toured the clinic, I held Admiral's calls and then we retired for the night. The next morning we took the Shinkansen to Osaka, where we caught our flights to get us home. We arrived back in Washington having been gone seven days.

ICELAND

Icelandic Airlines is the only airline that flies to Iceland—from anywhere. We flew from Baltimore with my Force Master Chief, Mike Stewart, my aide, Commander Tracy Malone, and my Public Affairs Officer, Commander Sheila Graham. We left Baltimore at midnight. The flight took five hours and because Iceland is four hours ahead of Eastern Time, we arrived there at 9:00 a.m., just in time for a whole day of activity. We went to a secure underground briefing room, where we were welcomed by the base commander, who offered some donuts and coffee for breakfast, and then the briefings about the base operations began. Tracy was in the back with a couple of feet of steel-reinforced concrete as a back support. The lights went out, the PowerPoint slides came on, and the drone of the briefing officer's voice began. In less than a minute there was a loud "thunk." The lights came on and Tracy was holding the back of her head. After it was determined she was all right, the briefings proceeded.

The mission of our base in Iceland was to keep an eye on the Soviet Navy as its ships and submarines passed from the Arctic Ocean into the North Atlantic Ocean. They had to pass through an area we referred to as the Greenland-Iceland-UK gap. We monitored every Soviet ship's and sub's passage with aircraft based in Iceland, a very sophisticated underwater listening system and satellite observations. We had the Soviets so bottled up they eventually stopped moving naval vessels through "the Gap." At the time of our visit they hadn't sent a submarine through there for over two years.

We had a small Family Practice hospital there that provided maternity care and could do minor surgery cases and short hospitalizations. The hospital physical plant was adequate. The Icelandic physicians provided specialty consultation, when needed. We provided routine dental care and oral surgery in an old physical plant in bad need of replacement. Because the Soviet Union collapsed in December 1991 and their navy was no longer a threat, we soon closed our base in Iceland and did not have to replace the dental clinic,

We got a short nap in the afternoon and then the medical staff hosted a potluck dinner for us. It was late May, only a few weeks from the summer solstice, so the days were quite long. The sun was below the horizon for only a few minutes. We went to one of the area's main attractions, the Blue Lagoon. We rented suits and spent an hour floating in the blue, hot water. The high mineral content made it possible to easily float, safe even for nonswimmers. After the hot bath I was ready for some rest, as we were to have an early morning flight to London. Some of my fellow travelers were avid golfers, so they, along with some of the hospital staff, headed to the base golf course, where they teed off after midnight.

London

While I had been floating around in the Blue Lagoon in Iceland, Deena and Grant had boarded a flight at Dulles Airport for London. Grant had just completed his second year at the Naval Academy and was on a month's leave. He chose to go to Europe with us because after my official duties ended I was going to take a week's leave and we were going to pick up a new car at the Mercedes factory in Stuttgart, Germany, then do some traveling through Germany and Austria. The two of them arrived at Heathrow in the morning and went to the hotel and got some rest. Meanwhile, I (along with my fellow travelers) was picked up by staff from our new medical clinic at West Ruislip, a Ministry of Defence site during World War II. This area had become the major housing area for the families of American Naval personnel in the London area.

After my day of tours and briefings Deena and I returned to 7 North Audley for a formal dinner. I had to wear my Navy Mess Dress uniform and Deena had to dress accordingly. The dinner was in what had been General Eisenhower's formal dining room during World War II. The Deputy CIN-CUSNAVEUR was the host. I was the senior officer present at the dinner. There was a line Rear Admiral there with his wife. Captain Marion Balsam, who was now the CINCUSNAVEUR Surgeon and had recently been selected for promotion to Flag Rank, and the Chief of Staff to the Deputy CINCUS-NAVEUR were there along with the Archbishop of Canterbury (I have no idea why he was there).

Dinner was preceded by a cocktail reception, the dinner about as formal as it gets. There were fried oyster appetizers, a soup, a salad, and the main course—Beef Wellington with Yorkshire pudding. There was a different wine with each course. I don't remember the desert. Perhaps the wine had taken a toll? Our host had a buzzer beneath the table at his seat. When he felt the table was ready he would push the button and the staff would trot in, clear the used dishes, and bring in the next course. After desert our host said the ladies were excused to go to the parlor while the gentlemen completed their business. Our business turned out to consist of brandy, polite conversation, and cigars. I partook only of the first two. After the cigars were finished we joined the ladies in the parlor. They had been engaged in similar carryings on but without cigars. Soon we thanked our host and headed back to our hotel.

The next day I started leave. We stayed a couple of days with Marion Balsam and showed Grant some of the sights in and around London before we flew to Stuttgart to pick up our new car. After Stuttgart we went to Ramstein Air Force Base and then on to Bonn. Here we visited my German counterpart, who took us to dinner, and we celebrated Grant's 21st birthday. From there it was on to Berlin, Dresden, Prague, Salzburg, Munich, and then home.

North of the Alps

North and south of the Alps is how I thought about Europe after the end of the Cold War and the collapse of the Soviet Union. The U.S. started rapidly removing forces from this area and closing the bases. Some of our troops moved to the south side of the Alps, but most returned to CONUS. Most of our forces that had been there since the end of World War II were finally coming home. I had been a DASD during much of the interim period between when the Berlin Wall opened and the Soviet Union ceased to exist. During that time I visited every U.S. military medical facility in the region, many on multiple occasions. We were planning for "moving day." Early in 1992 we began the move, and over the next two years we closed ten hospitals in Germany. We were left with one hospital there and one in England by the time I became Navy SG.

South of the Alps war had broken out in the ethnic regions in the Balkans that earlier had been under the yoke of the Soviets. We kept our bases close to the Balkans at full strength and used them to prosecute a war that many Americans had no idea was going on. After these wars ended in the mid–1990s, downsizing of bases and troop numbers in this region resumed. South of Rome though, we were expanding. We knew there would be further conflicts to the south. The Navy became the major force south of the Alps. I'll cover that in the following section.

South of the Alps

Rota, Spain

Our Naval Station at Rota, Spain, is aboard a Spanish naval base commanded by a Spanish Rear Admiral. Our senior officer at the Naval Station is a U.S. Navy Captain, clearly outranked by the Spanish Admiral. The Spanish control the gates to the base and the departures and arrivals by air. Beyond that, the U.S. runs the base. This may seem weird, but that is the way things are at many of our overseas bases. The reason for this is that the base remains sovereign territory of the host nation; we are tenants and the host nation is the landlord. We are there on a lease, called a Status of Forces Agreement, SOFA for short. These are time-limited "leases" and have to be renegotiated at or before their date of expiration or we have to leave.

Rota is west of Gibraltar in the province of Cadiz, on Spain's Atlantic coast. There is a small town known as El Puerto de Santa Maria on the banks of the Guadalete River near where the river enters the Atlantic. One night I was having dinner in a small restaurant on the riverbank, with shipmates from past assignments who were now stationed in Rota. One of them asked me if I knew what had occurred at this exact spot some 500 years ago. I was stumped and was told this was where three ships led by Cristóbal Colón spent the last night before they embarked on a search for a new and shorter passage to India. One of the ships was named after this port, the *Santa Maria*.

Our hospital in Rota was new and was quite modern. It operated on a family practice model, with a few specialties such as general surgery, internal medicine, pediatrics, and obstetrics to provide backup. The commanding officer, Nick Yamodis, was a neurosurgeon I knew from the time he was head of neurosurgery in San Diego. He, along with a Spanish employee, had a strong interest in medical information technology. Together they pushed CHCS to its maximum potential and beyond, making many additions and corrections to it that were deployed system-wide.

The hospital hosted a special event for us in a Bodega in Jerez, the sherry center. They served a great dinner followed by flamenco singing and dancing. We toured the facility. Oak barrels were stacked four high and filled with the juice from locally grown white grapes that, with aging, would gradually become sherry. The Bodega manager asked RADM Joan Engel and me to each sign the end of a barrel with a piece of chalk. After we had done so, he sprayed a covering of shellac over our inscriptions to preserve them. Someday I may drink a glass of sherry from "my" barrel.

While in Rota I got a call from the office of the Secretary of the Navy. He was flying to Naples for the groundbreaking ceremony for our replacement hospital there and had learned I was in Rota, so he wanted me to come for the event. Admiral Joe Lopez was now CINCUSNAVEUR and also would be attending. He sent a plane for me. I departed Rota for Naples before dawn with a box breakfast in my lap, the only passenger in a small jet. When I landed I was taken to Joe's quarters, the same place I had dinner with Admiral "Snuffy" Smith a few years earlier. After a sandwich for lunch we traveled from his quarters to the new hospital site in an armor-plated Mercedes lim-

After a tour of a sherry winery in Jerez, Spain, Joan Engle and I signed our names and rank on barrels with chalk. The manager, the gentleman standing next to Joan, sprayed the barrels with shellac to preserve our writings. The young man to the left was another visitor to the winery.

ousine. Heavily armed Carabinieri escorts accompanied us all the way with sirens blaring and red lights flashing. If cars didn't provide enough room for us to pass we drove on the sidewalks. We found our way through the incredible Naples traffic and got to the event in time. Someone made a speech in Italian, the Secretary spoke in English, a Navy chaplain and Catholic priest said some prayers. Then we all turned over a shovel of earth and it was over. After the ceremony Joe dropped me off at the airfield where the crew and plane were waiting for me. It's 1,148 air miles from Naples to Rota. I was back in time for dinner.

Souda Bay, Crete

Crete is the largest and most populous of the Greek islands. It is very mountainous, with several peaks over 8,000 feet. Our base was on the far western end of the island in Crete's second largest city, Chania. The Greeks have a naval base, air station, and hospital at Souda Bay, and we are tenants. This is where our ships and aircraft replenish supplies they need to carry out their assigned missions in the region. Tucked away in an inconspicuous building at the airfield is a U.S. Navy flight-line medical clinic with two flight surgeons and several corpsmen. They are responsible for maintaining the health of the Navy personnel there and certifying that flight crews are medically cleared to fly.

I visited the Crete Naval Hospital where our personnel requiring specialty services or hospitalization were sent. It is a modern facility with many clinical specialties. As I walked through it with an English-speaking physician I realized I could read the signs,

Παιδιατρική–pediatrics,

ορθοπεδική–orthopedics,

Οφθαλμολογία–ophthalmology,

Ωτορινολαρυγγολογία—otolaryngology,

δερματολογία—dermatology.

I was able to do this because over 30 years before, during my senior year in college, I had taken a course in Greek and Latin roots of medical terminology. Many of our medical terms come from the Greek language. I had learned the Greek alphabet and the sounds each character stood for and was still able to sound out the words.

Sigonella, Sicily

From Sigonella you can see Mount Etna, 25 miles away, snowcapped and with a steady emission of steam coming from its top. Sigonella is our "Hub of the Med." It has over 4,000 assigned personnel and serves large numbers of NATO personnel passing through, which creates a lot of work for the hospital. Naval Air Station Sigonella is a tenant command aboard an Italian Air Force Base and has over 30 U.S. commands and activities aboard. Not far from the city of Catania, it is near the center of the Mediterranean Sea and is well placed to support operations of the U.S. 6th Fleet, other military units, and U.S. allies and coalition partners

I addressed the hospital staff then toured the facility—again. This was a new commanding officer and he wanted to be sure I saw all the deckplate improvements he had instituted. He was new because I had relieved his predecessor a few months earlier due to his having created a command climate of fear. It had become so bad that the regional line commander, an Admiral in Gaeta, Italy, had requested I take this action.

Off-base housing remained a major problem in Sigonella, especially for junior enlisted. There was not enough on-base housing available to meet the requirement, so they were at the mercy of the Sicilian rental market. Home break-ins and theft were a common problem, and the local police were not effective at preventing or prosecuting this. I kept carrying that message back to Washington in hopes that something would be done. It took years, but eventually additional housing on base was constructed.

I had an officer to deal with individually, a general surgeon who had a bad outcome with a case. An investigation had been conducted and forwarded up the chain of command for review, with the recommendation that the officer be reported to the National Practitioner Data Bank. The case had been reviewed at BUMED by a board of medical officers that included a general surgeon, with a spilt decision between the members but favoring reporting. The general surgeon voted against reporting. I decided I would meet with the Sigonella surgeon while I was there. I decided not to report him. Given the notoriety of the case, I recommended that he be released from active duty, which was done.

That evening the command had arranged a dinner at an off-base restaurant famous for both the quality and the quantity of its food. Dinner was served family style, and dish after dish kept coming. None of us had ever seen so much food. There was free flowing local wine and after the tiramisu dessert, to aid digestion, an aperitif was offered. It was homemade limoncello. Sicily is famous for its citrus, so the limoncello was no surprise.

La Maddalena, Italy

I made a short flight from Sigonella to the southern end of the island of La Maddalena, then the one-hour drive to the north where the submarine tender *Simon Lake* was at anchor and we had a small shore facility with a clinic. For several years we had worked with the Italians to relocate the clinic from a rickety old three-story walkup building to a new purpose-built facility. This had finally occurred, a great improvement for this small, isolated base.

There had been two calamities at the base we called "LaMad" for short. One was a female sailor giving birth in her own berth on the ship. No one knew she was pregnant or that she delivered herself during regular working hours. After delivering, she put the baby and her bedding in a duffle bag and walked off the ship. After a week's search she was found in an Italian motel some miles distant from the ship. The baby was still with her, but it was dead. We had her returned to CONUS and she was discharged.

The other calamity involved a sailor aboard the ship who reported to sick call complaining of epigastric pain. The doctor was busy with another patient, so the corpsman had this sailor lie down on a bed and pulled a privacy curtain around him. A few minutes later the corpsman looked in on the sailor, who was dead. He had suffered a heart attack, despite being in good shape and in his mid-twenties. This is rare but not unheard of. I'd had a couple of other similar cases during my Flag career. The senior line officer in the area, a three-star Admiral, went ballistic and wanted the doctor court-martialed. I met with the Admiral and reviewed similar cases I had dealt with, going back to my time as CO in San Diego. The Admiral calmed down and did not tarnish this officer's reputation.

Gaeta, Italy

Gaeta is on a peninsula about an hour and a half drive north of Naples. As a DASD I, along with my Naval Academy classmate Bill Owens, had reached the limit of my fiscal authority when I financed the $3 million medical portion of a new facility in Gaeta.

The facility was a solidly built Italian warehouse dating from World War II. Bill had the money and authority to renovate the facility to provide the community with a small commissary, exchange, barber shop, beauty shop, and child day care center but lacked the authority to renovate any of the space to be a medical/dental facility. I had the authority to make renovations for a medical/dental clinic if the cost was $3 million or less. Voila! We joined forces.

The project was now complete and sat on top of a hill overlooking the bay. There was ample parking, and it was a real blessing for the personnel and families stationed there. We opened this facility in 1997, but it stayed open only until 2004 because the Navy left Gaeta and moved all of the activities to Naples. I was really proud of what we accomplished, and even happier that we got away with it.

Naples, Italy

Naples International Airport is in the Capodichino District and is also the location for the replacement Navy hospital for which I had earlier participated in the groundbreaking. The new hospital wouldn't be completed until 2003. We were fortunate to get it done that quickly. Italy moves at a slower pace than we do. Getting plans for a large construction project approved by the Italian government can take a decade or more. We had a twenty-year-old approved design for an Army hospital in the northern part of the country that we no longer planned to build. The Italians said if we would build from that plan we could proceed. In Italy you are going to find artifacts when you dig. We had to have archeologists on the site throughout construction, and when something was found work halted until the archeologists were through with their examinations. Many shards were found, and an ancient well dating from Roman times was uncovered. Work stopped, plans were revised, and corridors were rerouted around the well so future generations could see it.

The first Navy hospital in Naples, the one I previously visited, had been opened in 1967 in the Agnano section of Naples. The building had originally been the Hotel San Ramon in an area famous for its hot springs. It is in an "extinct" volcanic crater (or so they say). During the time we used this building as a hospital the steam vents were still active and the air was permeated with the smell of rotten eggs from the sulfur vents. Earth tremors occurred daily. Over the three-plus decades we operated this hospital there were many problems associated with the physical plant, and a lot of money was spent trying to correct them. Some of the problems with the plant were so severe that patient and staff lives were endangered.

On my trips there the staff members were incredibly hospitable. One time they took me on the fast ferry to dinner on the Isle of Capri! On another they hosted a banquet in a nearby hotel. Neapolitans love to eat and they have wonderful cuisine.

The Western Hemisphere

Puerto Rico

On my last visit to Puerto Rico the hospital was little more than a clinic with a few operating beds. They handled normal deliveries, but anything more complicated was sent out to civilian facilities. Although the crew was enthusiastic, it was my impression that we would be better off making the facility an outpatient clinic only and refer patients needing inpatient care to civilian hospitals. In 2004 the Navy closed the entire Roosevelt Roads base including the hospital.

Guantanamo Bay, Cuba

I went to Gitmo by military aircraft from the Navy terminal at Andrews Air Force Base. Travel time depended on the type of aircraft—a Gulfstream could make it in two hours, but other aircraft would take more than double that time. The most interesting "ride" I took there was on a Navy P-3 flown by a Navy Reserve Rear Admiral who had been a P-3 pilot in his early career. Once at altitude and out over the Atlantic, he shut down both outboard engines so we were flying in what the Navy called the "loiter" mode. This conserves fuel and the aircraft travels much slower. I came forward; they put me in the pilot seat and told me to fly the plane to Cuba. This isn't really hard to do with autopilot on. Then they turned it off and told me to keep the plane within 100 feet of a prescribed altitude. This was not easy.

When I first visited Gitmo, the migrant population there had increased to over 40,000 Cubans and Haitians. All of our dependents had been removed. On this trip we supervised and assisted in providing the healthcare for migrants and did the medical screening of them before they were evacuated. Over 90 percent were moved on to the U.S. On January 31, 1996, the last of them left the base and dependents began to return.

I took a helicopter tour of the fence line. There was a gunner on the side looking into Cuba, just a "precaution." I also visited the Northwest Gate.

There were still a handful of Cuban nationals working on the base. They lived in Guantanamo City just to the north of the fence line and they walked to the gate every workday. We'd pick them up with a van and take them to their workplace, then return them to the gate in the late afternoon. The most senior of them ran the galley in our hospital. He was a very nice man, spoke good English, and ran an excellent food service, one of the best galleys I ever ate in. He had an ancillary responsibility: at the end of every month he carried all the checks back into Cuba for the Cuban nationals who had worked for us and were now retired. Another activity at the Northwest Gate was the return of Cubans who had made it onto our base. Unless there was good reason to grant asylum, we'd return them to Cuba at the gate. When the Cubans picked the person up, they'd march him out to a flagpole on their side of the fence and make him sing the Cuban national anthem. This was good entertainment for the Marines on guard duty.

Me (left) with Force Master Chief Mike Stewart at the Northwest Gate, Guantanamo Bay Cuba, 1987 (courtesy U.S. Navy).

Every month the commander of our base would meet with his counterpart from the Cuban Army in the area. There was a hut at the gate where they met. Both were fluent in the other's language, so they'd always chat in the language of the person whose turn it was to bring the coffee and donuts. They'd talk about any Cubans who had recently visited and returned, then baseball and fishing.

The current Navy hospital opened in 1956. It has been kept in immaculate condition by the Cuban national custodial staff. It provides care to all those on our base. Gitmo was the first shore facility in which we installed telemedicine capability.

In 1997 I went to Gitmo for a change of command and retirement at the hospital. The retiring commander was a Captain who was on his fourth tour there. His change of command and retirement ceremony was notable in that when he started making his personal remarks I saw him close the notebook with his speech in it. He was in rapture talking about his career and his time at Gitmo. My aide, Tracy, had informed him that I had a 60-minute rule for ceremonies. At 60 minutes I would walk off the dais. I hadn't done it yet, but he was pushing his luck. I started glancing at my watch, figuring this was going to be the time I would have to make good on my rule. Then I looked heavenward and saw huge thunderheads were rapidly bearing down on us from the west. In less than a minute the clouds opened up in a tropical downpour. The audience and the Navy Band ran for the cover of the hospital, with me in hot pursuit, but I didn't get there in time. Now the event was over it was time for the reception the Cuban galley chief had prepared. Before I could partake. Though. I had to go back to the BOQ and completely change my clothes. I was soaked through; even my skivvies, shoes, and socks were soaked.

I returned to Gitmo in January 1998 at the request of Admiral Paul Reason, who was the four-star in charge of the entire Atlantic Fleet region. After all the Cuban and Haitian migrants had left he decided it was time to cut the base back to caretaker status. We had 6,000 personnel and their dependents there and his goal was to cut it back to no more than 1,500 people total, including active duty, civilian employees, and dependents. He wanted to know how many medical personnel would be required to take care of a force that size.

Gitmo had no local options. If there was a medical problem that exceeded our capability we couldn't just take the patient into town like we could at most of our other OCONUS locations. He hadn't thought of that. One doctor could easily provide care for 1,500 relatively healthy people, as long as none of them needed anything complex. If there were to be dependents at Gitmo the requirements would be much higher. Also, we still had a population of aging Cubans on base that we were responsible for. I visited the hospital again and the base command. Both the hospital commander and the base commander agreed with me: either we closed the whole base or we'd need to keep the hospital about the size it was. I went back and filed my report with Admiral Reason, and that was the last I heard of it.

That was January 1998. Three years and 8 months later, on September 11, 2001, everything changed. Gitmo had not been cut back to caretaker status and facilities that had been built to contain troublemakers during the Cuban and Haitian migrant period were still available to take in the first prisoners of war. Soon a new prison was built, and the prison census quickly rose to about 750.

Peru

In Peru I visited our research lab in Lima. Its function was similar to that of our lab in Cairo. It monitored emerging and reemerging diseases in this part of the world's equatorial region. Deena, my aide, Commander Tracy Malone, the director of the Navy Nurse Corps, Rear Admiral Joan Engel, and her husband Walt, my Public Affairs Officer, Commander Sheila Graham, and her husband Steve, and Captain Tom Contreras and his wife Gloria were also along on this trip. We were visiting Peru during what was misnamed the Japanese embassy hostage crisis, a misnomer because it wasn't the embassy that was being held hostage but the official residence of the Japanese ambassador to Peru. However, the media referred to it as the "Japanese embassy" and that is how it is conventionally known. Hostages were still being held there when we departed.

I visited the U.S. embassy to call on the ambassador and to see if there was anything we could do from our lab there to help them. He was very much aware of our lab's presence and the important contributions it made, points he continually emphasized to Peruvian officials. We could offer them little in the way of direct medical support, since our function was not clinical but research. They had a couple of fulltime family practice nurses who seemed to meet most of their needs.

My next visit was to our lab, Naval Medical Research Unit 6. In 1978 the idea for a tropical medicine program with joint participation between the U.S. and Peruvian navies began. This idea became NAMRU-6 in January 1983. It is the only U.S. military command in South America and is located on the grounds of the Peruvian Navy Hospital, Lima, in a separate building. NAMRU-6 is a level-3 lab, meaning it can handle all but the most virulent and contagious biologic agents. It conducts research and surveillance on a wide range of infectious diseases that threaten the region and that could rapidly spread beyond there given today's rapid means of transportation.

I visited the Peruvian Navy Hospital, which was familiar to me since I had previously visited our hospital in Beaufort. I went into the intensive care nursery, as the Peruvians knew I was a pediatrician and thought a visit there was in order. The hospital had opened in 1983, and the equipment in the nursery looked like what we had in Oakland when I was chief of pediatrics there. There had been numerous advances in neonatology over the past fourteen years, but this was like a time warp. I asked if I could see the unit's policies and procedures manuals. I figured they would be in Spanish, but I was wrong. They were in English and consisted of photocopies of the Beaufort policies and procedures manuals from 1983. I promised to try to get some up-dated manuals.

The entire command was present at Captain Wooster's that evening and all brought something special for dinner. The Wooster home was in a compound completely surrounded by a high wall topped with broken glass bottles set in cement with the jagged edges facing up. There was also an electronic alarm system protecting the entire property.

Bright and early the next morning a dozen of us went to the airport for the one-hour flight to Cusco. This city in the Andes, with a population then of 275,000, is at an altitude of 11,200 feet. On the flight we were served coca tea, a potent diuretic. This is important because, if you don't shed a lot of water, making such a rapid elevation ascent can cause pulmonary edema and heart failure. When we arrived in Cusco we were taken by bus straight to our hotel, where our rooms were ready. We were given some more coca tea, told to lie down for a few hours, and then come down for lunch. After that we took a motor van tour of the city.

The locals were all quite short and barrel chested. I had learned why during my days as a hematologist: their need for red blood cells was far greater than for those of us living at lower elevations. They needed extra red blood cells to carry enough oxygen to their tissues to survive at these altitudes. Their chests were large because the marrow cavities of their ribs and spine were much larger than normal, meaning these areas could produce more blood. The rest of the body was short, because there wasn't enough oxygen to both support life and grow.

On the tour we saw many historic sites in the city. We ascended to the highest point in the area, Inca Wasi, at 13,060 feet. At these altitudes some visitors passed out from oxygen deprivation. A highlight of the tour was the Cathedral of Santo Domingo, built between 1560 and 1664. During this time the city developed a distinctive style of painting known as the "Cusco School," and the cathedral houses a major collection of local artists of the time. The cathedral is best known for a Cusco School painting of the Last Supper depicting Jesus and the twelve apostles feasting on guinea pig, a traditional Andean delicacy. We were told you could get guinea pig in any restaurant in Cusco—the common local name for them sounded like *coo-we*. Guinea pigs are rodents. People raise them in their homes in cages as a food source, much like people raise chickens in the U.S.

That evening our group went to dinner in our hotel dining room. I looked over the menu, which conveniently provided English translations. One thing was certain: we would be served potatoes. Peru prides itself on cultivating over 3,000 varieties of potato, and at least three varieties are served at every dinner. I looked for an entrée and guinea pig was not listed. I asked and the waiter said, "Sure, you can get guinea pig anytime at any restaurant in the Andes." So I ordered it.

Soon we were all served our three varieties of potatoes and our entrée. I was the last to be served. There was a whole guinea pig, skinned, lying on its back with all extremities and head intact and perfectly cooked. The lady sitting next to me picked up her plate and went to the other end of the table where there was an empty seat. As she passed Deena she said, "It looks like Mickey Mouse."

It tasted like chicken.

The next morning we were off to Machu Picchu on the narrow-gauge train, a downhill run to 7,970 feet. Machu Picchu was built by the Incas around 1450 and abandoned a century later, at the time of the Spanish conquest. It is now a UNESCO World Heritage Site and in 2007 was voted one of the New Seven Wonders of the World.

When it was time to leave, buses took us down the mountain to the train. Then we were off on a 3,000-foot ascent back to Cusco and a quick, late afternoon plane ride back to Lima. A few hours later we were on a night flight back to Washington, via Miami.

Hawaii

I did not forget Hawaii, though it would have fit well in the Western Hemisphere section above. I had been there many times, but I decided to save it for the final section on travel that begins below.

Around the World

Part of this trip was another command performance from the Secretary of Defense, similar to the trip to China. This time it was a gathering of the leaders of the military medical components of the countries on the Pacific Rim to be held in the spring of 1997 in Kuala Lumpur (KL), Malaysia. The three Surgeons General of our military medical departments were asked to attend as keynote speakers at the opening plenary session.

A round trip to KL would be about 19,000 miles if there were direct flights. Since there were none, we checked to see if there were any places along the route we should visit. If we flew west, we could stop at Hawaii, Guam, our third research lab, NAMRU-2, in Jakarta, Indonesia, and Singapore, where we had a dental clinic that had never been visited by an SG or a chief of the Dental Corps as far as I knew. The Singapore military medical department provided support for our forces in that region of the world, so a visit with them made sense. From Singapore it was about the same distance home going east or west. Going west there were two more places we could visit, Diego Garcia and Bahrain. Getting transportation to those facilities would have to be on military charters from Singapore to Diego Garcia and from there to Bahrain. If available this would make our travel costs less then a round-trip ticket. Military air was available, so we elected to go all the way.

My aide, Commander Tracy Malone, Rear Admiral Joan Engel, and her aide, Commander Jennifer Towne, Captain Paul Tibbits, the commanding officer of the Navy Information Management Command, the BUMED Public Affairs Officer, Commander Sheila Graham, and Force Master Chief Mike Stewart accompanied me.

Hawaii

I'd been to Hawaii several times as a DASD, so I'd visited all of the military medical facilities on Oahu as well as some nonmedical commands. On this trip I visited the Navy clinic at Pearl Harbor, the clinic at Barbers Point Naval Air Station, which was in the process of being closed due to a BRAC decision, and the Navy clinic at Marine Corps Air Station Kaneohe Bay. I visited the Tripler Army Medical Center, where the second in command was a Navy Captain because of the joint nature of the facility. I also made calls on PACOM and CINCPACFLT.

On this trip a newly promoted Chief Petty Officer was assigned to me as an armed escort. We traveled between the facilities by helicopter because time was short. One day the chief and I boarded a Beechcraft C-12 and flew to the Navy's Barking Sands base on the southwest corner of the island of Kauai. Rear Admiral Joan Engel and Force Master Chief Mike Stewart accompanied me. Two Navy Reserve Captains who were commercial airline pilots doing their reserve duty flew the plane. All went well until we began our descent, when a crack appeared in the windshield. We rapidly descended and landed at the airstrip at Barking Sands. The plane was not serviceable, so the two pilots looked for a way to get us back to Oahu while we toured the base. The base had a helicopter just for these sorts of situations and pilots who could fly it. It was big enough for all of us to ride in comfortably. On the way back we got a sight-seeing tour of Kauai.

We flew through the Waimea Canyon, also known as the Grand Canyon of the Pacific, making a couple passes up and down the canyon. Then we made the 100-mile trip across the Pacific to Oahu. It was a beautiful day, so they had the passenger/cargo access doors on both sides of the helicopter fully open. We could look directly out and if we leaned over a bit, straight down. We spotted dolphins, sea turtles, gray whales, and even a couple of blue whales.

That evening we had a Luau with many of the staff from the medical clinics, PACOM and CINCPACFLT medical staffs, a great way to say "aloha." The next day we flew from Hawaii to Guam—which is farther than it is from Washington, D.C., to London—and it's over water all the way.

GUAM

When we landed on Guam the air was warm and humid. The average daily high temperature on Guam is 86° and the low 76° and it hardly varies a degree from that high and low all year. It also rains about 100 inches a year. This was an introduction to the temperature, humidity, and rain we would experience for the rest of the trip. I'd been to Guam once in 1992 when I was a DASD, so I was acquainted with our facilities there (which I covered in an earlier chapter). Neither the island nor our facilities had changed much.

I spoke to the staffs of both the Navy hospital and the Air Force Clinic at Anderson Air Force Base. Anderson was much busier than it had been during my first visit. In 1996 and 1997 about 7,000 Kurdish, Muslim, Iraqi, Iranian, and Turkish people were brought to the U.S. through Guam, but this didn't make the news. I spent a good deal of time talking with the Air Force personnel who were their primary providers. The Navy provided needed specialty consultations.

While there I swam in the ocean, something my father had enjoyed doing while he was there during World War II. He brought home quite a collection of shells, something that I think is not allowed now. The hospital CO had my group over to his quarters on Nimitz Hill for dinner. This was a spectacular location on the southern part of the island overlooking Agana Bay, where Chester Nimitz based his headquarters in January 1945. Here I saw my first brown tree snake. I had learned about these creatures from Senator Inouye when I asked why there was $4 million in my budget for them.

JAKARTA

To get to Jakarta we had to go to Denspar, the capital of Bali, on Continental Micronesia Airlines and transfer to a Garuda Airlines flight to Jakarta. Indonesia has the fourth largest population in the world, behind China, India, and the U.S. At that time its population was estimated at about 200 million. From west to east it spans nearly 3,200 miles, broader than CONUS. It has mountains rising to 16,000 feet, and its climate is hot and muggy.

Our purpose in Jakarta was to visit NAMRU-2, which at this time was involved with surveillance of febrile illnesses, avian influenza, Shigellosis, and drug resistant malaria in the area. To do this they had satellite labs in several countries in the region. We had a luncheon and meeting with the Indonesian ministry of health during which we discussed the problems of this emerging nation.

KUALA LUMPUR

We flew from Jakarta to Kuala Lumpur, Malaysia—again on Garuda Airlines. When we arrived at the headquarters hotel, Tracy said she would get us checked in and told me to hang back and grip and grin with the foreign military officers. I followed orders but kept an eye on her because I knew sometimes women weren't seen as equals in this part of the world. Sure enough, she appeared to be arguing with the Asian gentleman at the check-in desk. I went up to see what was going on. Tracy told me they were trying to give her the Presidential Suite and she was trying to convince them that I should have the Presidential Suite. The clerk looked at me and said, "Madam has Presidential Suite. Admiral has Honeymoon Suite." So we went and had a look. It was spacious and beautiful, and priced at the U.S. per diem rate.

At the plenary session I gave my remarks and attended some breakout sessions. Later we were taken on an escorted tour of the city, the metro area having a population of about 7 million. The city is the location of the Petronas Twin Towers, the tallest twin buildings in the world. Something I saw on the tour that immediately caught my eye was a huge monument reminding me of the Marine Corps War Memorial near Arlington National Cemetery. The monument is dedicated to 11,000 people who died during the 12-year Malayan Emergency (1948–1960). Malaysia's first prime minister was inspired to have this monument constructed after seeing the Marine Corps Memorial on a trip to Washington. He contacted Felix deWeldon, the Austrian designer of the Marine Corps Memorial, and asked him to design the monument for Malaysia. It opened in 1966.

SINGAPORE

Sheila Graham flew from KL back to Washington, as she had a compulsory meeting there to attend. The rest of us flew from KL on to Singapore, where the senior dentist at our clinic there met us at the airport. We had dental services in Singapore because the city didn't have enough dentists to take care of its rapidly growing population and to take care of our sailors' dental needs as well. Medical care was a different situation. Singapore had an excellent medical system and this is where we sent all of our medical problems that could not be handled at sea in the area, as well as those from Diego Garcia. The Singapore military also used our hospital information system, CHCS. Their medical care was on a par with ours. (We had to wait over the weekend until the military charter flight came through to take us on to Diego Garcia.)

Singapore is one of the cleanest and safest cities in the world. There is capital punishment for murder, some drug trafficking, and firearms offenses. It has four official languages—English, Malay, Mandarin Chinese, and Tamil. English is the "common" language and is taught in schools. Most government business is conducted in English. When we visited in 1997 we were told the population was 3.5 million. Today (2018) it is over 5.5 million. We had no trouble getting around. There is a superb subway and bus system. Cabs were plentiful and all cab drivers were required to speak and understand English.

We took a tour of the city that included visits to several of the old and new government buildings, and we stopped at the Raffles Hotel for a Singapore Sling in its world famous bar. One evening we took a trip to the Singapore Night Zoo, which doesn't open until sundown and stays open until midnight. Most of the animals are nocturnal, so the zoo uses low-intensity blue lights for illumination. Once our eyes adjusted, it was really spectacular. A tram took us around with excellent English speaking guides. There was a side benefit to the night zoo visit. Force Master Chief Mike Stewart is a dedicated carnivore. In this part of the world fish and fowl are the main forms of meat consumed. He had gone several days without red meat. In front of the zoo was a McDonald's. He said, "Just pick me up on your way out."

We also visited the Singapore botanical gardens and the National Orchid Garden within it. This is really a spectacular place. I doubt there is any other like it in the world.

Diego Garcia

Diego Garcia is in what is called the British Indian Ocean Territory, a five-hour flight from Singapore. We flew on an Air Mobility Command charter. An early version of a 747 configured with about a dozen first class passenger seats, all the rest of the cabin was filled with freight. The only flight attendant told me they had four planes, all old 747s, and they hauled stuff and a few people for the government all over the world. They did have a microwave meal—two choices—and an in-flight movie. Being the senior officer present, I was asked to pick the movie from a dozen choices. I chose to pass and sleep instead. The five-hour flight would be over water all the way.

When we landed it was about 2000 (8:00 p.m.) local time. As I exited the aircraft there were bright lights practically blinding me. When I got to the bottom of the stairs the base commander greeted me with a microphone in his hand and said, "Welcome to Diego Garcia, Admiral." I noticed there was someone with a TV camera, and I asked what was going on. The commander told me I was the highest-ranking military officer to visit the base

In Diego Garcia the Medical Clinic commanding officer issued Force Master Chief Mike Stewart, Rear Admiral Joan Engel, and me pith helmets, which are part of the standard uniform there (courtesy U.S. Navy).

in its history, as far as he knew. He presented me with a British-style pith helmet decorated with a U.S. Navy officer's insignia above the brim and a double strand of gold oak leaves on the brim. He had an appropriately decorated pith helmet for every member of our group.

There are 16 Royal Marines stationed at Diego Garcia to raise the Union Jack at dawn and lower it at sunset each day. One of the Marines played the piccolo and another beat a drum during the ceremony. The rest of the day the Marines spent in their club. The main mission of the island was to serve as a massive secure storage facility for war materials. The lagoon harbored many freighter hulls loaded with war material. We had more equipment aboard those vessels than it took to wage Desert Storm. Some of the material on the vessels was dated or deteriorative. There were over 3,000 stevedores on the island, mostly Filipinos, who did the hard physical work of removing and replacing this material. Navy logisticians directed the whole operation. During Desert Storm and subsequent periods of combat, Diego Garcia served as a frequent stopping-off spot for aircraft rest and refueling.

I addressed the entire staff, then Joan Engel met with the nurses, Paul Tibbits met with the physicians, and Mike Stewart met with the enlisted. The doctors were mostly Family Practitioners. The medical library was housed in a closet, and most of its contents were out of date. Paul Tibbits showed them how to use the Internet to get into the National Library of Medicine database and search for the latest material on any subject. This was new technology then, and it was a great leap forward for this command. For all the staff there was a tutorial on BUMED Instructions. It takes several three-ring binders to hold hard copies of all of these, and it is hard to keep them current. We had recently put all the instructions on a BUMED website, so Paul showed them how to access these. Joan Engel and Mike Stewart's discussions dealt mostly with career counseling.

We stayed busy with the command staff until after 0400. At that point they took us to the BOQ, where we could get a shower and put on clean clothes for our flight to Bahrain, which was due to depart just before dawn. I was in the Bob Hope Suite! Apparently he had brought his Christmas Show here once- upon a time and this was the room he stayed in.

Bahrain

We flew on another Air Mobility Command charter, a different aircraft flown by ATA Airlines, from Diego Garcia to Manama, Bahrain, which took a little over five hours. The aircraft was a relatively new 757 that was empty except for us. It had only coach seats, but we each got a whole row to ourselves plus pillows and blankets. We lifted off at the crack of dawn, 0600 (6:00 a.m.), and promptly went to sleep. When we landed our escorts took us straight to our hotel in Manama so we could get a couple hours of rest. We stayed at a hotel near the base because there were no visiting officer's quarters available. Something I noticed as we entered the hotel was that there were two guards at the front door in very fancy Middle Eastern military dress. One had a large-bore double-barreled shotgun and the other a very large automatic weapon.

Our first day's activity began with briefings at the Fifth Fleet Headquarters. The Fifth Fleet had been deactivated in 1947 and reactivated in 1995. It was responsible for Naval forces in the Persian Gulf, Red Sea, Arabian Sea, and parts of the Indian Ocean. Our base there was being expanded. The previous June a truck-bomb had been detonated at a housing tower complex in Khobar, Saudi Arabia, killing 19 U.S. Air Force personnel. Throughout the Middle East we were improving security on our bases. In Bahrain this was being done by moving the base perimeter out a quarter-mile from where it had originally been. The land used to do this had been "scraped"—all the structures on it had been removed.

Admiral Ron Zlatoper, whom I had known while he was chief of Naval Personnel, was now the Fleet Commander. He told me he and his wife were hosting a reception in my honor at their home that evening, but he wanted Tracy and me to get there an hour early so we could chat with him and his wife and have a chance to eat. He told us there would be a lot of people there, not just U.S. military personnel and people from our embassy, but a lot of locals as well. He said if we didn't get there early we'd get nothing to eat. He was right. Once the locals arrived there was no chance for us to get to the food.

The next day I toured four different hospitals in the city. There were two hospitals we sent personnel to since we had no inpatient capability in our clinic. The hospitals were quite modern and clean. The nurses were Muslim, spoke passable English, and were very polite. All the doctors spoke English. I spoke with some of our personnel who were patients and they were pleased with their care, including the food.

A local surgeon owned one of the hospitals. He took me to his office and had lunch brought in. The office was huge. There was a desk at one end, the hardwood floors were covered with multiple oriental rugs, and at the other end there was a full-sized grand piano. There were three violins on display, all made by the Stradivarius family. He played both the piano and the violin and had a teacher for both. He had gone to medical school in Germany and trained in surgery in London and still operated a couple of days each week. He asked if I could stay for the weekend. He had a yacht nearby and said we could go out and spend the night on the Persian Gulf. I declined his kind invitation.

That evening we ate an early dinner and all headed off to our rooms to try to get a couple of hours' sleep in a real bed before beginning our travel home, which would take about 20 hours. The hotel was nice enough to let us stay until 1:00 a.m. and not charge us for an extra day. When we left, the two guards were still at the front door.

Going Home

Before we left Bahrain I had to fix a problem. This trip was in early 1997 and the airlines had not converted yet to electronic tickets. We still had paper tickets with a voucher for each flight segment. These vouchers were as good as money to the airlines. My aide, Tracy, was the custodian of all the tickets. Travel still had to be reconfirmed. Our hotel said they would do this for us, so Tracy handed the tickets over to them. They were returned in an envelope later to her room.

When we got to the British Airways desk at the airport we discovered one of the ticket books was missing—Tracy's. We called the hotel, but they couldn't help us. We called our ticket agency back in CONUS and got a recorded message. The British counter agents said Tracy was confirmed for the flight, but she couldn't board without a boarding pass and they couldn't issue one unless we paid again for the ticket. Since the tickets were issued on United Airlines stock, they said we could straighten it out with United in London. In the meantime the only way Tracy could get on the flight was for us to pay for her ticket. I had a government issued American Express card, so I paid for it.

Our British Airways flight to London left Bahrain at 2:00 a.m. It took 6½ hours to get to London, and we arrived there about 6:30 a.m. local time. Our flight from London to Washington wouldn't leave until 11:00 a.m., so we had time for shopping, a second breakfast if we wanted it (we'd been served one on the flight), and sleep in airport waiting area chairs. I went to the United Airlines desk—no line this early in the morning. They said they couldn't do anything about it there; we would have to straighten it out through the travel agency in Washington. Out came the American Express card again and a new boarding pass was issued for Tracy for this last leg of the trip.

Force Master Chief Mike Stewart was with me. He and I both had a lot of miles racked up on United with our travels. I was ticketed in business class, Mike in the back. The agent asked why, with all Mike's miles, he didn't move up front with me. Mike said he couldn't do that, that if anyone moved up it should be Tracy. The agent knew we were finishing a very long trip and took pity on us. She asked how many were in our group and I said six. She said business class was nearly empty and she gave each of us a courtesy upgrade.

I asked Mike not to say a word to the others—we'd hold onto the boarding passes until it was time to board. What a nice surprise this was for all of them and a great way to end a very long trip. It was another 7½ hours home. There's a six-hour difference between London and Washington. We'd be home just after noon. While we were flying Tracy told me she had never flown anything but coach. We had flown a little over 25,000 miles; the equatorial circumference of the earth is 24,901 miles. We'd spent over 52 hours in the air. We made this trip in 17 days, and we'd gotten the day back we lost when we crossed the International Date Line.

After the trip we had to do battle with the ticket agency and American Express. Neither wanted to refund what we had to pay for Tracy's trip from Bahrain home. We got the Pentagon lawyers involved. They got American Express to iron this out with the travel agency and the airlines and clear the debit.

Preparing for Retirement

Near the end of January 1998 the Vice Chief of Naval Operations told me that the Navy was holding to the "gentleman's agreement" letter all Admirals signed at the time of our promotions that said we would submit our request for retirement after being in grade three years. It was time for me to go. That afternoon I sent in my letter to retire, requesting June 30 because that would be 40 years to the day from my "induction" day at the Naval Academy. Then I thought, *Why not retire at Annapolis, where I had first come in?* SG retirement ceremonies were usually held in conjunction with a change of office ceremony in front of the National Naval Medical Center, Bethesda, where I had relieved Don Hagen three years before, but it was my retirement ceremony and I could do what I wanted. I called Admiral Charles Larson, the superintendent, and asked him if I could have my retirement ceremony at the academy on June 30. He said, "Of course"—and in Memorial Hall.

On the way home that afternoon I stopped at Bethesda to see my urologist, Captain Kevin O'Connell. He had some bad news. A urine specimen I had provided a few weeks before contained a few cancer cells. I was admitted and cystoscoped in the operating room. No gross lesions were found, but the providers collected some random samples that also turned out positive. I was started back on the same medication regimen I had received seven years earlier: an infusion of 5-Flurouracil into the bladder every two weeks for six courses. The procedure wasn't all that unpleasant, but some of the medication was always absorbed systemically and it reduced my stamina. It also irritated my bladder and made me feel like I had to void frequently Travel was out of the question until the course of treatment was complete. By April my treatments were complete, so Deena and I flew to San Diego for a few days during Easter week to look at a house a friend had lined up that he thought would be ideal. It was a real fixer-upper but the right size—and one floor in a great neighborhood. We made a bid, and the seller accepted. The same friend then lined us up with an architect and general contractor.

Grant's graduation from the Naval Academy was on May 22. President Clinton would be speaking. Zachary Fisher, the founder and funder of the Fisher House Foundation, was hosting a dinner the night before on the hangar deck of the museum ship USS *Intrepid* at its mooring in the Hudson. Zach hosted one of these "soirees" every year and several hundred people always attended. The featured attraction this year was a speech by the Secretary of the Treasury, Robert E. Rubin.

Zach always wanted the three services Surgeons General to come to this event—in our dress uniforms. He would have us sit in front and introduce us to the gathering. I had always attended, but this year we couldn't find airline or rail transportation that would leave after the event and get me back in time to be in my seat for the graduation ceremony in Annapolis. My aide, Tracy, tried to explain this to him and he said, "I want the Admiral there, so I will send a plane for him." He did just that, a Gulfstream jet. It picked me up at the private terminal at Reagan National Airport and flew me to Teterboro Airport in New Jersey, flight time 22 minutes! A limo pulled up alongside the Gulfstream jet, I went down the aircraft's stairs into the limo, and we sped to the Intrepid Air, Sea and Space museum entrance. Dinner was served and the Secretary gave his speech. At its conclusion the guests were asked to remain until the Admiral (me) had departed, because he needed to get back to Washington to attend his son's graduation from Annapolis the following morning. The attendees stood and applauded. I went back to Teterboro in the limo, was dropped off at the plane's stairs, and twenty-two minutes later I was back at Reagan National Airport. A half-hour later I was home.

Grant's graduation was held in the Navy-Marine Corps Memorial Stadium. It was a beautiful spring day with clear blue skies. The Blue Angels flew over in their Victory formation. Grant graduated with merit, pretty good for a kid who had been hyperactive and on Ritalin. Bill Clinton shook hands with Grant, and he received his diploma from Admiral Charles Larson. Our three sons were all now fully out of the nest and commissioned officers in the United States Navy.

The Friday before my retirement ceremony we held a change of office ceremony in the Medal of Honor Hall at the Bureau of Medicine and Surgery. Dick Nelson relieved me as Surgeon General. After the ceremony Dick hosted a reception. After a few minutes I excused myself and went back to what had been my office. I held an awards ceremony for my staff and said thanks and farewell to them. Tracy received the Meritorious Service Medal and David Fisher the Legion of Merit. I picked up my remaining few personal effects and left.

On Monday, just before 1400 (2:00 p.m.), I put my sword on for the last time. Memorial Hall was filled over capacity for the ceremony. The Secretary of the Navy was there and some other Defense officials, members of Congress, about 40 of my Naval Academy classmates, some relatives, lots of friends, and the parents of a couple of children who had been my patients.

The official party consisted of me, Ed Martin, MD, who was the speaker and the chaplain, Captain John Fitzgerald, Chaplain Corps, U.S. Navy, who gave the invocation and benediction. My Chief of Staff, Captain David Fisher, Medical Service Corps, U.S. Navy, served as master of ceremonies.

Ed made some brief remarks and presented my personal award, the Navy Distinguished Service Medal. My oldest son, Steve, pinned Navy Wings of Gold on me, making me an honorary flight surgeon, with the blessing of the flight surgeon community. A Naval Academy classmate presented me a plaque for being the last member "over-the-side," and the Vice Chief of Naval Operations, Admiral Don Pilling, presented my retirement certificate and said I had served 32 years, 1 month, and 4 days. Force Master Chief Stewart presented a shadowbox with mementos from my career. I read my retirement orders and made a few remarks. I asked attendees to remember my fifteen classmates who had lost their lives in the Vietnam War and mentioned that their names were on a plaque behind me in the hall. The chaplain gave a closing prayer and the band played the Navy hymn. I left the dais to be piped ashore. The Navy Band struck up two familiar tunes, "I Love You, California" and "California, Here I Come."

A massive marble staircase leads from Memorial Hall down to the rotunda. Eight sideboys are posted on every other stair, four on each side.

I broke with tradition and, rather than sit for hours for an oil portrait, had several photographs taken and chose the best one to be transferred to canvas, which saved a lot of time and money. Traditionally the Surgeon General chooses three objects to have in the portrait. My selections, from left to right, are a statue of a male and a female Chief Petty Officer, a photograph of my family, and my Naval Academy class plaque (courtesy U.S. Navy).

Traditionally, a retiring officer went through alone then went back, picked up the waiting spouse, and went through again. I passed on doing it twice. Following the band's playing three Ruffles and Flourishes and eight bells being sounded, Deena and I went through together. In contrast to my thoughts three years earlier, this time they were of relief. My sideboys were:

Captain Paul Tibbits, Medical Corps, U.S. Navy;

Colonel Stuart Baker, Medical Service Corps, U.S. Army;

Captain David Maloney, Medical Service Corps, U.S. Navy;

Commander Tracy Malone, Nurse Corps, U.S. Navy;

Lieutenant Steve Koenig, U.S. Navy;

Major Alan Koenig, U.S. Marine Corps Reserve;

Ensign Grant Koenig, U.S. Navy;

Master Chief Michael Stewart, Hospital Corps, US Navy, Retired.

Our middle son, Scott, would have been a sideboy, but he was at sea.

The entire ceremony lasted 35 minutes.

That evening we hosted a dinner at our house. My BUMED staff were there, as were many staff who had worked with me during the four years I was in the Pentagon. My father's cousin Elmer Koenig; his wife, Ann; and son Alan; cousin Wayne and his wife, Norma; my scoutmaster from Salinas, Bob Bowman; and Tom Preston, the scoutmaster of the troop our sons had been members of in Oakland, were there. Doug Cunningham had been an early mentor in San Diego, Mike and Debbie Bohan and Ted and Bev Edwards, who had been stationed with us in Sasebo, came.

There was a portrait made of me to hang with all of the other SGs at Bethesda. I didn't pose for an oil painting as all previous ones had done. Instead a professional photographer took several pictures and we chose one.

14

Life After the Navy

As we left the National Capital area I had the best view of it I ever had—in my rearview mirror. We traveled across the northern states, through areas we had not been to before. We stayed at bed-and-breakfasts all the way. We visited some of Deena's mother's relatives in Saginaw, Michigan, and Deena's brother and sister-in-law drove over there from Sioux Falls, South Dakota. We drove across the Straits of Mackinac to Michigan's northern peninsula, spent a night in Fargo, North Dakota, then traveled through the Black Hills and Badlands into Montana and spent a night in Bozeman. We stopped long enough in Glacier National Park to hike down a trail to see a waterfall. On the way back up, with Deena leading, a bear cub ran across the trail and into the brush. I told her to back up and have a seat. A few seconds later the mother bear came crashing through the brush chasing her rambunctious cub, right where we had been standing.

We crossed the Continental Divide on the way into Kalispell, Montana, where we spent two nights with my sister and her husband. Farther on, in Washington, we visited Mount Saint Helens on our way to Vancouver, Washington, where we spent two nights with my father's cousin Elmer and his wife, Ann. We turned south and followed Interstate 5 into California's Central Valley, where it was stifling hot. We had reservations at a B&B near the coast and took a country road off I-5 toward the Coast Range. At the crest a heavy fog bank greeted us, and in a couple of minutes the temperature had dropped forty degrees. We spent the night in our last B&B on this trip and the next morning drove to Salinas to spend a day with my mother then take her to our oldest son's wedding in Calabasas.

Steve's betrothed, Dana, was Jewish, and I had been to Jewish weddings before, as well as many Christian and civil ones. They all seemed similar to me—women spend a lot of money on dresses they haven't been seen in before and will probably never be seen in again. Men wear what they are told, something from their closet if it still fits; or if the bride has declared formal wear for the male participants they rent it.

Our best friends from San Diego, Joe and Virginia Gistaro, drove up for the wedding. We had lived across the street from them from 1972 to 1980. Their son Joey and our son Steve had been best friends, and while Steve was in college at the University of San Diego and we were the National Capital Region the Gistaros' house was Steve's second home. Eventually Steve and Joey were in each other's wedding. While talking with Joe I noticed his speech was slurred but he was not drunk. I encouraged him to see his doctor. His slurred speech was due to Lou Gehrig's Disease (Amyotrophic Lateral Sclerosis). He lived less than two years.

After the wedding we put my mother on a plane back to Salinas, drove the last 125 miles to San Diego, and moved into temporary lodging. The next morning we went to see the progress on our house. There was still a long way to go. Even so, on October 18, Deena's birthday, the moving trucks came and we moved in. We were finished living out of suitcases.

Deena began working as a volunteer in the gift shop at the Navy hospital, an activity she has continued to this day with great enthusiasm. I did some consulting and was co-owner of a disabled veterans company and a member of several boards—philanthropic, government, community, and for-profit. I

Relaxing with Joe Gistaro (left) soon after I retired in 1998. Joe passed away from ALS about a year later.

continue my annual fishing trips. Roland Mayne, who organized them, passed away in 2007 and I have taken over this responsibility since that time. Deena and I have done a lot of traveling, with many trips to Europe, Africa, Asia, and Hawaii. Once, we circumnavigated the earth (a second time for me).

However, details of these activities await another book.

Appendix: Acronyms

AAMC • American Association of Medical Colleges

AFB • Air Force Base

ALL • Acute Lymphocytic Leukemia

AML • Acute Myelocytic Leukemia

ASD • Assistant Secretary of Defense

ASD-HA • Assistant Secretary of Defense for Health Affairs

BOQ • Bachelor Officers' Quarters

BRAC • Base Realignment and Closure

BUMED • Bureau of Medicine and Surgery

BUPERS • Bureau of Navy Personnel

BYU • Brigham Young University

CDR • Commander

CEC • Civil Engineer Corps

CHCS • Composite Health Care System

CIC • Clinical Investigation Center

CINCPAC • Commander in Chief, Pacific Command

CINCUSNAVEUR • Commander in Chief, U.S. Naval Forces, Europe

CIO • Chief Information Officer

CNO • Chief of Naval Operations

COMNAVMEDCOM • Commander, Naval Medical Command

CONUS • Continental United States

CRAF • Civilian Reserve Air Fleet

DASD • Deputy Assistant Secretary of Defense

DBA • Diamond-Blackfan Anemia

DoD • Department of Defense
DOPMA • Defense Officer Personnel Management Act
FEHBP • Federal Employees Health Benefits Program
FEP • Fitness Enhancement Program
FOT&E • Full Operational Test and Evaluation
GAO • Government Accountability Office
GMO • General Medical Officer
GMO • General Medical Officer
HPSP • Navy Health Professions Scholarship
HSETC • Health Sciences and Education Training Command
IG • Inspector General
ITP • Idiopathic Thrombocytopenic Purpura
JAG • Judge Advocate General
JMSDF • Japan Maritime Self-Defense Force
LCDR • Lieutenant Commander
MOOD • Medical Officer of the Day
NATO • North Atlantic Treaty Organization
NICU • Neonatal Intensive Care Unit
NIS • Naval Investigative Service
NROTC • Naval Reserve Officers Training Corps
OIC • Officer in Charge
PACC • Pediatric Acute Care Clinic
PACOM • Pacific Command
PAO • Public Affairs Officer
PDASD • Principal Deputy Assistant Secretary of Defense
PDASD • Principal Deputy Assistant Secretary of Defense
PLA • People's Liberation Army
RADM • Rear Admiral
RBCs • Red Blood Cells
RIO • Radar Intercept Officer
SAIC • Science Applications International Corporation
SES • Senior Executive Service
SITREP • Situation Report
SPR • Society for Pediatric Research

TAD • Temporary Additional Duty

TEC • Transient Erythroblastopenia of Childhood

UCLA • University of California Los Angeles

UCSD • University of California San Diego

UCSF • University of California San Francisco

USNR • United States Naval Reserve

USUHS • Uniformed Services University of the Health Sciences

VCNO • Vice Chief of Naval Operations

XO • Executive Officer

Index